Party Politics and Democratic Governance in India

About the Author

Alaknanda Shringare earned her M.Phil. and Ph.D. from Karnataka University, Dharwad. She has a research experience of five years, party politics, coalition government, and democratic governance being her areas of specialisation. She has worked as a lecturer in post-graduate department of Political Science, Goa University for two years. She has presented papers in a number of seminars and workshops. Also, she has published a good number of research papers in various journals of national and international repute.

Party Politics and Democratic Governance in India

Alaknanda Shringare

CONCEPT PUBLISHING COMPANY, NEW DELHI-110059

ISBN-13: 978-81-8069-569-8 **ISBN-10: 81-8069-569-7**

First Edition 2009

Published and Printed by

Concept
Since 1974

Concept Publishing Company
Regd. Office:
A/15-16, Commercial Block, Mohan Garden
New Delhi-110059 (India)
Phones : 25351460, 25351794, *Fax* : 091-11-25357109
Email : publishing@conceptpub.com,
website: www.conceptpub.com

Editorial Office:
H-13, Bali Nagar, New Delhi-110 015, India.

Cataloging in Publication Data--*Courtesy:* D.K. Agencies (P) Ltd. <docinfo@dkagencies.com>

Shringare, Alaknanda.
Party politics and democratic governance in India / Alaknanda Shringare. —1st ed.
p. cm.
Includes bibliographical references (p.).
Includes index.
ISBN 13: 9788180695698 ISBN 10: 8180695697

1. Democracy—India. 2. Political parties—India. 3. Political participation—India. 4. India—Politics and government—1947 - I. Title.

DDC 320.454 22

Foreword

Our experience of liberal democracy of the parliamentary variety in the last six decades presents us with many puzzles and paradoxes. On the one hand, we do not hesitate to praise it as an exemplary model in the context of the so-called third world, and, on the other, we take unhealthy delight in listing its major faults such as corruption, inefficiency and socio-economic injustice. We, therefore, need many empirical investigations into the truth of the claims and counter-claims. From this perspective, Dr. Alaknanda Shringare's work on popular participation and responsiveness in our liberal parliamentary democracy should be welcomed both by specialist scholars and laymen. Her focus on the political parties is also quite appropriate since the party system is the conduit between the elected government and the electorate. She also rightly singles out for her study the two crucial dimensions of the political parties in relation to their functionality within a democratic polity—their participatory and responsiveness potential. Having said that, I must also hasten to point out that the author's notion of democratic governance seems to be either too restricted or too imprecise. In this, she is simply a representative of our conventional academic culture which is obsessed with the legal structures and the political elite who manage them. The notion of democratic governance would be radically transformed if we shift our main focus from the rulers to the ruled. Also, the author could have supplemented her documentary data with strong empirical and hard fieldwork data. But theses do not take away from the strength and utility of her systematically structured account. They are mentioned here only to encourage the author to pursue further her study of

Indian democracy in a different direction so that this study will acquire a sharper edge and substance. Her writing is clear and analytically incisive, and it is indicative of a fresh and lively mind at work.

An interesting sociological dimension of her work is that she represents a new breed of scholars—women with a double mind, saddled with the twin responsibilities of being a housewife and a scholar. Though it is not yet visible in this work, this kind of new scholarship is bound to make a qualitative difference reflecting the sensibilities of women as scholars in a predominantly male-dominated landscape of our scholarship. While congratulating Alaknanda for her thoughtful and useful contribution to Indian political science, I must also unhesitatingly commend the supportive role of her family—her husband, her parents and her child.

6 April 2007,
Dharwad.

K. Raghavendara Rao
Retired Professor of Political Science
Mangalore University

Preface

India is passing through critical phase of crisis of governability. One of the main causes for this crisis is party politics. Concepts like governance, good governance, e-governance, etc., became buzz words in the 90s. However, no indepth study was made to understand the impact of party politics on democratic governance. Thus the need was felt to examine the role of party politics in determining democratic governance. Governance mainly deals with how power is exercised. If it is exercised in the interest of the people it is called democratic governance. People and political parties are two main centers of power in democratic governance. This study examines how these two power centers influence each other and in turn affect democratic governance.

The present study seeks to examine the relation between party politics and democratic governance in terms of participation and responsiveness. This study not only includes political parties' participation and responsiveness but also deals with popular participation and responsiveness. Role of people is significant in ensuring democratic governance. Political parties are intermediaries between people and government, and are crucial to democracy. They are controlled by the people. However, we cannot deny the fact that the primary aim of political parties is to capture power. Power politics had affected the functioning of political parties and thereby the quality of democratic governance. Thus there is an urgent need to study the impact of party politics on democratic governance and the present study is an attempt towards this.

I wish to express my gratitude to various individuals institutions, libraries and friends, who have helped me to complete this work.

At the outset, I extend my deep sense of gratitude to my guide, Dr. S.S. Patagundi, Professor and Chairman, Department of Political Science, Karnataka University, Dharwad, for his able guidance, constant encouragement and generous help, throughout the completion of my research work as well as during publication of this book.

I extend my sincere thanks to Dr. K. Raghavendra Rao, Professor of Political Science (retired), Mangalore University, Dr. K.S. Sharma, Principal (Retired), Sakri Law College, Hubli and Prof. S.N. Sangeeta, Professor and Head, Development Administration Unit, Institute for Social and Economic Change, Bangalore, for giving me their valuable suggestions and advice. I am thankful to the teachers in the Department of Political Science, Karnataka University, Dharwad, for their kind and active co-operation.

I thankfully acknowledge the assistance and co-operation of the members of the staff of the following libraries: Jawaharlal Nehru University, New Delhi, Parliament Library, New Delhi, Teen Murti Library, New Delhi, Indian Institute of Public Administration, New Delhi, Delhi University Library and ISEC Institute. I am also grateful to the librarian and the staff of Karnataka University Library for their help and co-operation in collecting data for my study. I also thank Karnataka University for giving me the permission to publish my thesis.

I would like to thank the Secretariats of the following political parties: Indian National Congress, Bharatiya Janata Party, Communist Party of India and Communist Party of India (Marxist).

I express my deep sense of gratitude to my colleagues, Sanjeev Kumar H.M., Subhash Patil, and V.B. Patil, Teacher fellows. I am helpful to Butani family and Smt. Maduri, for their co-operation while collecting data for my study.

I am grateful to my mother Sindhu and father Arvind Mandavkar who were a source of inspiration and encouragement for completing this work. I am also grateful to my in-laws Kamal and Pundalik Shringare, my brothers Abhijit, Amit and Pramod and my son Dhananjay for their co-operation. I would like to convey special thanks to my husband Pravin without whose help, cooperation and moral support it would not have been possible for me to complete my work.

A.P. Shringare

Contents

List of Tables

List of Abbreviations

AD	Akali Dal
AGP	Assam Gana Parishad
AIADMK	All India Anna Dravid Munnetra Khazgham
AIMC	All India Milli Congress
AITC	All India Trade Congress
BC	Backward Class
BJD	Biju Janata Dal
BJP	Bharatiya Janata Party
BJS	Bharatiya Jana Sangh
BSP	Bahujan Samajwadi Party
CPI	Communist Party of India
CPI (M)	Communist Party of India (Marxist)
DMK	Dravid Munnetra Khazgham
FB	Forward Block
FBL	Forward Block (Leninist)
FC	Forward Class
GP	Ganatantra Parishad
HM	Hindu Mahasabha
HVP	Haryana Vikas Party
INC	Indian National Congress
INC (T)	Indian National Congress (Tiwari)
IUML	Indian Union Muslim League
JD (U)	Janata Dal (United)
JKPDP	Jammu-Kashmir People's Democratic Party
JMM	Jharkhand Mukti Morcha
JP	Janata Party
JS	Jana Sangh
KEC	Kerala Congress
KMPP	Kisan Mazdoor Praja Party
LF	Left Front

LS	Lok Shakti
LSS	Lok Sevak Sangh
MBC	Most Backward Class
MDMK	Murumalarchi Dravid Munnetra Kazhgam
ML	Muslim League
MNF	Mizo National Front
MUL	Muslim Union League
NC	National Congress
NCP	National Congress Party
NDA	National Democratic Alliance
NF	National Front
NGO	Non Governmental Organisation
PMK	Puttali Makkal Kachi
PSP	Praja Socialist Party
PWP	Peasants and Workers Dal
RJD	Rashtriya Janata Dal
RJP	Rashtriya Janata Party
RLD	Rashtriya Lok Dal
RP	Republican Party
RPI	Republican Party of India
RPI (A)	Republican Party of India (Ambedkarite)
RRP	Ram Rajya Parishad
RSP	Rashtriya Samajwadi Party
RSP	Republican Socialist Party
RSS	Rashtriya Swayamsevak Sangh
SAD	Shiromani Akali Dal
SC	Scheduled Caste
SHS	Shiv Sena
SP	Socialist Party
SP	Samajwadi Party
SP	Samata Party
SSP	Samajwadi Socialist Party
ST	Scheduled Tribe
TC	Trinmool Congress
TDP	Telugu Desam Party
TMC	Tamil Manila Congress
UF	United Front
UPA	United Progressive Alliance

1

Introduction

Generally, democracy is accepted as the best form of government. In the words of Bryce, the most significant change in the last hundred years was the universal acceptance of democracy as the normal and natural form of government.[1] One of the main reasons for the popularity of democracy is the importance given to the people in the working of the government.

The primary aim of democracy is the welfare of the people. A democratic government has to function in the interest of the people. However, the main concern in this context is how a democratic government responds to the expectations of its people. A democratic government can fulfil the aspirations of the people through the political institutions like pressure groups, political parties, parliament, etc. A political party is one of the important institutional mechanisms available to the people through which they can best represent their interests and preferences. A political party is a channel between the people and policy makers. They are responsible for identifying policy alternatives.

Governance is defined as the manner in which 'power is exercised' in the management of the country's economic and social resources.[2] The primary concern of democratic governance is the welfare of the people. Political parties play a significant role in the governance of a country, for they are responsible for democratizing the process of governance. The interest and aspirations of the people are given preference in the policy making by the political parties. For democratic governance to be effective, there should be a good reciprocal relationship between government and people and this relationship is established by political parties. Thus, political parties play a significant role in democratic governance.

Statement of the Problem

Direct democracy is not workable today because of the vast size of the modern state. This has paved the way for the introduction of indirect or representative democracy. Political parties play a crucial role in indirect democracy, for among all the institutions, political parties are important and best available institutional mechanism to the people through which they can represent their interests and aspirations in an effective manner. Schattschneider declares that: "The only kind of organization that can translate into fact the idea of majority rule is the political party".[3] Political parties are necessary in order to organize and represent public opinion. Thus, political party is an institution, which expresses popular preferences.

In the words of Maurice Duverger, "Political parties are communities with general aims: they provide complete and coherent systems of thought about society; they aim at a total organization of national and even international life. This breadth of aim drives away from them many people who agree with them about some particular aim but not about the whole".[4] Giovanni Sartori thinks, "parties are instrumental to collective benefits, to an end that is not merely the private benefit of the contestants. Parties link people to a government...."[5] A political party is a part of the whole attempting to serve the purpose of the whole. It plays a significant role in democratic governance because the aim of democratic governance can be realized mainly through political parties.

The role of political parties in democratic governance is mainly classified into two forms, i.e., political parties' participation and their responsiveness. How political parties participate and the methods and techniques they adopt to win elections is crucial to understand. Contesting an election, campaigning, interest articulation and interest aggregation are some of the important functions of political parties. By performing these functions political parties participate in democratic governance. They are responsible for articulating and aggregating the interest of the people. They formulate the general policies and programmes based on which they contest elections. After getting power, it is the duty of a political party to put into practice the promised policies and programmes on which it contested and won an election. An effective responsiveness of a political party towards the interest and aspirations of the people determines democratic governance. The interest and aspirations of the people should be reflected in the policy making of political parties. The nature of party politics affects both political parties' participation and responsiveness. The party politics is nothing but an interaction among parties on different issues, policies and programmes. The style of functioning of the parties affects the party politics.

A study of political parties is crucial in this regard, which is incomplete without the study of political parties' participation and responsiveness. The two concepts, participation and responsiveness, are crucial for a proper understanding of the role of political parties in democratic governance. Thus both participation and responsiveness of political parties are equally important in democratic governance. It is through political parties' participation that the interests and aspirations of the people are articulated and aggregated. Based on the aggregated interests, political parties respond to various needs of the people, which, in turn, contribute to democratic governance.

Understanding popular participation and popular responsiveness is equally important in democratic governance because people play a crucial role in democracy. Popular participation and popular responsiveness strengthen democratic governance. People are responsible for electing their representatives. An active participation of the people may be an important indicator of their awareness about policies, programmes and promises made by different political parties. The act of understanding the means through which people participate in the political process is crucial in democratic governance.

Once the elections are over, generally the people hardly play any role. However, to ensure accountability of the political parties and to make them responsive towards the needs and interests of the people popular responsiveness is very essential. A democratic governance can be made meaningful by empowering, enlightening and engaging citizens in the process of self-governance.

Both political parties' participation and popular participation and political parties' responsiveness and popular responsiveness play a significant role in democratic governance because, a political party is an intermediate between the people and the government and the people are the soul of democracy. Without an involvement of people there is no democracy and a political party is one of the best available institutional mechanisms for the people to represent their will. For democratic governance to prevail, there should be a healthy interaction between these two. Political parties cannot claim significance over the people in democracy as they are accountable to the people and people need political parties for the best representation of their will. It is through the political parties that most of the people involve themselves in the process of governance.

Parliamentary form of government has been adopted in India after independence. As we know, political parties play a vital role in a parliamentary form of government. Without political parties parliamentary government is impossible.

In this study, an attempt is made to examine the nature of party politics in determining democratic governance in India. For this purpose, study of political parties' participation and responsiveness and popular participation and responsiveness during and after elections is very pertinent.

The present study is confined to the period from 1989 to 2004 mainly for two reasons. In the first place, before 1989 the problem of democratic governance did not attract much attention. The concept of governance was popularized during the 80s. In the second place, to make an in-depth analysis of the problem this study intends to confine its scope to the coalition era from 1989 to 2004.

Review of Literature

In recent years, the study of democratic governance acquired significance among the political scientists. Moreover, the study of democratic governance will not be complete without the study of party politics. Party politics determines democratic governance. It is through political parties that people participate in the government. Political parties give proper representation to the will of the people.

Indian Politics

Myron Weiner's book, *The Indian Paradox: Essays in Indian Politics*, covers four groups of essays on Indian politics. The first group of essays are the interplay between the violent struggle among India's linguistic, religious, caste and tribal communities and India's political institutions. He has also tried to explain why Indian democracy has thrived in spite of these ethnic conflicts and why management of conflict has become more difficult with the decline of the Congress Party organization and the weakening of federal structure. The central theme of the second group of essays are on public policies. It also studies the interrelationship of ideas and interests in shaping agricultural, industrial and preferential policies. The third section highlights Indira Gandhi's overwhelming electoral victory in 1971 following the split within the party. This section also deals with the determinants of political participation, the social bases of voter alignments and the emergence of two party system organized regional and ethnic identities. The fourth section describes the changes that have taken place in the mid-70s, making governance more centralized eroding the federal system. This section also deals with the reforms initiated by Rajiv Gandhi in later years. What has strengthened democratic institutions and what is the potential threat to these institutions is the subject of concluding essay.

V.A. Paipanandikar and S.C. Kashyap edited *Political Reforms: Asserting Civic Sovereignty* which is the result of the research conducted by Centre for Policy Research on political reforms. This book covers subjects like structural reforms of electoral system, multilevel governance, criminalization, communalization, casteism, corruption, popular control, poor administration, illiteracy, unrepresentative character of legislators, flaws in the organization and functioning of political parties and electoral law and processes, instability of government, etc. The first section of this book represents the study conducted on policy options in different areas undertaken by a group of eminent scholars and the second section provides the necessary and feasible political reform agenda and the desirable shifts in policies and priorities pursued by the state.

Anil Kumar Jana edited *Indian Politics at the Crossroads* which highlights nature and magnitude of India's political problems. The issues dealt with in this book by various scholars are: coalition politics, India's federal policy, regionalism in India, women's movements, electoral reforms, governability of contemporary India and participatory governance. This book also examines diversities of issues and concerns dealing with the basic problems of democratic governance.

C.P. Bhambhari, in his book *Indian Politics Since Independence*, focused his attention on political parties, federalism, the institutions of governance, the material foundation of Indian politics and the reality of global and Indian political economy. While discussing the roles of Pandit Jawaharlal Nehru, Indira Gandhi and political parties and social classes, the ideological issues of Indian politics like secularism have been analysed. This book is basically concerned with the problems of social transition through the active involvement of the Indian state.

Parth Chatterjee edited *State and Politics in India* which provides general introduction to the study of politics in contemporary India. It covers a wide range of subjects like parties and party system in India, centre-state relations, evolving trends in bureaucracy, local politics in India, India's minorities and women's issues, mainly violence against women.

Political Participation

R.P. Verma has edited a book entitled *People's participation in Indian Politics*, which deals with the concept of political participation and different modes of participation in general. It also studies the impact of social change on political participation of Indian masses in particular. It discusses voting behaviour as an expression of democratic system. The work examines the role of people in political development. Its emphasis is on people's role in Indian democratic system.

The main aim of Carole Pateman in *Participation and Democratic Theory* is to show that current elitist theories are based on an inadequate understanding of the writings of earlier democratic theories, that much relevant sociological evidence has been ignored and that the notion of participation still has vitally important place in a modern theory of democracy. Pateman examines theories of Schumpeter, Berelson, Dahl, Sartori, Eckstein, showing that they have misrepresented earlier writers. She then discusses the theories of Rousseau, J.S. Mill and G.D.H. Cole on the role of citizens' participation in a democratic political system. Chapter 3 and 4 relate the availability of empirical evidence to the traditional idea that participation is psychologically and educationally valuable and emphasize the importance of education in the process of political socialization. She concluded by discussing the impact of the empirical evidence on recent democratic theory and the extent to which it supports an alternative, participatory theory.

Governance

Goran Hyden and Michael Bratton have edited a book *Governance and Politics in Africa*. The main highlight of the book is on governance and politics in Africa but Goran Hyden in Chapter I discussed governance and related concepts and basic dimensions of the concept of governance like compliance, trust, accountability and innovation. He has also discussed the governance realm which according to him are bounded by four properties: authority, reciprocity, trust and accountability. He has talked about three principal empirical dimensions of governance: citizen influence and oversight, responsive and responsible leadership and social reciprocities. He has discussed governance in different regime types.

Mukesh Jain's book, *Excellence in Government—A Blueprint for Reinventing the Government*, aims at seeking a government that works for the people, cleared of useless bureaucracy and waste and freed from redtapism and senseless rules. The work focuses on providing effective governance through bureaucracy. A government's helplessness in providing basic needs and the people's expectations are examined in lucid language in part I, II, and III.

The work is meticulous in identifying the defects in government bureaucracy and suggests ways and means for improvement of the quality of management. It is a handbook and an excellent manual for managers interested in reinventing modern bureaucracies.

Laurence E. Lynn in his book, *Improving Governance: A New Logic For Empirical Research*, explains that policy makers and public managers around the world have become preoccupied with the question of how their goals can be achieved in a way that rebuilds public confidence in government. Yet, because of public policies and programmes which are being administered through a complicated web of jurisdiction, agencies and public private partnerships, evaluating their effectiveness is more difficult than in the past. Though social scientists possess insightful theories and powerful methods for conducting empirical research on governance and public management, their work is too often fragmented and irrelevant to the specific tasks faced by legislators, administrators and managers. Laurence E. Lynn, Jr., Carolyn J. Heinrich, and Carolyn J. Hill argue that theory-based empirical research when well-conceived and executed can be a primary source of fundamental, durable knowledge about governance and policy management. Focusing on complex human services such as public education they construct an integrative, multilevel "logic of governance", for the sophistication of power and relevance of their work.

Democracy and Governance

Atul Kohli's book on *Democracy and Discontent: India's Growing Crisis of Governability* attempts to understand growing crisis of governability in India. This study analyzes political changes that have occurred during the period of Indira Gandhi and Rajiv Gandhi from the late 1960s to the late 1980s. The material for the study was mainly gathered through the fieldwork in India in 1985 and 1986. Five districts were chosen as the units for understanding regional diversities at the local level. The districts chosen were the same, which were studied by Myron Weiner in his work, *Party Building in a New Nation: The Indian National Congress,* during early and middle 1960s. The reason for selecting the same districts may be to study the subsequent developments.

Atul Kohli concluded that the problem of governability at the centre was mainly based on local and national level trends. Atul Kohli attempts to explain how political process has been involved in the erosion of India's established pattern of authority.

S.K. Chopra edited a work, *Towards Good Governance*, which starts with an overview by three eminent public figures on their concepts and views on *Towards Good Governance*. This book mainly highlights the views of eminent personalities on the meaning of good governance, structural changes needed for good governance, the myths of good governance. Kishore Gandhi has given new meaning and models of good governance. This book also deals with constitutional aspects of good governance, the impact of political executives, administration and decentralization and science and technology on governance.

The literature mentioned above also reveals the fact that governance can be used in different contexts like administration, bureaucracy, politics, etc. The works examined above are confined to the role of bureaucracy in good governance, meaning and significance of governance; they provide insight on different aspects of governance, overview by eminent public figures, etc. They also highlight the significance of people's participation in Indian politics.

However, the above works indicate the research lacuna in respect of the role of political parties in democratic governance. There is a need to study the role of party politics in democratic governance because party politics plays an important role in democratic governance. The nature of party politics determines democratic governance. Therefore, it is necessary to examine the role of party politics in democratic governance.

Inter-relationship between Concepts

Party Politics and Democratic Governance

Democratic governance presupposes governance in the interest of people. Political parties are the means through which the interests and aspirations of the people are represented. Political parties are responsible for democratizing public policies. The role of political parties in democratic governance is determined by the means by which they participate in elections and respond to the interest of people by formulating public policies, laws, and the like.

The nature of interaction among political parties affects the nature of public policy formulation. Political parties are basic institutions for the translation of mass preferences into public policy.[6] While formulating public policy consensus building is very essential, it is also essential for maintaining stability and continuity in public policy. Here consensus does not mean just a uniformity of behaviour or total agreement. As it gives scope for debate and discussion, it strengthens democratic element of a political system. How political parties interact with one another to build consensus while formulating public policies is crucial for democratic governance.

The interactions among political parties can be classified mainly into two types: (1) intra-party interaction, and (2) inter-party interaction. Intra-party interaction means the interaction within a political party. Intra-party interaction is one of the important features of multi-party system. In multi-party system primarily due to the presence of a large number of political parties, often government formation by a single party becomes very difficult. Political parties have to ally themselves with one or more parties to form government. Most of the time, parties organize themselves under one common name and formulate a manifesto of their party, which is generally known as Common Minimum Programme. In this type of government (coalition government), political parties have to arrive at two types of consensus, namely, consensus on formulating Common Minimum Programme and consensus on formulating public policies. As parties in coalition government have their own ideologies, principles, policies and programmes, their arriving at consensus on issues of public importance is very difficult. Most of the time, their consensus is not based on any principle or value. Instead compulsion of sharing power may be the main reason for their arriving at consensus.

Equally important is the act of arriving at consensus in inter-party interactions. Inter-party interaction means the interaction among different political parties. However, having consensus among coalition partners is not enough for formulating public policies. The ruling party has to take into confidence the opposition parties for the effective formulation of public policies. Jawaharlal Nehru was successful in developing political consensus. The charismatic leadership of Jawaharlal Nehru and his style of functioning influenced substantially the interaction patterns among the parties in evolving consensus on most issues in public affairs.[7] He used to take both his party men and the leaders of opposition into confidence. One must say that the new political style which emerged after his death affected the process of consensus. The confrontation style of politics introduced by Mrs. Indira Gandhi led to the breakdown of consensual politics. When Rajiv Gandhi became the Prime Minister there was a ray of hope for the revival of consensus building. Though he made a good beginning, his style of functioning was almost like Mrs. Indira Gandhi's. In the post-Nehru era no government was totally successful in building consensus on public affairs.

Political parties have to observe certain norms for arriving at consensus. It is said, "Observance of certain norms for actors in the political process is a question of their orientation. One of the norms would be the subordination of the partisan approaches to the public policy issues in the interest of the people".[8] This democratic character of party politics makes its study crucial in democratic governance. Proper functioning of political parties is important for democratic governance. Thus, there is a close relationship between party politics and democratic governance.

The democratic style of working is crucial at arriving at a consensus on public policy issues. Moreover, formulation and implementation of public policy determines democratic governance. If political parties fail to arrive at consensus on public policy making the next best available method is majority principle. However, the majority principle is not as democratic as consensus. Consensus building is mainly dependent upon the nature of party politics. Thus party politics became one of the important determinants of democratic governance.

Participation and Responsiveness and Party Politics

Democracy presupposes party government. Without political parties there is no democracy. Political parties' main aim is to capture power. It is essential to understand how political parties participate and the methods they adopt to win elections. Every party tries to be the party of the masses, which works for the interest of the whole community. Usually political parties' interaction was formed in the form of allegations and counter allegations during the elections. Every political party mainly highlights the defects of other parties and the strength of its own party to attract voters.

The significant role played by voters in elections makes popular participation more important. Without popular participation, there is no meaning to the political parties' participation. Political parties are participating in order to attract the voters and ultimately to get power.

Popular participation makes party politics more active. Popular participation is mainly based on the way in which political parties approach the people. Participation of people is crucial for democracy. Of course, participation of the people in government is not direct. Modern democracy is based not on participation but on representation; it presupposes not direct exercise of power but delegation of power; it is not, in short, a system of self-government but a system of control and limitation of government.[9] Whatever be the mode of participation, popular political participation is essential in democracy.

After the elections, a majority party forms the government and minority party sits in opposition. Whether the parties are in the ruling or in the opposition, they are mainly the representatives of the people. They formulate public policies on behalf of the people. Therefore, their main aim while formulating public policies should be the welfare of people. Usually the ruling party or parties formulate the proposals of legislations and introduced them in the parliament. Here the role of opposition party is not less important in formulating policies. While formulating a public policy, the ruling party has to take into consideration the views and opinions of the other parties also.

Democratization of a public policy is mainly based on the nature of party politics. Both intra-party interaction and inter-party interaction play an important role in democratizing the policy making process. The responsiveness of political parties is evaluated based on the kind of policies formulated and their effective implementation. This mainly determines political parties' responsiveness.

An effective formulation of public policy is crucial in determining political parties' responsiveness. Congress under the leadership of Jawaharlal Nehru succeeded in arriving at both inter-party and intra-party consensus. This contributed as one of the important reasons for the effective responsiveness of Congress party towards the aspirations of the people. In the Indian context, the presence of leftist, centrist and rightist parties in parliament can be one of the reasons for the difficulties in arriving at consensus on basic policy decisions. Leftist parties in India uphold Marxist ideology. Their bend is mainly towards the upliftment of working class and minorities. For example, CPI, CPI (M) and Forward Bloc are the leftist parties. The centrist bend is in both ways. For example, Congress (I), which is considered the centrist party. The rightist parties inclination is more towards maintaining the *status quo* for capturing power. An example for this is the BJP. Every party has its own policies, programmes, principles, etc. In view of this, both inter-party interaction and intra-party interaction play an important role in arriving at consensus on any policy, which affects political parties responsiveness.

Feedback is essential for any policy decision making. Popular responsiveness can be a good feedback for policy decisions. Based on the feedback the existing policies can be altered or refined. In fact, popular responsiveness makes political parties more responsive towards people's interests. Thus, popular responsiveness contributes for the accountability and transparency, which are considered as the important prerequisites for democratic governance.

Conceptual Framework

Before proceeding to the discussion on the effect of party politics on the democratic governance in India an examination of the definition of various key concepts is necessary to understand their relevance to the present study.

Party

The term 'Party' is derived from the Latin word 'Partier', which means to share or divide. According to Giovanni Sartori, "A party is any political group that presents at elections, is capable of placing through elections, candidates for public office".[10]

According to the Dictionary of Social Science edited by Julius Gould and William Kolb, "A definition embracing all phenomenon that are regularly called party in this age is a difficult task unless it be reduced to its most general form, i.e., a party is a group framing general issues and putting forward candidates in elections".[11]

To Edmund Burke, "Party is a body of men united for promoting by their joint endeavours the national interest upon some particular principles in which they are all agreed".[12]

To E.J. Meehan, J.P. Roche and M.S. Stedman Jr., "In the simplest possible, a political party is an association whose goal is the acquisition of political power".[13]

Alan Ware defines political party as, "an institution that (a) seeks influence in a state, often by attempting to occupy positions in government, and (b) usually consists of more than a single interest in the society and so to some degree attempting to 'aggregate interests'".[14]

Politics

According to the Webster's New Twentieth Century Dictionary, politics means "prudent and sagacious in devising and pursuing measures."

To Avery Leiserson, "In dynamic manipulative terms, politics includes all the arts and processes of governance." [15]

According to Robert Dhal, "Politics, in its broadest sense, is concerned with the distribution of advantages and disadvantages among people".[16]

According to D.C. Pavate, "Politics is a game of capturing political power for the purpose of running the machinery of government in accordance with the definite and specific policy concerned".[17]

Party Politics

According to the Standard Dictionary of English Language, party politics is "politics engaged by, expressed through the medium of, or considered from the view point of political parties as distinguished from other interests (as geographical sections or economic classes)".

The Dictionary meaning of party politics is, "Political acts and principles directed towards the interest of one political party or its members without reference to the common good".

Responsiveness

According to Webster's New Twentieth Century Dictionary, "responsiveness is the quality or state of being responsive".

To Roland Pennock, "Responsiveness might be said to be the counterpart of influence. The person or group that influences is influential; the person or group on whom it is exerted is responsive".[18]

Political Participation

To David L. Sills, "Political participation will refer to those voluntary activities by which members of a society share in the selection of rulers and, directly or indirectly, in the formation of public policy".[19]

To Myron Weiner, "Some people define participation as only those acts of citizens that are defined by law as legitimate-voting, demonstrating, petitioning, lobbying, etc.,—excluding illegitimate actions. But in contrast, some radicals see illegal acts such as civil disobedience and other forms of mass confrontation as the only genuine acts of participation in a democracy."[20]

Democracy

Kenneth Janda, Jeffery M. Berry and Jerry Goldman, argued that, democracy, which means "authority in, or by, the people".[21]

According to Guy Hermet, "Democracy is not a type of society but is, more restrictively, a type of political system".[22]

To Samuel P. Huntington, "democracy exists where the principal leaders of a political system are selected by competitive elections in which the bulk of the population have the opportunity to participate".[23]

Governance

According to the Webster's Dictionary of the English Language, governance means control or authority.

According to the Oxford English Dictionary (1961) "Governance means to direct and control the actions and affairs (of the people, a state or its members) whether despotically or constitutionally. It also defines governance as the action or manner of governing or controlling, directing or regulating."

Party Politics and Democratic Governance

Democratic governance is mainly affected by the nature of party politics. Politics being an ancient part of human activity has been in existence since times immemorial. People have used the word politics in different languages to indicate an activity which implies the use of power by some people in favour of others or against others.[24] Aristotle's "Politics" is considered as first work on politics. Kautilya's "Arthashastra" puts forward the basic principles of politics. Religious works like the Bible, the Kuran, the Ramayana, the Mahabharata, etc., contain valuable political ideas and suggestions of various types.

According to Aristotle, politics was the affairs of the state. To Aristotle state was generally a city-state with small territory and less population where direct democracy could be practiced. However, slaves and foreigners were excluded from taking part into the affairs of the state. Thinkers like Polibius, Cicero, St. Augustine, Thomas Aquinas and others with some variations upheld the theme of Aristotelian thought. "Machiavelli's concept of politics can be described as politics of tricks and strategies for attaining one's goals or purposes. The contractualist looks upon politics as a matter of instituting a sovereign, ensuring law and order and ensuring a medium of peace and well-being of the people concerned. Hegel, Bosanquet, Green and Bradley represented the idealist traditions in politics".[25]

In the present study, party politics is used in the sense of interaction among political parties. Party politics is one of the important determinants of democratic governance. Intra-party politics and inter-party politics play a crucial role in the whole process of interest articulation and interest aggregation. Democratic governance is mainly concerned with how best the interests of the people are articulated and aggregated through the political parties. As political parties are crucial for democratic governance, participation and responsiveness of political parties are equally important.

Popular participation and responsiveness are crucial for democracy. To make political parties more responsive towards peoples' interests and aspirations, people should regularly participate in the affairs of governance and should be alert and vigilant. The quality, efficiency and effectiveness of these institutions of governance depend on the interest the citizens take in their institutions of governance.[26] Responsiveness of the people towards policy decisions makes political parties more responsive towards peoples' demands. Responsiveness of people tends to increase political parties' responsiveness and in turn contributes to democratic governance.

Objectives

The following are the objectives of the present study:

1. To understand democratic governance in India.
2. To examine linkage between political parties and democratic governance.
3. To analyze popular political participation and political parties participation in democratic politics.
4. To critically examine popular political responsiveness towards common issues of public importance and policy decisions of government and political parties' responsiveness to the aspirations of the people.

Political parties play a crucial role in the functioning of democratic political system. They represent the aspirations of the people. The responsiveness of political parties towards people is determined by the popular responsiveness towards issues of public importance and policy decisions of government. To understand democratic politics in

India a study of popular participation and political parties participation, and popular responsiveness and political parties responsiveness is essential.

Hypothesis

This study seeks to verify the following hypotheses:

1. Popular political participation in the democratic governance is not satisfactory due to the kind of party politics that prevail in India.
2. Popular political responsiveness adversely affects political parties responsiveness to fulfil the aspirations of the people.

Methodology

The methodology adopted in the study is mainly documentary. The data used in the study are from both primary and secondary sources. This study is based on primary sources of the data like party documents. Besides, this study is mainly based on secondary sources of the data like books, journals and newspaper clippings available in some of the leading libraries of India.

The Outline of the Present Study

The study is divided into seven chapters. The first chapter covers the statement of the problem and discusses the overview of literature, interrelationship between concepts, conceptual framework, objectives of the study, hypothesis, methodology and outline of the present study.

The second chapter examines the theoretical aspects of democracy, political parties, political participation and responsiveness.

The third chapter is dealing with the role of party politics in democratic governance. How best political parties are representing the aspirations of the people and also to find out the effect of party politics on democratic governance in India.

The fourth chapter mainly deals with political parties perception of governance.

In the fifth chapter, the focus is mainly on popular political participation and political parties participation in Indian politics.

The sixth chapter is concerned with popular responsiveness towards common issues of public importance and policy decisions of government and political parties responsiveness towards the aspirations of the people.

In the seventh chapter, the arguments of the study are summed up.

REFERENCES

1. Navin Chandra Joshi (ed.), *Democracy and Human Value,* Sterling Publishers Private Limited, New Delhi, 1979, p. 1.
2. Dilip Halder, Democratic Governance is no Panacea: The Experience of India and South Asia, *Indian Journal of Public Administration, 50(1)*, January-March 2004, p. 195.
3. Giovanni Sartori, *Parties and Party System: A Framework for Analysis,* Cambridge University Press, Cambridge, 1976, p. 28.
4. Maurice Duverger, *Political Parties,* Methuen and Company Limited, London, 1954, p. 107.
5. Giovanni Sartori, Supra no. 3, p. 25.
6. Giovanni Sartori, Supra no. 3, p. 28.
7. R.T. Jangam, S.H. Patil and S. S. Patagundi, *Political Analysis,* Oxford and IBH Publishing Company Private Limited, New Delhi, 1997, p. 156.
8. *Ibid.*, p. 158.
9. David L. Sills (ed.), *International Encyclopedia of Social Science,* MacMillan Company and The Free Press, Vol. 4, America, p. 115.
10. Giovanni Sartori, Supra no. 3, p. 64.
11. Julius Gould and William L. Kolb (ed.), *A Dictionary of Social Science*, The Free Press, New York, 1969, p. 482.
12. Edmund Burke, *Thoughts on the Causes of the Present Discontent (1770)*, in Louis L. Breduold and Ralph G. Ross (eds.), *The Philosophy of Edmund Burke*, University of Michigan Press, Ann Arbor, 1960, p. 134.
13. E.J. Meehan, J.P. Roche and M.S. Stedman Jr., *The Dynamics of Modern Government*, MacGraw Hill Book Company, New York, 1966, p. 28.
14. Alan Ware, *Political Parties and Party Systems*, Oxford University Press, New York, 1996, p. 5.
15. Avery Leiserson, *Parties and Politics,* Alfred A. Knopf Inc., New York, 1958, p. 4.
16. Robert A. Dhal and Dean E. Neubauer, *Reading in Modern Political Analysis,* Prentice-Hall, New Jersey, 1968, p. 33.
17. N.C. Sahani (ed.), *Coalition Politics in India,* New Academic Publishing Company, Jallandhar, 1971, p. 124.

18. J.R. Pennock, *Democratic Political Theory*, Princeton University Press, Princeton, 1979, p. 261.
19. David L. Sills (ed.), Supra no. 9, p. 252.
20. Myron Weiner, *Political Participation: Crisis of the Political Process*, in Leonard Binder and Other (contributors), *Crisis and Sequences in Political Development*, Addison Wesley Publishing Company, London, 1975, p. 1.
21. Kenneth Janda, Jeffery M. Berry and Jerry Goldman, *The Challenges of Democracy: Government in America*, Houghton Mifflin Company, Boston, 1992, p. 36.
22. Guy Hermet, Introduction: the age of Democracy, *International Social Science Journal*, 43(2), May 1991, p. 252.
23. Samuel P. Huntington's definition quoted in Guy Hermet, The Age of Democracy, *International Social Science Journal*, 43(2), May 1991, p. 252.
24. R.T. Jangam, S.H. Patil and S.S. Patagundi, Supra no. 7, p. 1.
25. *Ibid.*, p. 6.
26. Subhash C. Kashyap (ed.), *National Resurgence Through Electoral Reforms*, Shipra Publications, Delhi, 2002, p. 99.

2

Democratic Governance: Some Theoretical Issues

Theories of Democracy

Throughout history, men have grappled with the idea as to what is the best form of government. In quest of this ideal, they evolved different modes of governing themselves.[1] Most of the modes of government evolved contain in them some seeds of tyranny. Ultimately democracy is accepted in most of the countries as the best form of government.

Democracy has travelled through different stages of history. With every stage, a new concept of democracy was evolved and with it developed a new theory of democracy, which in turn enriched the subject of democracy. Few concepts in political theory are so enmeshed in controversy over scope and definition, as is the concept of democracy.[2]

Classical Theory of Democracy

The word democracy originated in the Greek writings around the fifth century B.C. 'Demos' referred to the common people, the masses; 'Kratos' meant 'power'.[3]

The democratic theory originated in Greek political thought. Greek thinkers, had placed democracy in the perverted form of government. Plato decried democracy because the people were not properly equipped with education "to select the best rulers and the wisest courses."[4] Aristotle placed democracy among perverted forms since it signified the rule of the mediocre seeking their selfish interests, not the interest of the state.[5] The theories of Plato and Aristotle had great influence on the subsequent theories. Classical theories of democracy were mainly concerned with the classification of government and possibilities of best form of governance. The theories of Hobbes, Locke, Rousseau and Montesquieu were important among them. They had given their own classification of governments for the sake of comparing different governments and to find out the best form of government among them and presented their own theories. The theories of these scholars were the product of their own time. Each thinker pleaded for a form of government which in their view is very pertinent to mankind and is described by them as democratic.

Direct versus Indirect Democracy

Direct democracy is one where citizens are taking direct part in the affairs of government. Direct democracy is possible in small and simple societies. These were in practice in Greek city-states. Though the theories of Hobbes, Locke and Rousseau were in favour of direct democracy, the theory of Rousseau is different from the theories of Hobbes and Locke. Rousseau though strongly advocated direct democracy, critically analyzed representative democracy. To Rousseau, "representative system is not democratic, because one's will can never be represented by another."[6] Philosopher Jean Jacques Rousseau contended that "true democracy is impossible unless all citizens gather together to make their own decisions and to supervise their government". Rousseau said that "decisions of government should embody the general will and 'will' cannot be represented."[7] He argued that in representative democracy people enjoy power only at the time of elections.

With the decline of city-states, there is also a gradual decline in the direct democracy and representative democracy is gaining prominence. It is obvious that the Greek style of democracy is inapplicable to modern conditions. Modern political societies are large societies, and the greater the number of the people involved, the less their participation can be effective and meaningful.[8] "While Greek democracy can be defined literally as a "government of the people over the people," modern democracy cannot be, for the people who are governed are not the same people who govern. Therefore, we should not be misled into believing that present-day "electoral participation" resembles the real participation of the Greek citizen and even less that the devices we call "direct democracy" (referendum, initiative, etc.,) can bridge the gap between the Greek and the modern formulas."[9] With this change from direct democracy to indirect democracy or representative democracy, there was also a gradual change in the theories of democracy.

Modern Theories of Democracy

With the emergence of representative democracy, political thinkers raised doubts about the success of democracy. In representative democracy, people's representatives formulate policies on behalf of the people. How far these representatives are successful in representing the interest of the people is the biggest question before the modern thinkers. A number of contemporary political theorists believe that we have come to rely too much on representative democracy and are now facing a weakening of citizenship of the sense of obligation to participate in civic life.[10] "At the beginning of the century the size and complexity of industrialized societies and the emergence of bureaucratic forms of organization seemed to many empirically minded writers on politics to cast grave doubts on the possibility of the attainment of democracy as that concept was usually understood. Mosca and Michels were two of the best known and most influential writers to advance such a thesis."[11] Both these scholars argue that in every society elites should govern. But, whether these elites especially political elites who are the chosen representatives of the people govern in the interest of the people or not is uncertain. If political elites take into consideration the interests and aspirations of the people, while formulating policies, that may lead to democratic governance.

To Shumpeter, "the basic problem of democracy is the need to institutionalize peaceful struggle among competing elites that offer the masses the opportunity to choose between alternative programmes even as they expose one another's weaknesses and failings."[12] Joseph Shumpeter and many others, both before and after him, were not wrong in regarding such a system as a mode of domination by elites.

As George Lavau has put it, "Democracy would develop as the autonomy of everyone and the autonomy of many different self-managed and ever expanding groups increased, there would be some who would always remain more active or skilful than the common run of citizens."[13]

However, given this largely unquestionable basis, the practical problem consists in measuring the degree of vulnerability or invulnerability of the ruling class in relation to the people who are required to express their approval or disapproval of it from time to time by their vote.[14] Dahl, though an advocate of Polyarchy, had critically analyzed representative democracy. According to him, elections are central to the democratic method because they provide the mechanism through which the control of leaders by non-leaders can take place; democratic theory is concerned with the process by which ordinary citizens exert relatively high degree of control over leaders.[15] When democracy operates through representatives its depth will depend partly upon the quality of the participation of the citizens in the election and partly upon the effectiveness of the influence of the constituents upon their representatives after election.[16]

"There are two major schools of thought about what constitutes democracy. The first believes democracy is a form of government. It emphasizes the procedures that enable the people to govern-mainly to discuss issues, voting in elections, running of public office. The second sees democracy in the *substance* of government policies, in freedom of religion and providing for human needs."[17]

The Procedural View of Democracy

"Procedural democratic theory sets forth principles that describe how government should make decisions. These principles address three distinct questions:

1. Who should participate in decision making?
2. How much should each participant's vote count?
3. How many votes are needed to reach a decision?"[18]

Who should participate in decision making?

According to the procedural democratic theory, all adults should take part in government decision making. Every citizen is allowed to participate in decision making. Only the foreigners, mentally retarded persons and those who are unfit to take decisions are excluded from participation. Procedural democratic theory is based on the principle of universal participation.

How much should each participant's vote count?

Universal participation is meaningless unless the vote of every citizen carries equal weight. There should not be such thing as votes of Prime Minister and other officials which carry more weight. Thus the second principle of procedural democratic theory is political equality.

How many votes are needed to reach decision?

"Procedural theory prescribes that a group should decide to do what the majority of its participants (50 per cent *plus* one person more) wants to do. This principle is called majority rule. (If participants divide over more than two alternatives and none receives a simple majority the principle usually defaults to plurality rule, in which the group should do what most participants want.)"[19] An article by Max Beloff in *The Fortnightly*, reached the striking conclusion that the time has come for a serious inquiry into the extent to which the principle 'of majority rule under a regime of universal suffrage is an adequate method of dealing with the ever more intricate and technical problems of a modern industrial society in a competitive world'.[20]

The three principles of procedural democratic theory, namely universal participation, political equality and majority rule are considered by many scholars as essential for democratic decision making. In small and simple societies like Greek city-states these principles can be met in a direct democracy. In representative democracy we adhere to these three principles to guarantee that elections are democratic. "But what happens after the election? The elected representatives might not make the same decisions the people would have made if they had gathered for the same purpose. To cope with this possibility in representative government, procedural theory gives us a fourth decision-making principle: responsiveness."[21] It is the duty of elected representatives to respond to the aspirations, demands and interest of the people. Democratic governance is concerned mainly with how best the representatives of the people will respond to the various demands of the people.

The Substantive View of Democracy

According to procedural democratic theory the decisions are based mainly on majority principle. But in some cases, for example, in case of India where the Hindu population is more, obviously more number of Hindu representatives are elected to the Parliament. There is possibility of Hindus claiming more benefits for the development of their own group sometimes at the cost of other groups. The substantive democratic theory claims an answer to this problem.

Substantive Democratic Theory

"Substantive democratic theory focuses on the substance of government policies, not on the procedures followed in making those policies. It argues that in a democratic government, certain principles must be embodied in government policies."[22] Substantive democratic theory stresses on taking into consideration civil liberties and rights while making decisions in democracy. But guaranteeing social rights and economic rights is also equally important in democracy. This divided the substantive theories into two groups namely conservative theorists and liberal theorists. "The political ideology of a theorist tends to explain his or her position on what democracy really requires in substantive policies. Conservative theorists have a narrow view of the scope of democratic government and a narrow view of the social and economic rights guaranteed by that government. Liberal theorist believe that democratic government should guarantee its citizens a much broader spectrum of social and economic rights."[23]

Liberal Theory of Democracy

For the liberals, "as they have been called since the term was first used in early nineteenth-century Spain—who in their scale of values put liberty first, democracy means institutions through which the freedom of the members of the politically organized community is realized. Liberal democracy is the correct expression with which to designate democracy as the organization of liberty."[24] Liberal Democracy may be taken to refer to the set of institutions—free elections, competing parties, freedom of speech—that make up the political system with which we are familiar in the West; or it may refer to the conception of democracy that underlies and justifies that system.[25] Equal liberty to all citizens is the main base of liberal democracy. According to the followers of liberal democracy this equality of liberties is guaranteed to the people through representative government. "It is the purpose of government, wrote Mill, to maximize the happiness of each individual. Men always act in their own interest as far as they know them, and getting them to know their interests is simply a matter of education, so the best assurance of good government is to give each man an equal share of political power, through the device of representative government."[26]

Believers in liberal democracy have generally given credence to the existence of a natural harmony of interests. "Like John Stuart Mill, they assumed that man was such a social animal, so sympathetic towards the needs and interests of others that—quite apart from consideration of "objective" right—he would be led to subordinate his special interests to the general welfare."[27]

Marxist Theory of Democracy

The followers of Marxist democracy criticize liberal democracy. "Marx himself believed in a natural social harmony. But for Marx this harmony of interests was something which could not be achieved as long as society permitted private ownership of the instruments of production."[28] Marxists believe that in every society there exist two classes, namely employees and workers, rich and poor, haves and have-nots and exploiters and exploited. As long as this distinction of class exists, democracy is not possible. Equality in some sense is basic to any conception of democracy.[29] In the long run the working class or the exploited class, which is in large number, revolts against the capitalist system. Furthermore it is held by followers of Marx that the revolution must be followed by the "dictatorship of the proletariat."[30] Ultimately, it leads to withering away of state where no class distinction exists, which leads to equality.

Elite Theory of Democracy

"The classical Elite Theory was at once anti-Marxist and anti-democratic for the elite theorists considered that both these values, democracy and equality, were not adequate to explain political phenomena. Historically, Elite Theory rose as a response to Marxism, a challenge to its ideology of equality. At the same time when Pareto and Mosca wrote, the liberal democratic political institutions seemed disintegrating."[31] Elites believe that in every society there exist some people who possess special qualities to govern. "According to Mosca, societies are ruled by minorities, by oligarchies and there is a ruling minority which holds power. The ruling minority justifies its rule by certain theories or principles which are acceptable to those who are ruled."[32] Thus, according to the elite theory, in every society we find two classes of people. First, the class that rules and second, the class that ruled. "The first class, always the less numerous, performs all political functions, monopolizes power and enjoys the advantages which power brings, whereas the second, the more numerous class, is directed and controlled by the first, in a manner that is now more or less legal, now more or less arbitrary and violent."[33] However, there is always a change in the ruling class, which is called by Pareto as circulation of elites. Pareto refers to circulation of elites which means the process according to which one elite is replaced by another.[34] "In an ideal society such changes would take place peacefully and not be accompanied by vast social upheaval-the demise of one governing elite and the rise of another usually meant the replacement of one dominant type of individual by another (Foxes by lions or *vice versa*) as the old regime had become too rigid or the political formula which had held society together, no longer proved effective."[35] "In a way, the elite theory is contrary to the democratic value such as equality. But the representative character of elites and the competition among the elites for replacement of one elite by another, indicate the democratic spirit. Elite theory believes in the rule of the best or excellent."[36]

From the above discussion, it has become clear, whatever the views of scholars on democracy, party plays a significant role in representative democracy. Parties form the most important part of the representative structure in complex democratic societies.[37] Democratic character of any government is mainly determined by the manner in which the input and output functions of a particular political system are performed: if a government is able to articulate and aggregate the interests and aspirations of the people in proper manner and is able to formulate policies in the interest and well being of the people, then its governance is considered as democratic governance. The role played by political parties is significant in democratic governance, because, it is an important institution responsible for articulating and aggregating the interest of the people. It is also responsible for formulating public policies. Parties play a crucial role in the interest formulation and interest aggregation. Ultimate concern of democratic governance is to ensure good governance. How far the political parties are able to exercise their power in the interest of people is the primary concern of this study. So an understanding of political parties is essential in this study.

Political Parties

The word party which is derived from part and refers to division or opposition within a body politic, first appeared in political discourse in the late Middle Ages.[38] As given by Giovanni Sartori, the term party came into use gradually replacing the derogatory term "faction", with the acceptance of the idea that a party is not necessarily a faction, that is not necessarily an evil, and that it does not necessarily disrupt the *bonum commune*, the common weal. To Voltaire, "Faction", he wrote, is an "parti saditieux dans un etate" (seditious party in a state). The term 'party' would thus seem applicable to the factions that are not seditious.[39] From the beginning of party theory, political parties have been described as gatherings of politically like minded people (by Edmund Burke and Sir Ernest Barker) or as social units with common goals, a division of roles, communication channels, and a hierarchical authority structure (by Samuel J. Eldersveld).[40]

The development of political parties is mainly linked with that of modern western democracy. As Daalder puts it: "The modern political party... can be described with little exaggeration as the child of the Industrial Revolution.[41] Modern parties such as Jacksonian Democrats in United States emerged when legislatures were institutionalized and, most important, when broad segments of the adult population gained the suffrage.[42]

According to Alan Ware, parties arose from two sources: (1) from within an existing legislature (as in the case of British Conservatives), and (2) by the mobilization of social groups and classes that had no representation in such legislatures and which sought to defend their own interests (one example being that of British Labour Party).[43]

To Ware, something to be recognized as a party, has to involve more persons than one. The goal of such parties may be different from each other. It may be the dissolution of an existing state rather than to exercise power within it or, its objective is to bring down a regime. And "there are political groups that call themselves parties, and which engage in some political activities with parties such as contesting elections but whose purpose is either to entertain or to ridicule politics as an activity."[44]

Sartori had also distinguished party into three types:

1. The party that remains external to and uninvolved with the sphere of government, the ambassador party, so to speak;
2. The party that operates within the ambit of government but does not govern; and
3. The party that actually governs, that takes on the governing or governmental functions.[45]

Direct democracy is not possible in modern times, as a result representative democracies are practiced by many states. Since three great ideals of progress came to be formulated during the French Revolution, namely, those of liberty, equality and fraternity, the world has witnessed the rise and development of a representative form of democracy and it is in this context that party system has grown and developed.[46] Political parties got more prominence in the representative government. No free and large country is without them. We cannot think of modern representative democracies without political parties. It may be one party system, two-party system or multi-party system; party system is bound to exist in every political system. Of all the forces and factors, the role played by political parties has been most effective in bringing about a radical change in the powers and functions of the parliament.

MacIver, in his treatise, "The Modern State" emphasized the importance of political parties. Defining political party as "an association organization in support of some principles or policy which by constitutional means endeavours to make the determinant; he asserted that a party seeks to do more than influence or support the government, it seeks to make it."[47]

Parties play a significant role in every democracy. To know why parties are playing such a crucial role in democracy it is essential to know about their functions. The kind of functions performed by political parties gave them significance in democracy. The first and foremost function of a political party is to influence the electorate. It is by their vote a political party can win the election.

Rod Mistry has given the following seven functions of political parties:

1. The parties unite, simplify and stabilize the political process.
2. Political parties generally compete for capturing power, they create stability out of chaos, they work as pressure groups.
3. Political parties provide levels between the government and its people.
4. They recruit political leaders.
5. They present issues, sets goals for the society.
6. Political party acts as a catalyst in the process of modernization.
7. They also perform social welfare functions.[48]

According to S.S. Patagundi, political parties perform the following functions:

1. Interest articulation and interest aggregation,
2. Expression of the will of the people,
3. Generation of ideas of common good, and
4. Acquisition of power.[49]

We can broadly classify the functions of political parties into two, participatory and responsive. In the participatory function of political party we can include contesting elections, campaigning, selection of candidates for election, interest articulation and interest aggregation, etc. and in the responsive functions we can include social welfare functions, providing stability, working as pressure groups, etc. However, it is not possible to separate these two functions into watertight compartments. Both the functions are interdependent. Participatory function has an effect on the responsive function. Winning elections is the aim of all political parties. To achieve this they participate in elections. Only by participating in elections, they cannot win. Winning elections mainly depends upon their performance. Moreover, performance of political parties is determined by their responsiveness.

How best a party is able to express the will of the people determines its future. Political parties are the intermediaries between the people and the government. They are concerned with the understanding of the grievances of the people and explaining them to the government.[50] Government policies should represent the will of the people. Competition for power is nothing but competition to win peoples' votes. And people vote for that party, which represents their interest in an effective manner. Responsiveness of political parties towards people is very crucial in winning elections.

Scholars like Rousseau and others view that representative government cannot effectively represent the will of the people. People are not allowed to take part in decision-making. Representatives may not properly represent the will of the people. However, one cannot neglect the reality of representative government. The capacity to govern will not be improved automatically by moving from 'single old government to new 'governance', for it depends primarily on mode of governing which incorporates representative politics, instead tries to avoid it. [51]

Governance

We have used the term governance to understand democratic governance. But, what do we mean by democratic governance? A clear understanding of democratic governance is not possible unless we study the concept of governance in detail.

The concept of governance is not new. However, it has gained particular significance in recent years when in the literature of African development among other things, the World Bank's (1989) identified the crisis on the continent as one of the governance.[52] 'Governance', has only recently entered the standard Anglophone social science lexicon and become a 'buzzword' in various lay circles.[53]

Richard Joseph at the Carter Center of Emory University in Atlanta was instrumental in helping to popularize the concept among Africans by conducting annual seminars under the auspices of the Center's African Governance Programme.

The Anglophone term 'governance' can be traced to the classical Latin and ancient Greek words for 'steering' of boats. It originally referred mainly to the action or manner of governing, guiding, or steering conduct and overlapped with 'government'.[54] For a long time, it was mainly limited to constitutional and legal issues. It has enjoyed a remarkable revival in recent years. It attracted the attention of scholars from various disciplines. "It is fair to say that since the end of 1970s, what the experts have been thinking about welfare state has also been applicable to governance. If one looks closely at the major international reports (OECD, 1981, 1984, World Bank, 1994) that have come out over the past two decades one can easily find a whole series of diagnoses, analyses and recommendations that parallels, in a striking way, those found in the literature on governance."[55]

According to Gerry Stoker, "governance is ultimately concerned with creating the conditions for ordered rule and collective action".[56] Rather, governance signifies "a change in the meaning of government, referring to a process of governing; or a changed condition of ordered rule; or new method by which society is governed".[57]

Bob Joseph has identified two closely related meanings of governance. "First, governance can refer to any mode of co-ordination of inter-dependent activities. Among these modes, three are relevant here: the anarchy of exchange, organizational hierarchy, and self-organizing 'heterarchy'. The second more restricted meaning, is heterarchy (or self-organization)... ."[58] One of the main features of heterarchy is interdependence of various agencies, institutions and systems which are operationally autonomous from one another. This is a familiar form of governance in many different contexts. Each system has its own operational logic. The overall development of the system can be possible by taking into consideration their own internal codes and logics and adjusting them to the outside controls.

The main idea is that in an increasingly complex world where different sub-systems are emerging, the state has lost its capacity for action.[59] Democratic governance to be effective should respond properly to the demands of the people. State finds it difficult to adjust itself to the demands put forward by the civil society which are too numerous and too contradictory. Social disorder, cultural cleavages, community pluralism are some of the problems faced by the state. In the old theory of governance, the state was very powerful and possessed all necessary resources to resist social pressures. With increasing globalization and with it increasing uncertainty, state's power has diminished.

To Franscois-Xavier Merrien, the solution to this problem can be found by forming partnership with private sectors. The state must act as a mediator between public and private sectors by occupying an essential place in development. This he considers as a new theory of governance. Thus, public-private partnership, industrial, districts, trade associations, statecraft, diplomacy, interest in 'police'(Polizei), policy communities and international regimes all involve aspects of what is now termed 'governance'.[60] In the new governance process development and welfare is not the sole concern of the state. The state has to work along with the private sectors and voluntary organizations. Thus, private sector, public sector and voluntary associations and organizations together form new governance process. Thus the "new (good) governance is characterized by the move away from supervision to contracting out; from centralization to decentralization; from state that redistributes to the state that regulates; from public services management to management following market principles; and from state 'guidance' to co-operation between the state and the private sector."[61]

Goran Hyden defines governance as "the conscious management of regime structures with a view to enhancing the legitimacy of the public realm."[62] To Hyden public realm encompasses both state and society. A government to be legitimate must be responsive to the needs of the people. The main aim of all governments should be the welfare and well being of the people. To achieve this aim the governmental structures and institutions should work in the interest of the people. The political party is one of the important institutions available to the people through which they elect their representatives who on behalf of people formulate the policies. The policies should be in the interest of the people. For this, participation of people in the decision making process is equally important. In representative democracy, direct participation of people in decision-making is not possible. People by organizing themselves in trade unions and in various organizations and associations can influence the outcome of the decision. Thus, not only the management of the governmental structure but non-governmental structure is equally important in democratic governance.

Goran Hyden in his book, "Governance and Politics in Africa" has provided four properties, namely, trust, reciprocity, accountability and authority, which bound the realm of governance. "Trust refers to normative consensus on the limits of action present in a political community. It is sustained by socialization into the rules and not a contract. Indicators of trust in political community are the extent to which individuals and groups in society cooperate in associations that cut across basic divisions such as ethnicity, race, religion and caste."[63] The differences of ethnicity, race, religion, and class are bound to exist in every society. In spite of these differences, there is a sort of co-operation among the individuals and groups in the society, which is the indicator of trust.

Reciprocity refers to an interaction among members of political community. Freedom of individuals to form associations to defend and promote their interests is an important indicator of reciprocity. Authority is mainly concerned with effective leadership who can very effectively implement the policies and be able to solve specific problems affecting them. Accountability refers to the control that people exercise on their leaders. Citizens judge political decisions along two lines: (1) how effective they are in solving specific problems affecting them; and (2) how these decisions are carried out.[64] The four variables mentioned above are considered by Goren Hyden as prerequisites for effective governance.

Effective governance can maintain the stability of the system. "But the real test of governance comes in situations where regime changes are needed to meet new demands or deal with new problems. The study of governance then involves the identification of the conditions that facilitate good governance and by implication, effective problem solving."[65] Hyden has suggested three conditions mentioned below:

1. *Citizens Influence and Oversight*

It refers to,

(a) *Degree of Political Participation*: To what extent people are able to take active part in the political affairs of the state.

(b) *Means of Preference Aggregation*: By participating in the political process people express their preferences about public policy. They not only express preferences about public policy but also see to it that they are properly aggregated for effective policy making.

(c) *Methods of Public Accountability*: It refers to the means, which are available to the people, and which hold governors accountable for their decisions and actions.

2. *Responsive and Responsible Leadership*

Responsiveness and responsible leaders refers to the attitudes of political leaders towards their role as public trustees.[66]

(a) *Degree of respect for civic public realm*: Political leaders have to give proper respect to aspirations of the people while policy making. Attitude of political leaders towards people and their ability to represent the aspirations of the people depends on the degree of respect for civic public realm.
(b) *Degree of openness of public policy making*: Political leaders should be ready to share information with citizens. They have to educate the people regarding the policies made in their favour. This knowledge is essential on the part of citizens to have effective control over leaders and policies.
(c) *Degree of adherence to rule of law*: Laws are meant not only for the people but they are also applicable to the leaders in the same way. Every act of people and leaders should be within the framework of law.

3. *Social Reciprocity*

It refers to the type of interaction between the individuals and group of individuals. Social reciprocities refers to the extent to which citizens or groups of citizens treat each other in an equal fashion; how far such groups demonstrate tolerance of each other in the pursuit of politics; and how far voluntary associations are capable of transcending the boundaries of such primary social organizations as kinship, ethnicity, or race.[67]

(a) *Degree of political equality*: Different groups in the society have their own interests different from the interests of other groups and how far these various groups treat others in an equal fashion.
(b) *Degrees of inter group tolerance*: Degree of political equality mainly determined by how these various groups demonstrate tolerance of each other's interests.

(c) *Degree of inclusiveness in associational members:* It deals with how far the associations bring people of similar interest together in spite of their differences because of kinship, ethnicity, race, etc.

Hyden is of the opinion that these indicators differ from country to country depending on the circumstances. Hyden in his classification has very systematically analyzed the role of an individual, group and leader in the process of governance.

Hyden has given the classification of regimes into four types, namely, communitarian, libertarian, corporatist and statists. By this classification, he has tried to identify the challenges to effective governance in different regimes. In the communitarian regime, community demands are not properly aggregated and articulated because of the hard civic public realm. Limited public resources on the other hand make effective governance hard, if not impossible.

In the libertarian regime, crisis of governance is mostly because of two reasons. "The first is the inability of the those in leadership positions to aggregate citizens preferences in an effective manner so as to deliver authoritative decisions. The second reason is the tendency for the utilitarian values to get enriched in such a way that citizen interest in politics wanes."[68]

The corporate regime which consists of various groups faces crisis of governance, when the interest of one community comes into clash with that of other or when the interest of any one is neglected by other groups. With so many differences among groups arriving at consensus on policy issue becomes very difficult.

In the statist regime where power is concentrated in the state, the leaders can become increasingly arrogant and unresponsive by ignoring citizens' control dimension.

Dimensions of Effective Governance

Joachim Ahren has given four dimensions of effective governance according to four principles in his book, *Governance and Economic Development: A Comparative Institutional Approach.* They are accountability, participation, predictability and transparency.

Accountability

"Basically, accountability means making politicians and bureaucrats responsible for their actions and overall government policies and avoiding the capture of the state by narrow interests. With respect to policy reform, accountability refers to the design of development—enhancing reform programmes, making these congruent with their implementation and enforcement and eventually ensuring an efficient use, stewardship, and allocation of resources."[69] In democratic governance politicians are accountable to the people. Politicians who are representatives of the people are elected by the people. Hence they are accountable to the people for their actions in the government and for the overall governmental policies. Accountability ensures effective governance as it avoids the capture of the state by narrow interests.

Participation

"Participation is often an objective of development in itself because it is expected to enhance citizens' independence, autonomy, and self-reliance. But participation also plays a critical role in strengthening governance structures. More specifically, it reinforces accountability because it provides the means by which citizens may exercise influence and control over decisions and actions of their governors."[70] For effective governance, participation is essential because participation ensures accountability. By active participation, people can make their representatives accountable or answerable to them. This in turn makes the representatives more responsive towards the needs and aspirations of the people. Thus, "...the right to participate is an essential element of democratic government, inseparable from such other attributes of democracy as consent, accountability, majority rule, equality, and popular sovereignty."[71]

Predictability

Predictability relates to the clearly-defined laws and policies that regulate the economy and society as a whole, to the clear and explicit communication of the laws and other rules to the business sector and private actors (including citizens' rights and duties) as well as to their consistent and impartial application and enforcement.[72]

To enhance predictability, effective organizations and institutions are required. As we all know the values of society are always changing. With this change there is also a change in the attitude of the people towards particular things. So, it necessitates that the existing laws must have some amendment procedure to adopt themselves to the changing conditions if they want to serve their purpose.

Transparency

The transparent provision of information on policy making and implementation (in association with clear and straightforward decision-working procedures) help to reduce opportunities for corrupt behaviour, improves the analysis and articulation of public policy choices, and enhance their acceptance.[73]

"These four principles are clearly interrelated and reinforce each other. Institutional arrangements that further these principles are expected to provide those incentives that are conducive to effective policy making and developmental outcomes."[74]

Governance is mainly concerned with how political power is exercised in the society. If the power is exercised in the interest of the people, it may lead to democratic governance. As in the representative democracies power is exercised by the political parties, their participation and responsiveness is crucial to democratic governance. They should be responsive towards the interests and demands of the people. Responsiveness of political parties is mainly ensured by their effective participation. Popular participation and responsiveness is equally important for democratic governance. Unless and until people actively participate in the political affairs and respond towards policy decisions of government we cannot ensure democratic governance. Because, "first of all, democracy cannot be foisted upon people. They must have the desire to be self-governing. Along with the desire for self-government must go the willingness to assume the responsibilities it entails. Democratic rights cannot be realized without the acceptance of their correlated duties; with the right to self-government go the duties of active citizenship."[75]

e-Government and e-Governance

The prefix 'e' suggests that an activity is 'electronic' or digital in nature. Thus, e-government would simply refer to the use of electronic information and communication technologies in all kinds of government activities. The key word in e-government is not electronic but government, and e-government would be regarded as an alternative and complementary approach to government administration and service delivery, as well as a means to redefine the way it interacts with citizens and the private sector.[76] Electronic (or e) government is the process of transformation of the relationships of government with its constituents—the citizen, the business—and between its own organs, through the use of the tools of Information and Communication Technology (ICT).[77] Thus e-government activities focus on four forms of interactions: Government-to-Citizen (G2C), Government-to- Business (G2B), Government-to-Government (G2G) and Government-to-Employee (G2E).

With the development of ICTs there have been improvements in the efficiency and effectiveness of the service delivery to the citizens. It also ensures transparent government, as the information is easily available to the citizens about the policies and programmes of the government. This information makes possible the active participation of the people in the governmental activities. "The ODA, World Bank and UNDP reports have laid down 'participation', 'legitimacy', 'accountability', 'transparency', and 'competence' are the essential features of good governance. The major objective of ICT should thus revolve around the outlined essential in order to bring about efficiency, responsiveness, openness and participation in governance and arrest corruption at different levels."[78] In this context SMART government has gained popularity, which stands for, Simple, Moral, Accountable, Responsive and Transparent government. Essentially 'SMART' captures all the important attributes of good governance.[79]

"ICTs, especially the Internet, enable gathering of model legislations and policies at international and national levels on any subject and the experience of nations and regions in the implementation of those laws and policies. It is, therefore, possible to formulate new policies or modify/review existing laws and policies in a quicker time frame and in a more informed manner."[80] With the development of ICTs, the people will be informed as never before. "They can build powerful learning as well as opinion-and-value articulating groups by lateral communication on the Internet. These powerful opinion bodies will actually run the political system and the governance of nations."[81] Thus with the help of ICTs, people will be in direct communication with the government or their representatives. This helps in democratizing the process of governance. "Internet will make democracy real. Complete access to all required knowledge, free consultations among people and unhindered communication channels for them to let their minds be known are the key to political power for the people."[82]

Most often, the word e-government and e-governance are used interchangeably. So, it is essential to know the difference between the two. "But whereas the government is the formal apparatus for this objective, governance is the outcome as experienced by those on the receiving end... . e-government can be more productive version of government in general, if it is well implemented and managed. E-governance can evolve into participatory governance if it is well supported with the appropriate principle, objectives, programmes and architectures."[83] In other words, we can say that e-government is the electronification of the government processes.

"E-governance has different interpretations:

- E-governance implies a smoother interface between the government and citizens.
- E-governance is nothing but good governance. The 'e' is only a tool.
- E-governance is to enhance the use of Information technology and to help enhance peoples' lives.

E-governance enables active citizen involvement by:

- Informing the citizens
- Representing the citizens
- Encouraging the citizens to vote
- Consulting the citizens
- Encouraging in participation from the citizens."[84]

"India's information technology vision has passed through a series of formulation processes. However, Shri Atal Bihari Vajpayee, India's former Prime Minister has provided the political will and support. This has motivated the bureaucracy and the private sectors to embrace information technology."[85] In order to give scope to the use of information technology in governance, the 'Centre for E-governance', a new division within the Ministry of Information Technology, was set up on 15 August 1999. The year 2001 has been declared by the information and technology minister as 'the year of e-governance'. This indicates the commitment of the government to develop information technology in all sectors of the Indian economy. When we are considering the e-governance of India we cannot neglect Andhra Pradesh. "The state of Andhra Pradesh had designed e-government architecture in 2000 and published the standards at its web site www.ap-it.com in February, 2001. The standard document was updated in April 2002. The architecture and standards were 'mandated' for all major e-government projects-through an executive order though not a regulation or legislation."[86] But the efforts of Andhra Pradesh government towards developing an e-government architecture in 2000 was neither comprehensive nor complete. "It was heavily biased towards defining technology standards and identification of core business processes and e-government initiatives. It fell short of building a service-oriented-Architecture that included Process, People and Technology in the right proportion."[87]

It was not only the case with Andhra Pradesh but in most of the developing countries e-government projects have failed. A survey done by 'egov4dev' during 2002 revealed that only 15 per cent of the e-government projects in the developing countries are really successful while 50 per cent are partial failures and 35 per cent are total failures.[88] In most countries including India, the digital divide remains the primary barrier to the take-off of electronic government services. Peoples' habit of utilizing ICT is more likely to be exposed on the receiving end rather than initiating ones. According to surveys conducted by different agencies in year 2003, India has 1,65,80,000 persons accessing the Internet.[89] Robert Schware, Lead Informatics Specialist, the World Bank, remarked that, "The failures and partial success of e-governance initiatives should be studied to make better use of technology for governments to deliver services to citizens." He said "33 per cent of all e-governance initiatives in developing countries had failed, while 50 per cent had succeeded partially."[90]

Efficiency of e-governance can be understood in terms of information the people get which enables them to make good choices about government and makes government more accountable. Thus, it also helps in empowering the people.

Participation Theory

From Aristotle to John Dewey, political philosophers have extolled popular participation as a source of vitality and creative energy, as a defence against tyranny, and as a means of enacting the collective wisdom.[91] Participation ensures accountability and responsiveness of the representatives. The first modern observer to consider seriously both practical and theoretical significance of the citizen participation in politics was Alexis de Tocqueville.[92] According to one writer, 'meaningful participation may be defined as occurring when a person has a sense of his involvement in a total experience, a sense of where his efforts fit into an overall plan, when he identifies with respect to the accomplishment of the goals, and has stake in the results of the total experience.'[93]

Right to participation exists in almost all kinds of democracies. It is one of the major elements of democratic governance. Procedural theory of democracy considered participation as one of the important principles of democracy. Most of classical writers advocated direct democracy with the maximum participation of people in the affairs of the state. Some of the modern writers were not in favour of maximum participation of the people. The popularity of the concept provides a good reason for devoting some attention to it, but more importantly, the recent upsurge for demands for more participation can raise a central question of political theory; the place of 'participation' in modern, viable theory of democracy.[94]

Significant role of participation in democracy made some scholars give participatory theories of democracy. Among them, the theory advocated by Rousseau, J.S. Mill and Cole is very important. Rousseau might be called the theorist par excellence of participation, and an understanding of the nature of the political system that he considers in *The Social Contract* is vital for the theory of participatory democracy.[95] In his theory, he has given more importance to the participation of individuals in the political process. To Rousseau, for a participatory system favourable economic conditions such as economic equality and economic independence are very essential. He has not advocated absolute economic equality but he has argued that the inequalities prevailing in the society should not lead to political inequality. According to him, there should be a situation where no citizen shall be rich enough to buy another and none so poor as to be forced to sell himself.[96]

Rousseau believes that the voice of majority cannot be easily the neglected by the leader. As the leaders are accountable to the people, the leaders should take into consideration the will of the majority. To him general will which is based on the will of the majority is always rightful because it promotes the happiness of majority of people. The will of each individual is merged in the general will and contributes for effective decision making. Rousseau's participatory system makes two points clear; first, that 'participation' for Rousseau is participation in the making of decisions and second, that it is, as in theories of representative government, a way of protecting private interests and ensuring good government.[97] By participating in decision making process individuals can protect their private interests and contribute to democratic governance.

The theory given by Rousseau forms the basis for participatory theory of democracy given by many scholars. The major limitation of Rousseau's theory is that it is confined mainly to the city states. The theories given by J.S. Mill and Cole are not confined to city-states but highlight the modern political system.

J.S. Mill was very much influenced by the theories of his father James Mill, and also by the theories of Jermy Bentham and de Tocqueville's "Democracy in America". To Mill one of the greatest dangers to democracy is the sinister interest of the holders of power. "He says in *Representative Government*—which expressed the principles 'to which I have been working up during the greater part of my life'—that one of the greatest dangers of democracy lies in 'the sinister interest of the holders of power: it is the danger of class legislation... And one of the most important questions demanding consideration...is how to provide efficacious securities against this evil'."[98] The necessary condition for democratic governance is the promotion of right kind of individual character through right kind of institutions. Only participatory institutions can develop such characters. Mill like Rousseau believes that with the development of such qualities the political system acquires self-sustaining character. He remarked that political sophistication and public spiritedness are necessary qualities of representative government.

"Mill argues that, it is no use having universal suffrage and participation in national government if the individual has not been prepared for this participation at local level; it is at this level that he learns how to govern himself. A political act, to be done only once in a few years, and for which nothing in the daily habits of the citizen has prepared him, leaves his intellect and his moral dispositions very much as it found them."[99]

A discussion of Cole's theory is significant in this regard because it is connected with the modern industrialized society. Rosseau's theory of participatory democracy is of little relevance today but Cole attempted to translate the insights of Rousseau's theory to suit modern conditions.

Participation constitutes a major part of his theory. By associating with other individuals men learn how to adjust their self-interest with community interest and arrive at certain decisions that are commonly acceptable to all. "'I assume', he says, echoing Mill's criticism of Bentham's political theory, 'that the object of social organization is not merely material efficiency, but also essentially the fullest self-expression of all the members.' Self-expression 'involves self-government' and this means that we must 'call forth the people's full participation in the common direction in the affairs of the community'"[100] Such decisions are in the interest of the larger community as a whole. This involves fullest freedom to the individual citizen who participates in decision making because the laws, which he is supposed to obey are self imposed and not forced on him externally.

Associations got more prominence in Cole's theory. The theory of association got significance in his theory of democracy. According to Cole, real democracy can be possible only when it is conceived in terms of functions and purposes. Moreover, the associations have to function in such a manner which should lead to the fulfilment of their interests for the attainment of which it was formed. By pursuing the objects of associations, it is possible to pursue general object of a community as a whole. The decisions arrived at the associations are represented in the parliament by the representatives of the associations.

In Cole's view, existing forms of representation are misrepresented for two reasons. First, because the principle of function has been overlooked and the mistake of assuming that it is possible for an individual to be represented as a whole and for all purposes instead of his being represented in relation to some well-defined function has been made. Secondly, under the existing parliamentary institutions the elector has no real choice of, or control over, his representative, and the system actually denies the right of individual to participate because 'having chosen his representative, the ordinary man has, according to that theory, nothing left to do except to let other people govern him'.[101] Cole argues that functional representation is the best form of representative government where there is the constant participation of the ordinary man in the conduct of those parts of the structures of Society with which he is directly concerned and which he has therefore the best chance of understanding.[102] If the representation is organized on functional basis an individual can certainly, advise, criticize and if necessary recall the representatives.

The participatory theory of democracy is mainly based on the notion that we cannot separate the individuals from institutions. The existence of a national institution at the center is not the sufficient condition of democracy. The success of such institution depends on the maximum participation of all the people. Moreover, this is possible only through social training, which he gets by participating in other spheres of activities as Cole pleaded for guild socialism and J.S. Mill advocated the role of associations. By participating in such institutions individuals attitude and psychological qualities can develop, which contribute to the maximum participation at the national level. Therefore, for a democratic polity to exist meaningfully it is necessary for a participatory society to exist, i.e., a society, where all political systems have been democratized and socialization through participation can take place in all areas.[103]

Variables Affecting Political Participation

Forms of participation differ from country to country. The concept of participation, which depends on many variables, is very complex. Therefore, it may be difficult to develop a general theory of participation or evolve an approach to this ideal. Individual's action to participate or not to participate is mainly influenced by the environment in which he lives. Three types of environments, namely, social environment, psychological environment and political environment, play a crucial role in determining political participation.

In the social environment, we can mainly include education, occupation, income, age, race, religion, sex, mobility and residence. "Research in the United States and elsewhere shows that most of these variables correlate to some degree with participation. In general, participation tends to be higher among the better-educated, members of the higher occupational and income groups, the middle-aged, the dominant ethnic and religious groups, men (as opposed to women), settled residents, urban dwellers, and members of voluntary associations."[104] But, the influence of these factors on participation varies from one political cultural context to another. For example, if we say participation tends to be higher among the better educated in some countries, this may not be so in some other countries.

In the psychological environment man's need for power, competition, achievement, affiliation, aggression, status, money, prestige, sympathy, responsibility and such other factors are responsible for participation. Political observers throughout the ages have variously attributed man's political activity to his need for power, competition, achievement, affiliation, aggression, money, prestige, status, recognition, approval, manipulation, sympathy, responsibility, in short, to virtually every need that impels human behaviour.[105] While the relation between the cognitive states of low self-esteem are strongly correlated with political apathy.[106]

It was a general belief that national and international crisis makes people participate in the political environment. Scholars who tested these hypotheses found that election turnout did not increase during crisis, but the popularity and unpopularity of a candidate had an effect on the election turnout.

In addition to the general variables touched on, the party system, the nature of the campaign, and issues and ideology are three areas that shape participation in modern societies.[107]

Dimensions of Participation

Sidney Verba, N.H. Nie and Jae-on Kim had given five dimensions of participation.

1. *Type of Influence Exerted*

Citizen activity can affect the behaviour of governmental leaders in two ways: They can communicate information about the preferences of citizens and/or they can apply pressure on political leaders to conform to these preferences.[108] It may be the gain or loss of votes or some material loss or reward.

2. *The Scope of the Outcome*

Verba, Nie and Kim argue that most of the time political scientists focus mainly on the policies of the government, which have a collective impact and affect entire society or a large segment of it. Importance is given to government policies, outcome of an election, a tax reform bill or governmental decision on foreign policy and many others, the outcome of which has a collective impact on all citizens. "But governments do not make decisions only about broad social policies. Often they produce outcomes that will affect only a particular citizen or his immediate family. The government issues a zoning variance to an individual so that he may enlarge his home, provides a licence, grants an exemption from the army because of family hardship, provides a job, offers agricultural assistance, or agrees to provide a better water supply to a given home."[109] Thus, they argue that rather than emphasizing more on having collective impact on all citizens the political scientists also have to highlight on those policies or acts, which though not have much impact on collectivity but may have an intense impact on the individual or his family.

3. *The Conflict Dimension*

As governmental benefits are limited, activity by one group to obtain something for itself may injure the interests of others.[110] The policies of the government are always not in favour of all the people. The governmental benefits are limited. The activity of one group to attract the attention of the government to fulfil its own interest may injure the interests of others. This leads to the conflicting situation in the society.

There are views that conflict dimension is related to the scope of potential outcome. "The wider the impact of the outcome, the more likely is it that there will be opposing groups active in relation to it. If the governmental outcome that the participants seek has a narrow impact, having a noticeable effect on the participants alone and affecting others only indirectly, this increases the likelihood that the participatory situation would involve just one set of participants attempting to achieve one particular policy outcome."[111]

4. *The Cooperative Dimension*

This refers to the extent to which individuals work along with others. To what extent individuals cooperate with other individuals in the attainment of their interest determines cooperative dimension. Collective action of individuals is likely to bring fruitful results. "Effective political action often depends upon the ability of citizens to work collaboratively. This dimension also relates to the potential outome."[112]

5. *Initiative Required*

"This dimension is similar to the criterion for differentiating political acts that has been the usual one within the literature: How "difficult" is the act? We are interested in the amount of time and effort needed for an act of participation, but more so in how much initiative is needed by the individual in choosing when and how to act."[113]

Modes of Political Participation

Verba, Nie and Kim have given four modes of political participation. They are as follows:

1. *Voting*

It is the most popular mode of participation. Citizens cast their vote in elections. The citizens elect their leaders mainly through voting. In order to gain votes leaders adjust their policies according to the demands of the people. Voting determines election outcome. It exerts influence over leaders through pressure: Leaders adjust their policies in order to gain votes, and of course, the vote determines who holds elective office.[114]

2. *Campaign Activity*

Next to voting, campaign activities are more popular. It can communicate more information about the participants preferences because campaign activists are a more clearly identifiable group with whom candidates may be in close contact.[115] Campaigning is the second variable which contributes to political participation. Campaigning should be face-to-face. The effect of campaign on participation is also dependent upon the popularity, character and charisma of the candidate.

3. *Citizen-initiated Contacts*

This involves popular participation in between elections. Individuals with particular interests in mind contact the government official to discuss these interests or to make these interests known to the government. Here, individuals choose their own agenda, time and substance of the act of participation. "Here we have the individual *vis-à-vis* the government, or some small segment of the government. He determines the timing, target, and substance of the act of participation. This type of participation—which we call citizen, initiated contacts—represents a third type of political activity."[116]

4. *Cooperative Activity*

Cooperative activity is significant because it can combine information about citizens' preferences (since citizens come together to work on a particular issue) with pressure (since leaders are more likely to respond to a number of citizens than to a lone contractor).[117] It is a group activity to solve their problem. Cooperative activity may get effective response because leaders are under pressure from a large number of citizens. This may not be so under citizen-initiated contacts. Most of the time the outcome of cooperative activity affects a large number of people.

The characteristics of these four modes of activity in relation to the dimension of participation are listed in Table 2.1.

From Table 2.1 it is clear that voting exerts high pressure on leaders but communicates little information about individual preferences. While communal activity and particularized contacts communicate high information about individual preferences but, exerts low pressure. While, campaign activity exerts high pressure but some campaign activities communicate lot of information about individual preferences and some others less.

Table 2.1: Modes of Political Participation

Mode of Activity	Type of Influence	Scope of Outcome	Conflict	Initiative Required	Cooperate with Others
Voting	High pressure/low information	Collective	Conflictual	Little	Little
Campaign activity	High pressure/low To high information	Collective	Conflictual	Some	Some or Much
Communal activity	Low to high pressure/high information	Collective	May be yes/May be no	Some or Much	Some or Much
Contacting official on personal matters	Low pressure/high information	Particular	Non-conflictual	Much	Little

Source: Sidney Verba, Norman H. Nie and Jae-on Kim, *Participation and Political Equality*, Cambridge University Press, Cambridge, 1978, p. 55.

The scope of outcome is collective in the case of voting, campaign activity and communal activity. The scope of outcome is confined to a particular individual in case of particularized contacts. Voting and campaign activities create conflicting situations. People are divided on the basis of party and group interests. The interest of one group may collide with that of the other. Communal activity sometimes creates conflicting situation. But, particularized contacts are non-conflicting.

For voting little initiative is required but for contacting officials for personal matters a lot of initiative is required on the part of the individual. For voting and particularized contacts little cooperation of other individuals is required. But, it may be more or less, same kind of initiative is required in case of campaign and communal activity.

"Rush and Althoff have presented a political participation scale, where they have divided the political activity into ten hierarchically placed levels. These are in the following descending order:

(i) holding of administrative and political office,
(ii) seeking political or administrative office,
(iii) active membership of political organization,
(iv) passive membership of a political organization,
(v) active membership of quasi-political organization,
(vi) passive membership of a quasi-political organization,
(vii) participation in public meetings, demonstrations,
(viii) participation in informal political discussions,

(ix) general interest, and
(x) voting."[118]

More number of people participate in voting than in holding of administrative and political office.

"Milbrath's conceptual analysis of political involvement includes the following activities:

1. Voting;
2. Discussion and opinion leadership;
3. Wearing a button or putting a sticker on the car;
4. Petitioning political leaders;
5. Making a monetary contribution;
6. Attending a political meeting;
7. Campaigning;
8. Active party membership;
9. Soliciting political funds;
10. Office-seeking and holding; and
11. Protests and demonstrations."[119]

Milbrath's Hierarchy of Political Involvement was given by Anthony M. Orum in his book, *Introduction to Political Sociology*.

Gladiatorial Activities
- Holding public and party office
- Being a candidate for office
- Soliciting political funds
- Attending a caucus or strategy meeting
- Becoming an active member in a political party
- Contributing time in a political campaign

Transitional Activities
- Attending a political meeting or rally
- Making a monetary contribution to a party or candidate
- Contacting a public official or a political leader

Spectator Activities
- Wearing a button or putting a sticker on the car
- Attempting to talk another into voting a certain way
- Initiating a political discussion
- Voting
- Exposing oneself to political stimuli

Source: Anthony M. Orum, *Introduction to Political Sociology*, Prentice-Hall, New Jersey, 1978, p. 286.

According to Milbrath more number of people participate in spectator activities; and as we move upward peoples' participation tends to decline.

By actively participating "citizens pool their information and their insights, deliberate together, criticize each others ideas and arrive at a collective and near unanimous decisions."[120] By active participation, people will be motivated to get more information and also feel more responsive. According to the textbook model of democracy, an alert, informed and wise citizenry rationally assesses the men who offer themselves for election, chooses the best, and removes or reappoints them after carefully weighing their performance.[121]

Modes of Political Parties Participation

Of all the influences on participation, the influence of party is the most potent one. It is an important institution, through which people make their preference known to the government. The following are the important modes of political parties, participation:

1. *Participating in Elections*

The main function of political parties in this mode of participation is to contact the voters and register them, select candidates for election, organize the campaign and educate the voters regarding the issues and how to vote. The more active forms of participation include formal enrolment in a party, canvassing and registering voters, speech writing and speech-making, working in campaigns, and competing for public and party office.[122]

2. *Interest Aggregation*

"Every political system has some way of aggregating the interests, claims and demands which have been articulated by the interest groups of the polity. Aggregation may be accomplished by means of the formulation of general policies in which interests are combined, accommodated, or otherwise taken account of, or by means of the recruitment of political personnel, more or less committed to a particular pattern of policy."[123] A political party is an institution that (a) seeks influence in a state, often by attempting to occupy position in government, and (b) usually consists and so to some degree attempts to 'aggregate interests'.[124] Interest aggregation is the activity in which the political demand of the individuals and groups are combined by the political parties into policy demands.

3. *Interest Articulation*

As every political system has some way of aggregating interests it also has some way for articulating interests, claims and demands. Political party is an important institutional mechanism, which performs the work of interest articulation. The party system aggregates interests and transforms them into a relatively small number of alternative general policies.[125] To occupy position in government the political party has to seek votes. If votes are to be sought, grievances must be attended to, and demands must be, to some extent, satisfied.[126]

Pennock in his book *Democratic Political Theory* has discussed relation of various types of democratic theory with participatory theory.

1. *Motivational Theories*

The radical individualism would not favour the attempts to increase participation. Individuals can participate for the sake of participation but if he feels that he had certain desire which the polity can satisfy, then he can exercises his democratic right for the attainment of the same. "The rational man theorist is quite conscious of the costs of political action and is likely to conclude that they would exceed the probable reward. He is not likely to assume, although logically he might, that citizens will place a positive value on political activity for its own sake. Also this theorist is forced, by his assumption of the incommensurability of values, to accept the valuation that each citizen places upon the satisfaction of desires and the costs of achieving such satisfaction."[127] But, the radical individualist is not likely to assume that institutions are so perverted that revolutionary action by a self-selected minority is required to effect substantial change and to create the conditions for the rational behaviour.[128]

To Tocquevilly, individualistic participation is simply a means to attain self-protection and self-advancement, and he does not feel the necessity of encouraging political participating.

The modified individualists do not seem to differ substantially from the radical individualist in respect of political participation. The modified individualists participate in the political activity for the sake of participation and are more responsive to the appeals of vote.

The romantic individualist believes that the individual has great potentialities for development. Mill stressed the role of political activity in contributing towards the development of individual personality. They believe that political participation contributes to the individual development.

The public interest theories believe that participation gives recognition to individual interest which might otherwise be neglected. "Beyond this, he has a special concern for those interests—they might be called political externalities—that tend to be overlooked by individuals acting independently. For this reason, he would favour enough participation of people to get them involved in thinking and talking about public policies so that the interests satisfaction, which may be produced by joint activity and common accomplishments are given due recognition, not to mention the private interest but economic externalities, such as polluted atmosphere or water supply."[129]

The rights and duties theorists are some what similar to the public interest theory but have a bit more lenience towards individual interest. They demand enough participation to protect private rights of an individual.

The collectivists, mainly egalitarian collectivists support extensive political participation because it contributes to the development of community as a whole.

2. *Power Theories*

According to Pennock, Democratic Elitism is not in favour of participation of all people in government. Always in every society, a small group governs. "The elitist is not only content with representative government, he believes that the process of selecting representatives provides an important, not to say crucial, opportunity for those who possess the best political talents to be selected for governing, while allowing the less active and less politically qualified sufficient power, by choosing between competing elites, to protect and advance their interests. The elitist puts little stock in the value of participation as a means of contributing to individual development."[130] He sees it as a tool, which the average man can use when he sees the need for it. Policies are formulated by representatives of people. People do not have any role in making policies. Elitist believes that running the government is not the job of all citizens. It requires special skill to perform that job and this skill is possessed by a minority group in the society.

But, if the policies are not in the interest of the people then they can ask for a change in the policy.

The populists' ideology is opposite to that of elitists. While elites give importance to a few people in the society who posses special quality to rule, the populists favour general, active and informed participation of all. Their concern is more on the wisdom of the people. They believe initiatives and referendum are most acceptable methods to the individuals. "Somewhat paradoxically, the populist tends to favour centralization, especially as between legislature and chief executive. The legislature, a deliberative body, tends to develop ideas of its own to 'refine' the popular will, perhaps beyond recognition. An elected chief executive, on the other hand, is seen more as the chosen instrument of the people."[131]

The constitutional democrats do not attach any special importance to participation. Whatever freedom the individual enjoys to participate should be within the limits of constitution.

To the social pluralist popular participation in all kinds of organized groups, though it has not any political objectives is important. They contribute to the development of the personality of individual and concern for the interest of others. "In his view, human wants, needs, and values are (and he might add 'ought to be') so various that they cannot receive adequate expression through a single set of institutions. Moreover, they must have outlets through associations that are not solely, or perhaps even mainly, political. This variety of groupings is important not only to provide for people of different natures and for the differing interests and purposes of the same people, but also to check the abuse of power."[132] The role played by non-governmental organizations through which people participate in the political affairs of the country is important. Not only do they give representation to the various interest of the people, but they also act as a check on the abuse of power. Theorists of this type would, like the populists, favour the widest possible distribution of actual political power, but with emphasis upon a great deal of decentralization and with the aim of changing the participants fully as much as changing the governmental output.[133]

Responsiveness

Apart from participation, the concept of responsiveness is also equally important in understanding the democratic governance. All the above mentioned theories of democracy are revolving around participation and responsiveness in one way or the other. However, responsiveness is mostly used in the criticism of democracy's operation. One of the main criticisms of democracy is that it is not sufficiently responsive.

The dictionary meaning of responsiveness is "reacting easily and readily to suggestions or appeal". The word 'responsive' has to do with responding or answering. In representative democracy, there is a possibility that the aspirations of the people are not properly represented. The elected representatives might not make the same decisions, which the people would have done if they would have gathered for the same purpose. To cope with this problem the procedural theory of democracy has given the principle of responsiveness. Responsiveness means following the general contours of public opinion as complex pieces of legislation are formulated.[134] Responsiveness might be said to be the counter part of influence. The person or group that exerts influence is influential; the person or group on whom it is exerted is responsive.[135] In democracy, people are influential and government should be responsive to the aspirations of the people. Democratic governance is concerned with how best government responds to the aspirations of the people. Unless and until the government responds to the aspirations of the people adequately, it cannot be called democratic. It is very difficult to arrive at consensus on public affairs. In this respect, society is divided. Each group in the society has its own perception with regard to the issue of public importance.

This is one of the major problems in understanding public opinion. As a result, it may be difficult to understand the popular responsiveness on issues of public importance. Pennock has pointed out such problems as follows: firstly, he points out the problems of splintered wills and demands. "It is not only that wills or demands, even when they exist and are known, are often splintered, so that no majority supports any one proposal; but also, popular demands may conflict with each other. The same people may demand lower taxes and increased benefits of services entailing increased expenditures. Or two pressures (demands), while being in the strictest sense compatible with each other, may lead to mutually self-defeating results."[136] In every society different groups pursue their own interest and demands and try to fulfil them. Such demands may co-operate or contradict with the demands of other groups in the society. Majority people may or may not support proposal on public affairs. Some groups may agree to a proposal but there are some who hold totally opposite views on the proposal. This creates a situation in which government finds it difficult to decide which proposal is legitimate. Negligence of any such proposal may affect governance.

The second problem is that in democratic society there may be a number of problems (demands). But how far these proposed demands are reasonable? "Demands, desires, may vary greatly in their intensity. Is the responsive government simply to count demands, or should it somehow measure their strength? And how should it respond to a situation in which 35 per cent of the electorate strongly favour a certain proposal, 55 per cent mildly oppose it, and the remaining 10 per cent are indifferent?"[137] Responsiveness provides no answer to such questions.

The third problem identifies by Roland Pennock is concerned with the defect of representative system. "To whom should government be responsive? To the majority of 'the people'? Apart from the fact that on most issues no such majority exists, if we are speaking of representative government, as for practical purposes we must be, this question raises issues regarding the role of the representative."[138] Representative system may not properly represent the will of the people. If government responds to the majority will then the question arises, who compose this majority? Whether it consists of all the people or only representatives of the people? In a representative government the role of people is only to elect the representatives and not to participate in decision-making. And the representatives who are supposed to respect the will of the people may not give proper representation to the aspirations of the people. How then can we expect effective responsiveness from government?

The fourth problem in democracy's task of being responsive to the popular demands is that in some cases, representatives of the people themselves decide what is in the interest of the people and such decisions are enforced. "Moreover, it appears that even apart from any conscious governmental policy to influence opinion, in fact public opinion often changes to accord with existing public policy. It would be highly unrealistic to think that government acts simply in response to wants and demands."[139] Pennock believes that in representative democracy it is highly unrealistic to believe that government is acting in accordance with the wants and demands of the people. More often people are satisfied by something other than what is wanted. The wants of the people are satisfied by their very expression what is called as 'expressive demands' by Pennock.

By the above discussion about the difficulties in responsiveness, it is quite clear that what people want is not simply responsiveness but responsiveness to needs, wants, demands grievances, aspirations or preferences. However, the question is, should democracy give the people what they want? The demands of the people may or may not be reasonable. Do the legislators represent genuine aspirations or opinion of majority of the people? Unless the legislators represent the genuine aspirations, it is not possible to expect the effective responsiveness of governance. Without this, governance cannot be democratic.

Generally, legislators belong to one or the other political parties. Therefore, the responsiveness of government is significantly influenced by the political parties. Performance of political parties is mainly judged by the type of policies formulated by them. By responding towards the policy outcome of the government, people are providing feedback to a particular policy. Popular responsiveness contributes to political parties responsiveness. Awareness about the particular issue and ideology of parties affect the quality of popular responsiveness. Data indicate that the politically aware are usually better able to relate their social values to their political opinions to achieve stable, internally consistent belief systems; and to comprehend and act upon the constitutional rules of the game.[140] Popular responsiveness is required to democratize the governance process.

Political Parties Responsiveness

Governance is the capacity to establish and sustain workable relations between individuals and institutional actors in order to promote collective goals.[141] Here, individuals are the citizens and institutional actors are the political parties, various public and private institutions and voluntary organizations, etc. Political parties constitute a major institutional actor in democratic governance. They function as the important mediators between the people and the policy makers. Effectiveness of any policy primarily is determined by the nature of interaction among political parties.

As given by Giovanni Sartori, parties can only be linkages between the people and a government. During the eighteenth century, the English began practicing party government. However, what the English started practicing during the eighteenth century was not actually party government, but responsible government. In this government, ministers are responsible to parliament, also called the parliamentary system. Burke made this point clear. His stance was: "The virtue, spirit and essence of a house of commons consists in its being the express image of the feelings of the nation. It was not instituted to be a control upon the people."[142] The government can become democratic when people legitimate its position in all respects have control over the policy outcome as well as their leaders.

A government responsible to the house also becomes, in the long run, a government responsible to the people and thereby a responsive government, a government attentive to, and influenced by the voice of the people.[143] Responsiveness of political party to the aspirations of the people legitimates its position in all respects.

People aspire to have democracy in order to get good governance in which people can choose the representatives and have control over them. They should also possess the right to affect the decisions. Democratic governance is the government of the people, which works for the fulfilment of the interest of the people. By the above mentioned theories of democracy, participation, responsiveness, governance and political parties, it becomes clear that party politics is the main determinant of democratic governance and political parties, participation and popular participation, and political parties, responsiveness and popular responsiveness in the political process are the main pillars on which the whole democratic structure is based.

REFERENCES

1. Navin Chandra Joshi (ed.), *Democracy and Humane Values*, Sterling Publishers Private Limited, New Delhi, 1979, p. 1.
2. Hillman M. Bishop and Samuel Hedel, *Basic Issues of American Democracy*, Appleton-Century, Crotts, Inc., New York, 1951, p. 23.
3. Navin Chandra Joshi (ed.), Supra no. 1, p. 36.
4. O.P. Gauba, *An Introduction to Political Theory*, Macmillan India Limited, New Delhi, 1995, p. 287.
5. *Ibid.*, p. 288.
6. Leslie Lipson, *The Democratic Civilization*, Oxford University Press, New York, 1964, p. 43.
7. Kenneth Janda, Jeffrey M. Berry and Jerry Goldman, *The Challenges of Democracy: Government in America*, Houghton Mifflin Company, Boston, 1992, p. 39.
8. David L. Sills (ed.), *International Encyclopedia of Social Sciences*, Macmillan Company and The Free Press, p. 115.
9. *Ibid.*, p. 115.
10. Kenneth Janda, Jeffrey M. Berry and Jerry Goldman, Supra no. 7, p. 39.
11. Carole Pateman, *Participation and Democratic Theory*, Cambridge University Press, Cambridge, 1970, p. 2.
12. Pratibha Kagalkar, A *Comparative Study of Socialism and Democracy*, Himalaya Publishing House, Mumbai, 1996, p. 103.
13. Guy Hermet, The Age of Democracy, *International Social Science Journal*, March 1998, 115, Blackwell Publishers, UNESCO, p. 253.
14. *Ibid.*, p. 253.
15. Carole Pateman, Supra no. 11, p. 7.
16. Pratibha Kagalkar, Supra no. 12, p. 126.
17. Kenneth Janda, Jeffrey M. Berry and Jerry Goldman, Supra no. 7, p. 37.
18. *Ibid.*, p. 37.
19. *Ibid.*, p. 38.
20. T.F. Utley, J.S. Stuart Maclure (ed.), *Documents of Modern Political Thought*, Cambridge University Press, New York, 1957, p. 33.
21. Kenneth Janda, Jeffrey M. Berry and Jerry Goldman, Supra no. 7, p. 39.
22. *Ibid.*, p. 41.
23. *Ibid.*, p. 42.
24. Massimo Salvadori, *Liberal Democracy*, Pall Mall Press, London, 1958, p. 6.
25. David Miller, *Deliberative Democracy and Social Choice*, in David Held (ed.), *Prospects for Democracy*, Stanford University Press, California, 1993, p. 74.
26. J. Roland Pennock, *Liberal Democracy: Its Merits and Prospects*, Rinehart Company, Inc., New York, 1950, pp. 17-18.

27. *Ibid.*, p. 125.
28. *Ibid.*, p. 125.
29. *Ibid.*, p. 125.
30. *Ibid.*, p. 125.
31. Vijay Laxmi Pandit, *Elites and Urban Politics: A Case Study of Delhi*, Inter India Publication, New Delhi, 1984, pp. 8-9.
32. S.S. Patagundi, *India's Foreign Policy: An Elitist Perception*, Uppal Publishing House, New Delhi, 1995, p. 18.
33. Vijay Laxmi Pandit, Supra no. 31, p. 2.
34. S.S. Patagundi, Supra no. 32, p. 19.
35. Vijay Laxmi Pandit, Supra no. 31, p. 4.
36. S.S. Patagundi, Supra no. 32, pp. 20-21.
37. Robert A. Dahl and Dean E. Neubauer, *Readings in Modern Political Analysis*, Prentice-Hall, Inc., New Jersey, 1968, p. 87.
38. Seymour Martin Lipset, *The Encyclopaedia of Democracy*, Vol. III, Routledge, London, 1995, p. 925.
39. Giovanni Sartori, *Parties and Party System: A Framework for Analysis*, Cambridge University Press, Cambridge, 1976, p. 17.
40. Peter H. Merkl, *Modern Comparative Politics*, Holt, Rinehart and Winston, Inc., U.S.A., 1970, p. 265.
41. Giovanni Sartori, Supra no. 39, p. 19.
42. Seymour Martin Lipset, Supra no. 38, p. 925.
43. Alan Ware, *Political Parties and Party System*, Oxford University Press, New York, 1996, p. 12.
44. *Ibid.*, p. 35.
45. Giovanni Sartori, Supra no. 39, p. 19.
46. Keerat Joshi, *Elections, Party System and Defections*, in Subhash C. Kashyap (ed.), *National Resurgence Through Electoral Reforms*, Shipra Publications, Delhi, 2002, p. 121.
47. D.D. Khanna and Gert W. Wreck, *Principles, Power and Politics*, MacMillan Company, Delhi, 1999, p. 243.
48. Roda Mistry in Subhash C. Kashyap (ed.), Supra no. 48. p. 133.
49. S.S. Patagundi in Subhash C. Kashyap (ed.), Supra no. 48, p. 155.
50. *Ibid.*, p. 155.
51. Ali Kazancigil, Governance and Science: Market-Like Modes of Managing Society and Producing Knowledge, *International Social Science Journal*, 115, March 1998, p. 72.
52. Goran Hyden and Michael Bratton (ed.), *Governance and Politics in Africa*, Lynne Rienner Publishers, America, 1992, p. 5.
53. Bob Joseph, The Rise of Governance and the Risks of Failure: The Case of Economic Development, *International Social Science Journal*, 115, March 1998, p. 29.

54. *Ibid.*, p. 30.
55. Francois-Xavier Merrien, Governance and Modern Welfare State, *International Social Science Journal*, 115, March 1998, p. 59.
56. Gerry Stoker, Governance as Theory: Five Propositions, *International Social Science Journal*, 115, March 1998, p. 17.
57. *Ibid.*, p. 17
58. Bob Joseph, Supra no. 53, p. 29.
59. Francois-Xavier Merrien, Supra no. 55, p. 57.
60. Bob Joseph, Supra no. 53, p. 29.
61. Francois-Xavier Merrien, Supra no. 55, p. 59.
62. Goran Hyden and Michael Bratten (ed.), Supra no. 52, p. 6.
63. *Ibid.*, p. 12.
64. *Ibid.*, p. 14.
65. *Ibid.*, pp. 14-15.
66. *Ibid.*, p. 15.
67. Goran Hyden and Michael Bratton (ed.), Supra no. 52, p. 16.
68. *Ibid.*, pp. 17-19.
69. Joachim Ahren, *Governance and Economic Development*, Edward Elgar Publishing Co. Limited, U.K., 2002, pp. 133-134.
70. *Ibid.*, p. 134.
71. David L. Sills (ed.), Supra no. 8, p. 253.
72. Joachim Ahren, Supra no. 69, p. 135.
73. *Ibid.*, p. 136.
74. *Ibid.*, p. 136.
75. J. Roland Pennock, Supra no. 26, p. 212.
76. Y. Pardhasaradhi, Information Technology for Governance and Efficiency, *The Indian Journal of Public Administration*, 50(1), January-March 2004, p. 317.
77. J. Satyanarayan, *e-Government: The Science of the Possible*, Prentice-Hall of India, New Delhi, 2004, p. 1.
78. Alka Dhameja and Uma Medury, ICT and Governance: The Socio-Economic Concerns, *The Indian Journal of Public Administration*, 50(1), January-March 2004, p. 317.
79. J. Satyanarayan, Supra no. 77, p. 2.
80. *Ibid.*, p. 14.
81. Kiran Bedi, Paraminder Jeet Singh and Sandeep Srivastava, *Government@net: New Governance Opportunities for India*, Sage Publications, New Delhi, 2001, p. 21.
82. *Ibid.*, p. 21.
83. J. Satyanarayan, Supra no. 77, p. 22.
84. Murli Dhar Tiwari, *Education and e-Governance*, MacMillan India Limited, Delhi, 2001, p. 15.

85. *Ibid.*, p. 18.
86. J. Satyanarayan, Supra no. 77, p. 43.
87. *Ibid.*, p. 45.
88. *Ibid.*, p. 5.
89. Y. Pardhasaradhi, Supra no. 76, p. 275.
90. *The Hindu*, November 6, 2004.
91. David L. Sills (ed.), Supra no. 8, p. 253.
92. R.P. Verma (ed.), *People's Participation in Indian Politics*, Rajat Publications, New Delhi, 2002, p. 308.
93. David L. Sills (ed.), Supra no. 8, p. 253.
94. Carole Petmen, Supra no. 11, p. 1.
95. *Ibid.*, p. 22.
96. *Ibid.*, p. 23.
97. Carole Pateman, Supra no. 11, p. 24.
98. *Ibid.*, p. 28.
99. *Ibid.*, p. 30.
100. *Ibid.*, p. 36.
101. Carole Pateman, Supra no. 11, p. 37.
102. *Ibid.*, p. 37.
103. *Ibid.*, p. 43.
104. David L. Sills (ed.), Supra no. 8, p. 256.
105. David L. Sills (ed.), Supra no. 8, p. 257.
106. *Ibid.*, p. 259.
107. *Ibid.*, p. 260.
108. Sidney Verba, Norman H. Nie and Jae-on Kim, *Participation and Political Equality*, Cambridge University Press, Cambridge, 1978, p. 310.
109. *Ibid.*, p. 310.
110. *Ibid.*, p. 311.
111. Sidney Verba, Norman H. Nie and Jae-on Kim, Supra no. 108, p. 312.
112. *Ibid.*, p. 312.
113. *Ibid.*, p. 312.
114. Sidney Verba, Norman H. Nie and Jae-on Kim, Supra no. 108, p. 313.
115. *Ibid.*, p. 313.
116. *Ibid.*, p. 314.
117. Sidney Verba, Norman H. Nie and Jae-on Kim, Supra no. 108, p. 315.
118. J. Roland Pennock, Supra no. 26, p. 440.
119. Dhirendra K. Vajpey, *Modernization and Social Change in India*, Manohar Publications, New Delhi, 1979, pp. 73-74.
120. J. Roland Pennock, Supra no. 26, p. 443.
121. David L. Sills (ed.), Supra no. 8, p. 262,
122. *Ibid.*, p. 253.
123. Gabriel A. Almond and James S. Coleman (ed.), *The Politics of the*

Developing Areas, Princeton University Press, New Jersey, 1970, pp. 38-39.

124. Alan Ware, Supra no. 43, p. 5.
125. Gabriel A. Almond and James S. Coleman (ed.), Supra no. 123, p. 37.
126. Giovanni Sartori, Supra no. 39, p. 21.
127. J. Roland Pennock, Supra no. 26, p. 446.
128. *Ibid.*, p. 446.
129. *Ibid.*, p. 447.
130. *Ibid.*, p. 449.
131. J. Roland Pennock, Supra no. 26, p. 450.
132. *Ibid.*, p. 451.
133. *Ibid.*, p. 452.
134. Kenneth Janda, Jeffery M. Berry and Jerry Goldman, Supra no. 5, pp. 39-40
135. J. Roland Pennock, Supra no. 26, p. 261.
136. *Ibid.*, p. 262
137. *Ibid.*, p. 262.
138. J. Roland Pennock, Supra no. 26, pp. 262-263.
139. *Ibid.*, p. 263.
140. David L. Sills (ed.), Supra no. 8, p. 261.
141. Joachim Ahrens, Supra no. 69, p. 121.
142. Giovanni Sartori, Supra no. 126, p. 19.
143. *Ibid.*, p. 20.

3

Democratic Governance in India

Political parties play a crucial role in the functioning of representative democracy. They articulate and aggregate the interests of people. Parties are simply the means through which the people make the governmental system of their choice work and realize their collective purpose.[1] "Political parties constitute one set of political institutions that can help narrow the gap between the growth in politicized demands and governmental effectiveness. Well organized parties thus become especially crucial."[2] Political parties have become an integral part of democratic governance.

Though there is no reference of political party in the Indian Constitution, they continue to play an influential role in the Indian democratic governance. The first reference of political party in the Constitution of India can be found in the tenth schedule to the Constitution. Political parties are crucial for democratizing the process of governance. The nature of party politics determines the effectiveness of democratic governance in terms of promoting the well being of the people.

Democratic Governance in India

Democratic governance mainly relates with how power is exercised in the society. If power is exercised in the interest of the people then it leads to democratic governance. "The first step towards democratic governance is to select representatives of the people by secret ballot, as such, is a number game and the rule of this game is majority rule. Ideally, the candidate elected as the representative is supposed to have combined hopes, aspirations and choices of the maximum number to the maximum extent. If he can satisfy the electorate by his performance as a functionary in the structure of democratic governance he is expected to be re-elected, if not, dropped."[3]

The political parties contesting the elections are accountable to the people and play an important role in democratic governance. Democratic governance is ensured when political parties are made accountable and answerable to the people in the real sense. There should prevail transparency in their actions and they should participate fairly and actively in the governance process. Participation, transparency, accountability, responsiveness, consensus oriented, legitimacy, are considered as important elements of democratic governance. Under this brief overview, we can study the Indian democratic governance under three main phases. Firstly, governance during the Nehruvian period, secondly, governance in the post-Nehru period and thirdly, governance since 1989. The changing nature of party politics played an important role in these three phases. It was the change in the nature of party politics that gave importance to the process of governance in India.

As the nature of party politics determines democratic governance, the study of inter-party politics and intra-party politics becomes crucial. Political parties have to represent the interest of the people. Their main aim is to capture power. To capture power, a political party has to compete with other parties. It has to compete for mobilizing the support of the people. Political parties are mainly regarded as the mediators between the people and the State. They are responsible for democratizing the process of governance. Party politics takes a central position in democratic governance. Political parties are responsible for formulating public policies. Public policies have a direct bearing on the democratic governance of a country. To what extent political parties are able to fulfil this responsibility is a crucial question to deal with.

Governance During Nehruvian Period

Kohli (1990) links the crisis of governability in India to the organizational decline of the Congress.[4] To Rajni Kothari, "India had a functioning system of governance which was basically the Congress System."[5] Post-independent India saw the emergence of One-Party Dominant system. Institutions and practices of democracy found considerable acceptance during the first phase, which was dominated by Nehru and which lasted from the mid-1950s to late 1960s. Besides from Nehru's own commitment to democracy, India benefited in this phase from the presence of two very important institutions: a well functioning civil service and a popular ruling party, the Indian National Congress (or Congress).[6]

In the first three general elections, which were held in 1952, 1957 and 1962, Congress got thumping majority. Because of its numerical strength, its bargaining capacity in the parliament was high. No doubt, the Congress had to face both inter-party and intra-party conflicts. However, the Congress under the leadership of Nehru was able to resolve conflict and was successful in building consensus. The charismatic leadership of Jawaharlal Nehru and his style of functioning influenced substantially the interaction patterns among the parties in evolving consensus on most issues in public affairs.[7] A government to be responsive should be based on consensus.

The Congress placed before the country a bold programme of economic and social development. Congress was successful in mobilizing the support of the masses after independence. It inherited a historical consensus, a considerable organizational base and a widespread feeling of trust and confidence.[8] These were euphoric times in India as new beginnings always are. Although many difficult problems confronted the new government, people had great trust in the capacity of their leaders to solve these problems. It is worth noting here that precisely the period (1952-1965) which saw the development of democratic institutions and a wide diffusion of democratic norms and practices, also saw a modest but uniform rate of growth of the economy, at around four per cent peryear.[9]

People developed confidence in the system of governance. The new elite committed itself to the challenge of development. "Nehru's great achievement in the political sphere was that he helped the rise of a system that was so democratic in operation when he could have easily opted to hold all power in his own hands and justified it in the name of national interest. However, he made this process of democratization incumbent upon personal equations which he worked out with a whole array of people."[10] But he made no attempt to institutionalize this process through structural reforms.

Governance During Post-Nehru Period

Table 3.1 shows that during the first three general elections Congress was in a dominant position. However, the fourth general election weakened the position of the Congress due to several reasons, important among these being the death of Nehru, India's defeat at the hands of China and inflationary trends in Indian economy.[11] With the death of Nehru much has changed. Most important the States' capacity to govern (i.e., the capacity simultaneously to promote development and to accommodate diverse interests) has declined.[12] The economic condition was considerably deteriorated, and the target of economic growth remained unfulfilled. The breakdown of the One-Party Dominant system beginning slowly from 1957 onwards lowered the ability of the Congress party to absorb and assimilate various small groups and movements.

Along with this decline, order and authority are being eroded. Since the mid 1960s, the surface manifestation of this process has been widespread activism outside the established political channels that often has led to violence, a problem compounded by the state's growing incapacity to deal with the pressing problems of law and order, corruption and poverty.[13]

Governance During 70s and 80s

The second major phase during the 1970s and 1980s was dominated mainly by Nehru's daughter, Indira Gandhi. Indian politics during this phase became considerably more turbulent, even temporarily threatening democracy.[14] This phase "was witness to increasing tensions between the contestants in the political process on account of the breakdown of the consensus that had been so evident in the earlier years. With non-Congress governments being voted to power in the States, the insecurity of the Congress leadership at the Central level increased.[15] Indira Gandhi started building her image within the party primarily by adopting a populist strategy. She and her supporters did not feel the need to build a strong party organization. She also did

Table 3.1: Seats Won by Political Parties in the Lok Sabha from 1952–1965

Party	*1952*	*1957*	*1962*	*1965*
Congress	364	371	361	284
Communist	26	27	29	
Socialist Party	12			
Jana Sangh	3	4	14	35
PSP		19	12	13
SP (Lohia)		7	6	
KMPP	9			
Ram Rajya Parishad	3		2	
Hindu Mahasabha	4	2	1	
Muslim League	1	1	2	2
Akali Dal	4		3	3
Jharkhand Party	3	7	3	
Republican Party	2	7	2	1
RSP	3	1	2	1
Forward Bloc	1	3	2	2
Lok Sevak Sangh	2	1	1	1
Ganatantra Parishad	5	7		
Janata Party	1	3		
Peasants and Workers Party	2	4		
Krishikar Lok Party	1			
Bangla Congress				1
Eastern and Indian Tribal Union		1		
Travancore Tamilnad Congress	1			
Commonwealth Party	3			
Tamilnad Toilers Party	4			
Swantantra			22	44
DMK		2	7	25
Hill Leaders Congress			1	1
Hariyana Lok Samiti			1	
Naga Vidharbha Andolana Samiti			1	1
CPI				23
CPI (M)				19
SSP				23
Socialist Unity Centre				1
National Conference (Kashmir)				1
Jana Kranti Dal				3
Independents	35	27	20	29

Source: Harts Hartmann, *Political Parties in India*, Meenakshi Prakashan, Meerut,1971, pp.181-201.

not encourage internal democracy in the Congress party. Elections within the Congress Party might have produced leaders who would not have supported Indira Gandhi, and in order to avoid such power challenges, Indira Gandhi let Congress's organization decline.[16]

However, as the drive to centralize political power in New Delhi has intensified, the political support to sustain it has declined. The highly factionalized, but once mighty Congress, with its strength based on the districts and in the state capitals, was reduced by Mrs. Gandhi in many states and districts to bodies of persons oriented more towards the favour of her emissaries from New Delhi than toward local support bases and state political leaders.[17] The weakening of party organization further weakened Congress party's hold on local politics and gradually its effects can be seen on central politics too. Because systematic mechanisms for recruiting the competent and committed, and filtering out those who cannot serve the organization's purpose, simply do not exist, the quality of local leadership has declined.[18] There is also a decline in the capacity of the party to articulate and aggregate the interest of the people in a proper manner. Party leaders are more loyal to High Command than to the people. As a result, it became less responsive to the needs and aspirations of the people. Significance of the Congress declined as it failed to be the party of the masses. The Congress system, which had provided a functioning system of governance started declining mainly because of lack of intra-party democracy.

Responsiveness of party towards people started declining. This was confirmed by its defeat in 1977 general elections. Indira Gandhi had established a pattern of personal dominance in the working of Congress party, the Cabinet, the Parliament, etc. Routine administration came to be executed by a 'loyal' and politicized bureaucracy; and populism came to the forefront in Indian politics. This resulted in structural change towards erosion of institutional rule in India. As a result, intra-party democracy of the Congress declined to a considerable extent. Thus, the Congress lost its significance as an important institution for maintaining the linkage between the policy makers and the people. "The first tendency was the scramble for office in a typical Westminster model of state management in which legislative and ministerial position became more important than party positions. This led to a structure of factional manipulation within the state and district organs of the dominant party, gradually making fresh entry into it more and more difficult and thus turning it into a closed shop (except occasionally through the intervention of leaders from higher levels)."[19] "Much the same happened to the other parties most of which, with the exception of the communist parties, followed the pattern set by the Congress. Increasingly accent was placed more on the manipulative capabilities of a leader or a would-be candidate for a legislative seat and less on participation in the party's programme of 'constructive work' as was the case during the independence movement and for some time after independence."[20]

With her 'Garibi Hatao' populist slogan, Indira Gandhi became more popular among the people. The populist methods adopted by Indira Gandhi gave her electoral victory. Attaining the majority in the parliament became the basic concern of all parties. Every party competes with other parties with populist techniques to win elections. Gradually, the values that governed the functioning of political institutions were undermined. Populist politicians with a considerable sway over the minds of the people who, however, have both failed in producing viable political institutions and through them delivered the goods to the people.[21] But, such populist techniques worked well for some time but failed to achieve long term objectives. The agitation in Gujrat, J.P. Movement, the judgement of the Allahabad High Court on Indira Gandhi's election and above all, imposition of National Emergency in 1975—all these factors contributed to the defeat of the Congress in 1977 elections. The efforts of Congress since 1978 to restore its governance at the Centre had not succeeded. Indira Gandhi's assassination in the mid 1980s and that of her son Rajiv Gandhi a few years thereafter, brought an end to the era of Congress dominance via family rule.[22] Their hold on power is so personalistic that their legitimacy did not run deep. With the authoritarian style of functioning of Indira Gandhi, people could hardly see any future of democracy in the hands of the Congress.

Democratic Governance Since 1989

It was argued by many that the challenges that Indian democracy faced in the 1990s are distinct. An altogether new phase in Indian politics started with the emergence of coalition governments. The election results of 1989, 1991, 1996 and 1998 returning hung parliament confirm this new trend in Indian politics.

The institutional decline of the Congress party has not been offset by the development of an alternative national party.[23] It paved the way for region based multi-party system. The party system has entered into a phase of transition since the second half of 1980s and a new 'regionalized' multi-party system is gradually emerging in which all India parties based in various states compete for power at the Centre.[24] With the rise of regional parties the significance of national parties started declining. It has become difficult for any single party to attain majority in the Parliament. It is true that the splintering and fragmentation of party system is, to a large extent, responsible for political instability leading to difficulties in governability.[25] The third and current phase that began around 1990s has thus been characterized by a variety of national level political experiments to find a substitute for the old Congress party rule.[26]

The year 1989 marked a new beginning in Indian political system. With the emergence of coalition politics there was a change in the governance of the country. Since 1989, coalition politics has become a common feature of Indian democracy. It has also changed the nature of party politics.

Governance is not an independent variable but it is a direct function of the policies and actions of the government.[27] It is essential to have good governments to have good governance. The governments should be able not only to formulate the policies but also to translate these policies into action through an accountable administration. The primary accountability rests with the representatives who most often are the members of one or the other party. Accountability gives legitimacy to the government. When the accountability of the leaders itself is in question then there is no room for legitimacy. However, in India, "accountability if at all exists, is to the party or the party high command and not to the people."[28] When there is neither accountability nor legitimacy, then there is no scope for responsiveness. Therefore, an understanding of democratic governance involves an analysis of the functioning of political parties. By taking the examples of coalition governments, we attempt to analyze the perspectives of political parties on democratic governance and to how much our leaders succeed in providing accountable and responsive governance after 1990s.

In 1989 for the first time, government was formed with the support of right and left parties by putting an end to one-party dominant system. To defeat the mighty Congress the non-Congress parties formed an alliance. National Front government was formed under the leadership of V.P. Singh with the support of Janata Dal, Congress (S), DMK, TDP and Assam Gana Parishad. This time the BJP supported the government from outside.[29] After the 1989 elections, when no political party won an absolute majority in the Lok Sabha, the BJP decided to give the National Front a chance to form the government at the centre. The main aim behind supporting the National Front was to keep the Congress out of power. As the National Front government had no clear mandate it was dependent on the support of BJP.

The decision to implement Mandal Commission Report created widespread violence in the country and weakened the coalition. BJP that had supported the coalition from outside, faced a classic dilemma. If it were to back the government on the issue of job reservations, the party risked the loss of its traditional urban base and if it opposed Mandal, it risked losing a large chunk of backward Hindu voters concentrated in the rural areas. The party leadership came to the conclusion that only purely religious issues could unite the Hindus, irrespective of caste/class divisions.[30] Ayodhya campaign was the only remedy and the temple was the only issue which could match the multi-dimensional challenge of Mandalism.[31] Devi Lal made V.P. Singh as the leader of the National Front with the hope of getting some rewards. When things did not turn out as expected, he and his son Om Prakash Chautala became responsible for aggravating the violence, which was created because of the Mandal issue. Amidst all this confusion, the BJP withdrew its support to V.P. Singh government.

Taking the advantage of the situation, Congress leader Rajiv Gandhi announced that his party was willing to extend its support to Janata Dal minus V. P. Singh. Chandra Shekhar, then a member of Janatal Dal found his way to realize his long cherished dream of becoming the country's Prime Minister. Soon after the resignation of V. P. Singh, Chandra Shekhar formed the next government with the support of Congress and its allies. Anxious to retain his chair at any cost, Chandra Shekhar conceded Congress demands one after the other. "Personally presenting some remarkably fresh and even pragmatic ideas, Chandra Shekhar could not escape the pressures of Rajiv Gandhi's Congress, either in policy making or even in personnel appointments. His greatest problem was the fast disappearance of financial reserves and the inability to fashion any economic policies, even a budget."[32] For the first time in Indian history, the budget was postponed. This was primarily due to the kind of party politics that prevailed then. The country went without budget until Narasimha Rao government produced interim budget in July 1991.

Instead of becoming responsive towards the needs and aspirations of people, the political parties gave priority for partisan gains. Instead of becoming genuine representatives of the people, they became formal representatives of the party. Inter-party and intra-party conflicts dominated the proceedings of the Parliament without throwing light on the grievances of the people.

When Prem Singh and Raj Singh were arrested by the Delhi Police for their unauthorized presence outside the then Congress President's 10, Janpath residence, Congress insisted on the government to take adequate action into the probe. Chandra Shekhar promised remedial action but only after a proper enquiry.[33] Though the assurance was given by Chandra Shekhar of remedial action the Congress went on insisting on the issues, which led to the adjournment of Lok Sabha twice for want of quorum. Maybe the Congress thought that they could use it as a pressure point for some other purposes, but it was too much for Chandra Shekhar. Chandra Shekhar became adamant and submitted his resignation on March 10, 1990. The motives of the Congress were not good from the beginning and Rajiv Gandhi soon pulled the rug, leaving Chandra Shekhar hanging in mid-air, thus precipitating the 1991 general elections.[34]

"The Indian party system, from the elections to the dissolution of the 1989 Lok Sabha was afflicted with a paralysis of the will to govern. With no clear mandate for any one party, the two minority governments in the Ninth Lok Sabha displayed no imagination or skill in working out the delicate task of governing a highly complex democracy."[35] There was also a certain degree of ungovernability making the party system, most evident in the breakdown of normal institutional process of politics in some states or parts thereof due to ethnic fundamentalism, class radicalism and Naxalite violence, as well as the growing criminalization of politics, political and administrative corruption, and electoral violence.[36] The above example shows how each and every issue is politicized by the political parties to gain more power. One or the other ally of the coalition is always ready to pull the rug under the government.

Because of this politics played by the political parties the process of democratic governance has become difficult. As government kept on changing in Delhi, it looked as though no one could take charge of policy-making, not to speak of implementation.[37] It was rightly pointed out by Alesina and Tabellini that in relation to public debt, "uncertainty about who will be appointed in the future prevents the current government from fully internalizing the cost of leaving debt to its successors... By leaving debt to the future, today's government can force its successor to 'pay the bills."[38]

"...the problems of governance, compounded by a financial crisis leading to root-and-branch changes in the economy, dominated the thinking and energies of the country throughout 1991."[39] The 1990s saw the emergence of a severe economic crisis. Economic crisis and persistent fiscal deficits budget by state year after year made the state to take to increased borrowing which resulted in increased interest payments. NF government rather than taking measures to reduce economic crisis it launched populist policies worsening the economic situation. The New Economic Policy enunciated by the Congress in 1991 was seen widely as "a shift from the Congress policy of Nehruvian Socialism or mixed economy to the policy of market economy with less state or administrative control, liberalization of the economy, privatization of the large and bulky public sector and an eagerness to invite both foreign capital and technology in a big way."[40] The Congress party which slowly started liberalizing its economic policy opted for globalisation influenced by external developments such as "...collapse of Soviet bloc as a result of failure on the economic front, while China marched forward triumphantly as it integrated with the global economy and took to the path of the market, held little future for the socialist model that India had thus far followed. The combination of domestic economic crisis and the external collapse at the command economy model served 'to change the mindset' in India."[41] It was believed that the compulsions which made India to act according to the dictates of IMF and World Bank are more due to the failure of democratic governance than the external pressure. "The pressure was always there from industrially developed nations of the West for opening India's economy in the interest of the expansion of their capital and commodity markets, but India could withstand that till, 80s of the last century. Since India could not set her house in order, mainly because of the all pervading corruption, democratic governance failed miserably making India surrender to accept reform measures with humiliating terms."[42]

While justifying his reputation as a consensus seeker, the new Prime Minister moved fast and steadily to transform India's economic system, even though no consensus on this was possible within his own party.[43] BJP criticized the economic policies on populist ground. "Indian industries resist the policy of inviting foreign companies and find the BJP concept of '*Swadeshi*' a relief. The Left was critical of the new economic policy and the conditionalities imposed by the IMF and the World Bank. It organized rallies and protests against the new policy. However, the Left government in West Bengal did not lag behind in inviting foreign capital and technology to its state."[44] Both Janata Dal of V.P. Singh and Lok Dal of Chandra Shekhar were not in favour of them. Narasimha Rao's government was accused of abandoning the national consensus and the great legacy of Nehru and founding fathers.

However, very soon the promise of faster economic growth inherent in the liberalization process has been clouded by several factors.[45] The Security Scam and scarcity of competent economists to examine, evaluate and articulate policy alternatives were some of the problems in front of the government. There is also lack of consensus on what measures to take and given the health of the Indian economy, most measures are bound to be politically uncomfortable and unpopular.[46] All these have contributed for the slow down in the economic process.

According to I.K. Gujral, India is facing crises of governance mainly due to new economic policy. According to him, the new economic policy had four negative impacts on Indian society. "They have created new inequalities and sharpened the traditional ones, thereby lending new edges to social and political turmoil and disorder. Secondly, they have enlarged the width and depth of corruption. Thirdly, they have brought into being a flood of narcissist self-indulgence by a relatively small, but not insignificant affluent consumer middle-class whose glittering life style has immensely sharpened the age old universal social contradictions in India. Finally, they have expanded people's expectations and aspirations for the glitters of good living without generating either enough national resource or enough national will to rapidly develop our vast depressed human resources, exposing to national and international limelight the gaping faultiness in our chosen models and pathways of development."[47]

Congress ceased to be the predominant party in 1996 elections. It was primarily due to internal feuds, corruption, etc. Congress realized the slow and steady decline of its position. Over the years, it has become more interested in patronage than good government. It concentrated more on urban rich than rural poor. In 1996 elections, the voters' message was clear that the Congress had lost its way. The poll outcome of Lok Sabha 1996 is given in Table 3.2.

The Congress party faced double dilemma because on its own it could not form the government and if it could not support the UF coalition BJP may form government. This became a compulsion on the part of Congress to support the UF government to keep the BJP out of power. "Yet, during the election campaign the harshest rhetoric by the UF parties was directed against Congress—including charges of corruption and of having sold out the poor of India to the greed of multinationals. Policy differences, personality clashes and memories of the 1996 election campaign prevented Congress from joining the UF government as an active partner."[48]

Table 3.2: Lok Sabha 1996 Poll Outcome

Party	*Seats*
Congress (I)	140
BJP	161
Janata Dal	46
Congress (T)	04
Janata Party (S)	05
Shiva Sena	15
Samata	09
SP	16
LF	51
TMC	20
MPVC	01
BSP	11
HVP	03
Others	56
Independent	08
Total	**541**

Source: *Asian Survey*, 36 (3), March 1997, p. 1.

The greatest weakness of the United Front was its total dependence on the Congress for survival, which supported UF from outside. These coalitions had no homogeneity of outlook and the motives of the dominant partner were suspected right from the start. No wonder, they could not pursue strong, consistent and long-range policies, and fell a prey to their internal contradictions.[49]

"Kesari had gambled on engineering defections from the ranks of UF member parties and there by forming a new Congress (I)-led government. But the principal constituents of the UF rejected his blandishments, and Kesari was only able to bring about the ouster of his nemesis, Deve Gowda, from the prime minister's post."[50] Kesari also agreed to support the UF because it was assumed that if fresh polls were declared, people were not either for authoritarian and corrupt Congress or for the communal and disruptive BJP. But the tenure of I.K. Gujral did not last long. The Congress withdrew its support and midterm elections became inevitable.

"The political uncertainty that characterized India during the year exacted a toll on economic growth and foreign investment. Fearful of possibly abrupt shift in economic policy, foreign investors approached the Indian market with increased caution."[51] Since the beginning of the reform process the Janata Dal, BJP and especially the Left Front had been bitter critiques of economic liberalization. They vowed, therefore, to overthrow the economic policy reforms if they came to power which threatened Congress party's claim that the reforms were here to stay since they were based on a national consensus.

When UF government was formed Janata Dal and Left parties were partners in the coalitions. They are fully aware of the fact that they cannot impose their will on other partners. The UF partners adopted a common approach and formulated joint programme promising a strengthened public sector. In realizing their joint programme, CPI (M) general Secretary Surjeet declared that no privatization would be allowed as the public sector was the foundation of the country's industrialization and had a continuing vital role to play.[52] More importantly, UF was dependent on Congress for support in order to come to power and stay in power and that a necessary precondition for such a support was the continuity of economic reforms initiated by the Congress government. Though UF partners stressed on strengthening public sector in their CMP, to stay in power they adopted economic liberalization. Thus most of the time formulation and continuity of economic policies depend at the convenience of political parties rather than based on national interest.

The UF government could not achieve much in the public affairs as most of the time it was worried about maintaining its power at the center. For accountability and responsiveness stability is a necessary condition, though not the sole condition. An unstable and shaky government can hardly be a responsive and responsible government if it does not have time to function without constant interference or leg pulling partners.[53]

The 1998 election resulted in a hung Lok Sabha. Table 3.3 indicates the position of parties in Lok Sabha. BJP succeeded in forming the government with the help of parties like Akali Dal, AIADMK, BJD and other regional parties. "These alliances were made possible in part by the fact that there appeared to be no other party in opposition to form a government. Also, the BJP managed to portray itself more credibly as a moderate party of the right that eschewed—for the time being at any rate—aspects of its Hindu nationalist agenda that had contributed to its pariah status."[54]

The 'national agenda' of the BJP-led government declared "Our first commitment to the people is to give a stable, honest, transparent and efficient government, capable of accomplishing all round development." But, how do we hope the government to accomplish or how much time shall it take to act on the promise? What we find in practice is that this coalition government of thirteen parties is constantly engaged in keeping its head above the relentless bickering and tussels among the partners in the government.[55]

BJP's survival depended very much on the mercy of its smaller allies, particularly the AIADMK under Jayalalitha. During the 12 months support to the coalition government, Jayalalitha raised many issues like the imposition of President's Rule in Bihar, George Fernandes, statement, labelling China as enemy number one, the delay in passing the women's reservation bill, amending the Constitution to allow the states to have their own quota of reservation beyond fifty pecent and the setting up of a committee to make all languages listed in the eighth schedule as national languages.[56] She kept three major demands as a pre-condition for continuing her party's support to the government. They included, to reinstate Naval Chief Admiral Vishnu

Table 3.3: Election Results of 12th Lok Sabha 1998

BJP and Allies	*Seats*	*Party*	*Seats*
BJP	**182**	**INC (I)**	**141**
Pre-poll Allies	**73**	**Allies**	**25**
ADMK	18	RJD	17
SAP	12	RPI	04
BJD	09	MUL	02
SAD	08	KCM	01
TC	07	RJP	01
SHS	06		
PMK	04	UF Parties	99
LS	03		
MDMK	03	CPM	32
HVP	01	SP	20
JP	01	CPI	09
TRC	01	DMK	06
JD	06		
Post-Poll Allies	**13**	**RSP**	**05**
TMC	03		
HLDR	04	FBL	02
ANC	02	AIICS	01
MSC	01	TDP	12*
SD	01	NC	03*
Independent	05		
Others	**10**		
BSP	05		
ASDC	01		
MIM	01		
PWP	01		
SJRP	01		
VMF	01		

* TDP and NC out of UF after poll.

Source: Arun Kumar, *On Coalition Course*, Gyan Publishing House, New Delhi, 1998, p.13.

Bhagwat, to divest George Fernandes of the Defence portfolio or to shift him to another ministry and to set up a Joint Parliamentary Committee to look into the corruption charges in defence deals. "The AIADMK chief Jayalalitha accused the Prime Minister in April for not showing any interest in solving the problems of Tamil Nadu, nor did he consult the alliance partners on important issues like the Pokhran Tests, Cauvery Water dispute, Power Tariff, Regulatory Authority and a host of other matters including the inept handling of the national security. She finally declared that because of all this, she was forced to pull out the Vajpayee government."[57]

During this period Vajpayee managed to get some of the opposition parties support on important issues. "On the one hand, some elements within the Congress offered to cooperate with the BJP government to implement such important pieces of legislation as the Women Reservation and Insurance Reform Bills, on the other hand, Congress was tempted to block every piece of legislation in order to make the BJP government appear ineffective. The net result was a logjam in Parliament that underscored the high costs of a fragmented parliamentary system."[58] In 1998, Indian economy was weakened. "For one, coalition governments with weak internal cohesion meant that pressing economic problems have been secondary to the exigencies of government survival. Additionally, the inherent instability of such governments also meant that the frequency of government turnover increased, and with it, the time horizon of political actors has been shortening. As a result, even when government intentions and instincts have been in the right direction, they have been undermined by inexperience transmuting into ineptitude."[59]

NDA formed the ministry after the 1999 elections. But, "Inter-party relations in the NDA, both in the parliamentary and federal arenas of politics, have been more volatile. Unity has been sought to be maintained by power-sharing arrangements in the union cabinet and in politics in the states."[60] NDA under the leadership of the BJP was successful in completing its full term from 1999 to 2004. It was the personality of Vajpayee which held the NDA partners together. But, its achievement in the sphere of public welfare is not satisfactory which is confirmed by its defeat in 2004 general elections.

The rise and fall of NDA proved the fact that it is not easy to deceive the people of India only by attractive promises. They are capable of judging the performance of the political parties by the works they have done. Fed up with the Congress rule and unstable coalitions people of India found some hope in the NDA government. They were attracted by the promises of efficient, transparent, accountable and responsive government. However, during its rule it proved no different from other parties. Perhaps this might have made the people to turn towards the Congress party, which was out of power for eight years.

Table 3.4: General Election Results 2004

Party	Contestants	Won
INC	417	145
BJP	364	138
CPM	69	43
BSP	435	19
CP!	34	10
NCP	32	9
SP	237	36
RJD	42	24
DMK	16	16
SHS	56	12
BJD	12	11
JD (U)	73	8
SAD	10	8
PMK	6	6
TDP	33	5
JMM	9	5
MDMK	4	4
JD (S)	43	3
RLD	32	3
AIFB	10	3
RSP	6	3
AITC	33	2
AGP	12	2
JKN	6	2
MUL	10	1
JKPDP	3	1
NPF	3	1
KEC	1	1
MNF	1	1
SDF	1	1

Source: http://archive.eci.gov.in/GE 2004/index-ge.htm

Congress party had accepted the coalition trend in the country and by aligning itself with other parties it started appealing to the sentiments of the poor which were so far neglected by the ruling NDA. BJP became so confident of its victory in the fourteenth Lok Sabha that it committed a number of mistakes that proved to be an advantage to the Congress party. The BJP was highlighting more on the issues of Bofors and Sonia Gandhi's foreign origin. It believed: "Once the issues of Bofors and Sonia Gandhi's foreign origin are raised, the NDA government's failure—its unending record of corruption scandals, its dismal performance in the agriculture and social service sectors, its indifference to the problem of growing unemployment, its callous disregard towards farmers' suicides, its apathy to the sufferings of common people—recede into the background. The only thing that catches the media's attention is the response of the Congress to the BJP's attacks on Sonia Gandhi."[61] However, things turned out differently. Congress party's acceptance of coalition logic and Rahul Gandhi's entry into politics also contributed to its victory. In order to lift the sagging prospects of the party in the State, Rahul Gandhi was fielded from Sonia Gandhi's parliamentary constituency, Amethi, while she would shift to neighbouring Rae Bareli.[62] UPA under the leadership of Congress formed the government. Left parties have given outside support to the Congress-led UPA government.

In a federal system, it is natural to accept the existence of regional parties, which stand for the promotion of social and economic justice for particular region. However, if they contest parliamentary elections, they will send a handful of representatives and there will be no party having an absolute majority in the Lok Sabha.[63] Since 1989, India has been facing the same problem. Alliances were made with parties having no common ideology or objective. Political parties form alliances without the least regard for ideology or policy issues.[64]

The government itself need not be a coalition of parties. What is needed is a government that is able to govern with a unity of purpose and stability of policies.[65] A significant reduction in the number of parties, howsoever desirable, is simply not possible, given the dynamics of present-day politics, what with castes, religions, regions and ambitions and egos of leading players playing dominant roles. What one could realistically hope for is (i) a viable coalition with a genuine power sharing culture and (ii) issue-based co-operation between the ruling side and the opposition in the national interest.[66]

Indian political system is being controlled by the parties' and individuals' desire for power. The recent example for this is the AIADMK, which was part of a coalition led by BJP (1998), but could overnight switch over to talk about forming a coalition with Congress (I).[67] The present alliances are neither based on ideology nor have any common objective to cement them together. They are merely short-term tactical arrangements established by ambitious politicians that are rooted in the exchange of mutual benefits and the compulsions of power".[68] Consensus politics, conciliatory gestures and the spirit of co-operation is on the decline; the respect for conflicting views and dissent have faded away.[69] All these situations are hampering the process of democratic governance in India.

Party politics has become one of the main difficulties in democratizing the process of governance. Interaction among political parties within and outside coalition are obstructing the policy making process. Political parties within the coalition are always ready to grab the opportunity to overthrow the government. Political parties outside the coalition are creating deadlocks in the proceedings of the parliament in order to make the government ineffective. Important policies were hardly discussed in the parliament. Arriving at consensus on most of the policies has become very difficult task due to the nature of party politics. In such a situation where every political party is concerned mainly with capturing power we hardly hope for achieving democratic governance.

"Although democracy is understood as a self-rule, we are practically ruled by our representatives. Certainly there is a considerable gap between the aspirations of our rulers and our own aspirations. This gap is creating problems and tensions in our social and political life."[70] In such a situation, people should make government accountable and responsive to the needs of the people. If government has to perform well, it is the political parties that have to perform well. Welfare of the people should be their main concern for which they are in power. Today, we hardly find any party that is service oriented. When citizens cast their vote, they expect the candidate for whom they vote to work and serve the nation and citizens honestly and faithfully. Based on their performance people decide whether to re-elect them or not. Thus, through elections the representatives are made accountable to the people. When the electoral system itself is suffering from a number of deficiencies, how can the people hold their representatives accountable? Money, mafia and muscle power play an important role in electoral politics. Booth capturing, rigging, false and bogus voting, etc., are the common features of our election process. There are routine references of such incidents in many of the states in India. In such a situation, it is difficult to ensure accountability and responsiveness of the representatives. With such a system, people may turn to be apathetic towards politics. Good people are living away from politics. They consider politics as a dirty game. No doubt through violent agitations, riots and protest movements some people show their dissatisfaction with the system and attempt to draw the attention of the government. Most often, such movements are suppressed with the help of military/police forces, as they are very less in number.

There are high promises from the political parties to win the election and very little performance in the government in accordance with the promises.[71] The danger had occurred because the rulers who are representatives of the citizens do not represent the will of the society but work for their 'individual will' and petty interests. By getting elected they get power and as soon as representatives get power, citizens become helpless.[72] Rajni Kothari, in his writings elaborately discusses this aspect and cautions the people that an alert and vigilant public opinion alone can serve our democracy.[73] For a healthy democracy, people have to react on policies and decisions of the government. A government reflects the thinking of society. As Daniel Webster said, "nothing will ruin the country if the people themselves will undertake its safety; and nothing can save it if they leave that safety in the hands of others."[74]

Globalization and Governance

Globalization and governance are the new coinages of today's international community. The expression of globalization can be found in the writings of French and American scholars in the 1960s, which has become a buzz word in 1990s. It is primarily due to its ambiguous nature we cannot find cogent theory of globalization. However, Mohit Bhattacharya had given three schools of thought of the phenomenon of globalization.

(i) The hyperglobalizers' views of globalization as a new era in which people are increasingly subjected to disciplines of the global market.

(ii) The sceptics consider the hyperglobalism thesis as myth. They "confirm only heightened levels of internationalization among national economies in terms of overtime world flow of trade, investment and labour."[75] The sceptics do not believe that in the global world, national governments or state sovereign is being undermined.

(iii) The transformationalists believe that globalization is a powerful force which has the ability to reshape modern societies and the world order.

In its contemporary usage the concept of globalization has come to reflect "a widespread perception that the world is being rapidly moulded into a shared social space by economic and technological forces and that development for the one region of the world can have profound consequences for the life chances of individual or communities on the other side of the globe."[76]

Globalization in simple terms means integrating the economy of the country with that of the world. After 1980s most of the developing countries faced acute economic crisis which compelled them to liberalize their economy as per the international compulsions. The integration of developing countries into the world economy has given rise to the emergence of complex negotiations between governing elites and international agencies to bring about socio-economic change. These forces of integration are potentially positive developments. It was hoped that they would provide an environment conducive to global economic prosperity in general and the aspirations of the developing countries in particular. Unfortunately, the system did not work in this way.

The governance idea initially broached by the World Bank and later further elaborated by the OECD countries, had its origin in the early nineties of the last century, when the foreign donors' basic interest had been to lay down conditionalities for receiving foreign aid.[77] The components of governance like accountability, transparency, participation, responsiveness, legitimacy, development and human rights are very much pleasing and attractive. By insisting that it exists to sponsor 'fairness', justice, liberty, an independent judiciary, respect for human rights and inefficient and corruption free bureaucracy and by insisting that there were the basic requirements.... For a modern state, the Bank is certainly open to the charge that its objective is to impose modern western democracy by means of economic incentives.[78] However, the underlying philosophy is to restrict aid to developing countries by imposing conditionality.

If developing countries are to follow open economic policies in these turbulent times, they need great confidence in a shared commitment to establish trading rules that are fair to developing countries.[79] The Asian crisis had added worries and uncertainties and raises fears that the present international financial system is inherently unstable. There is an urgent need to search for an appropriate architecture for an international financial system which could increase confidence in its stability. There is need for much better regulation and supervision of the financial system in all countries, based on common set of norms and standards.[80]

Governance also draws our attention to a shift in responsibilities and stepping back of the state. In the new governance process initiated by the World Bank and IMF, responsibilities are shared between public, private and voluntary sectors. Thus, the developing countries are facing domestic as well as external crisis of governance.

Globalization and Governance in India

"The increase in the assertion of identity and their political mobilization and the economic reforms effected in the shadow of globalization, are arguably two of the most significant trends in Indian politics and society in the last decade of the twentieth century. In their different way both have had important consequences for the way in which the role of the state and problem of governance are approached and conceptualized."[81]

In India, "the state is a strong interventionist force not only for maintaining order but, more importantly for engineering social and domestic development."[82] Though the state is the chief controller and regulator of the economy, planned economic transformation and development led to the growth of private corporate sector or capitalist development. "Capitalism is developing in India in a conscious manner and the state is its promoter because capitalists are controlling the state through multiple linkages and alliances."[83] Political arrangements were clearly dominated by an educated and nationalist elite. The class elite, landed and caste elites were equally influential. The dominant political elites, moreover, practiced a reconciliatory approach towards the competing elites, while professing the hope that they would be able to bring the poor and the oppressed masses into the mainstream of India's modernizing political economy.[84] People had confidence in the ability of the elites and their developmental programmes.

Gradually the capacity of the states to promote development and accommodate diverse interest declined mainly because of the following reasons:

(i) Members of higher class and caste graduallv lost their capacity to influence those below them in the socio-economic hierarchy. Because, the state became democratic but the administration remained largely authoritarian under the influence of higher class and caste people.

(ii) Decline of One-Party-Dominant system led to the emergence of multi-party system which is dominated by the regional parties. Emergence of regional parties made formation of government a difficult task. No single party is in a position to form government on its own. It has to ally itself with one or more parties to form government. Political parties with different ideologies and interest made governance more difficult. Coalition governments without coalition culture added problems in governance.

(iii) The relentless march of globalization, mandating economic deregulation and liberalization, represent exogenous imperative that has contributed heavily to the emasculation of the state, if not always to its retreat.[85] Ashok Malhotra in his paper, *Good Governance* presented at General Discussion Forum for the RBAP-RR Meeting said globalization as one of the major weaknesses of Governance in India.

The seeds of globalization were evident in early eighties in India in the form of government concessions to foreign capital, allowing MNCs to enter a number of crucial sectors and impact of liberalization process. India faced problem of balance of payment after 1980-81. Policies were formulated to attract the MNCs to overcome the economic crisis. However, they did not achieve much success in attracting the private capital. India faced acute economic crisis in 1990-91, which pushed India into adopting structural adjustment programme of the IMF and World Bank. Since then India had been pushed towards globalization.

Thus, the gradual decline in the nation-state's capacity to provide effective governance increased the importance of public sector and voluntary organizations. Institutions of local government (such as panchayats); civil society organization (ranging from social movements to non-governmental and from cooperatives to civic associations); and private corporations as well as other market institutions are all relevant actors in the new lexicon of governance.[86] In such a governance process the state is not totally losing its power. Though it is associated with the private sector and voluntary organization, it continues to be supreme. The actors have a significant degree of autonomy yet, government steers the whole process, which should be in the interest of the people. Mahbub-ul-Haq who developed the concept of humane governance, in his Human Development Report (1999), said: "The concept of humane governance puts people at the centre for all governance policies, stratégies and actions."[87]

Mahbub-ul-Huq stressed that the governance should always be in the interest of the people. What is needed is to "bring back human concerns to the centre of regulating both the State and civil society; of recovery of the basics and of first principles, thus recreating an ethical order which is a source of values."[88] This cannot be achieved by market economies. To Rajni Kothari: "Civil society's ordering of politics and governance is, in my view, the take-off point for humane governance."[89] The role of NGOs, self-help groups, different organization and movements of the people are crucial in this regard. The government should share its power with these voluntary agencies which make governance more humane and democratic.

"Such sources of regeneration in terms of being able to provide an alternative lie more in the South than in the North, more in women than in men, more in the marginalized than in the powerful, more in ethnic identities and submerged civilization than in dominant culture. It is precisely those groups and segments of human society which were rendered dispensable with the projects of the State, they become indispensable as political and ethical sources for humane governance."[90] Thus, peoples' participation is crucial to make governance more democratic.

REFERENCES

1. V.A. Paipanandikar and Subhash C. Kashyap (ed.), *Political Reforms:*

Asserting Civic Sovereignty, Konark Publishers Private Limited, 2001, p. 273.

2. Atul Kohli, Democracy and Discontent: *India's Growing Crisis of Governability*, Cambridge University Press, Cambridge, 1991, p. 30.
3. Dilip Halder, Democratic Governance is no Panacea: The Experience of India and South Asia, *The Indian Journal of Public Administration*, 50(1), January-March 2004, pp. 208-209.
4. Pradeep K. Chibber, *Democracy Without Associations: Transforming the Party System and Social Cleavages in India*", Vikas Publications, New Delhi, 1999, p. 178.
5. S.K. Chopra (ed.), *Towards Good Governance*, Konark Publishers Private Limited, Delhi, 1997, p. 21.
6. Atul Kohli (ed.), *The Success of India's Democracy*, Cambridge University Press, New Delhi, 2001, p. 6.
7. R.T. Jangam, S.H. Patil and S.S. Patagundi, *Political Analysis*, Oxford and IBH Publishing Company, New Delhi, 1997, p. 156.
8. Rajni Kothari, *Politics and the People: In search of Humane India*, Vol. I, Ajanta Publications, Delhi, 1989, p. 6.
9. Rajni Kothari, *Democratic Polity and Social Change in India*, Allied Publishers, New Delhi, 1976, p. 11.
10. *Ibid.*, p. 15.
11. Hans Raj, *Indian Political System*, Surjeet Publications, Delhi, 1990, p. 110.
12. Atul Kohli, Supra no. 2, p. 5.
13. *Ibid.*, p. 5.
14. Atul Kohli (ed.), Supra no. 6, p. 7.
15. Sandeep Shastri, *The Indian Journal of Political Science*, 63(1), March 2002, p. 94.
16. Atul Kohli, Supra no. 2, p. 190.
17. Paul Brass, *The Politics of India Since Independence*, Cambridge University Press, Cambridge, 1990, p. 33.
18. Atul Kohli, Supra no. 2, p. 188.
19. Rajni Kothari, Supra no. 9, p. 26.
20. *Ibid.*, p. 26.
21. Rajni Kothari, *Memoirs: Uneasy is the Life of Mind*, Roop and Company, New Delhi, 2002, p. 157.
22. Atul Kohli (ed.), Supra no. 6, p. 9.
23. Atul Kohli, Supra no. 2, pp. 5-6.
24. Zoya Hassan (ed.), *Parties and Party Politics in India*, Oxford University Press, New Delhi, 2002, p. 151.
25. V.A. Paipanandikar and Subhash C. Kashap (ed.), Supra no. 1, p. 278.
26. Atul Kohli (ed.), Supra no. 6, p. 9.

27. S.K. Chopra (ed.), Supra no. 5, p. 33.
28. Dilip Halder, Supra no. 3, p. 209.
29. D. Devanathan, Strengthening Coalition Experiment at Center, *Third Concept*, January 1999, p. 26.
30. Yogendra K. Malik, Bharatiya Janata Party: An Alternative to the Congress (I)?, *Asian Survey*, 32(4), April 1992. p. 333.
31. M.L. Ahuja and Sharada Paul, *1989-1991 General Elections in India*, Associated Publishing House, New Delhi, 1992. p. 71.
32. K. Shankar Bajpai, India in 1991: New Beginnings, *Asian Survey*, 32(2), February 1992, p. 208.
33. M.L. Ahuja and Sharada Paul, Supra no. 31, p. 77.
34. Attar Chand, *Prime Minister: H.D. Deve Gowda*, Gyan Publishing House, New Delhi, 1997, p. 24.
35. Mahendra Prasad Singh, "The Dilemma of the New Indian Party System: To Govern or Not to Govern?", *Asian Survey*, 32(4), April 1992, pp. 307-308.
36. *Ibid.*, p. 308.
37. K. Shankar Bajpai, Supra no. 32, p. 207.
38. Baldev Raj Nayar, *Globalisation and Nationalism*, Sage Publications, New Delhi, 2001, p. 187.
39. *Ibid.*, p. 207.
40. Atul Kohli, *India's Democracy: An Analysis of Changing State-Society Relation*, Orient Longman, New Delhi, 1988, p. 236.
41. Baldev Raj Nayar, *Globalisation and Nationalism*, Sage Publications, New Delhi, 2001, p. 148.
42. Dilip Halder, Supra no. 3, p. 212.
43. K. Shankar Bajpai, Supra no. 32, p. 209.
44. Atul Kohli, Supra no. 39, p. 236.
45. Ramashray Roy, India in 1993: The Struggle of Economic Reform, *Asian Survey*, 34(2), February 1994, p. 200.
46. *Ibid.*, p. 201.
47. R.N. Prasad, *Governance of India: Issues and Perspectives*, Concept Publishing Company, New Delhi, 2002, p. 33.
48. Ramesh Thakur, A Changing of the Guard in India, *Asian Survey*, 38(6), June 1998, p. 606.
49. Attar Chand, Supra no. 34, p. 25.
50. Sumit Ganguly, Asia in 1997: Another Year of Turmoil, *Asian Survey*, 38(2), February, 1998, p. 127.
51. *Ibid.*, p. 137.
52. *Economic Times*, 19th April, 1996.
53. Subhash C. Kashyap (ed.), *National Resurgence Through Electoral Reforms*, Shipra Publications, New Delhi, 2002, p. 23.

54. Devesh Kapoor and Bhanu Pratap Mehta, India in 1998: The Travails of Political Fragmentation, *Asian Survey,* 39(1), January/February 1999, p. 164.
55. Sisir Dhar, The Ailing Political Life of India, *Janata,* 53(23), September 13, 1998, pp 9-10.
56. Meenu Roy, *Electoral Politics in India,* Deep and Deep Publications, New Delhi, 2000, pp. 23-24.
57. *Ibid.*, pp. 27-28.
58. Devesh Kapoor and Bhanu Pratap Mehta. Supra no. 51, p. 167.
59. *Ibid.*, p. 168.
60. M.P. Singh and Rekha Saxena, *India at the Polls,* Orient Longman, New Delhi, 2003, p. 15.
61. Purnima S. Tripathi, On the defensive, *Frontline,* 21(9), May 7, 2004, p. 8.
62. Purnima S. Tripathi, With Dogged Determination, *Front Line,* 21(8), April 23, 2004, p. 33.
63. *The Hindu,* June 3, 1999.
64. *The Hindu,* April 28, 1999.
65. *The Hindu,* April 28, 1999.
66. *The Hindu,* December 6, 1999.
67. *The Hindu,* April 28, 1999.
68. Sudha Pai, Party System under Transformation, *Asian Survey,* 38(9), September 1998, p. 850.
69. D.P. Bharthwal (ed.), *Indian Administration Since Independence,* Bharat Book Centre, Lucknow, 2003, p. 7.
70. Bharat Jhunjunwala, *Governance and Human Rights,* Kalpaz Publications, Delhi, 2002, p. 126.
71. G. Palanithurai, *Peoples Perception of Politics,* Kanishka Publishers, Delhi, 1995, p. 19.
72. Bharat Jhunjunwala, Supra no. 67, p. 127.
73. G. Palanithurai, Supra no. 71, p. 60.
74. Navin Chandra Joshi (ed.), *Democracy and Human Values,* Sterling Publishers Private Limited, New Delhi, 1979, p. 23.
75. Mohit Bhattacharya, Globalization, Governance and Development, *The Indian Journal of Political Science,* 62(3), September 2003, p. 352.
76. *Ibid.*, p. 351.
77. *Ibid.*, p. 355.
78. Anthony Pagden, The Genesis of 'Governance' and Enlightenment Conceptions of the Cosmopolitan World Order, *International Social Science Journal,* 115, March 1998, p. 7.
79. rrmeet.undp.org.in
80. *Ibid.*

81. Niraja Gopal Jayal and Sudha Pai, *Democratic Governance in India: Challenges of Poverty, Development and Identity*, Sage Publications, London, 2001, p. 11.
82. Bhabani Sen Gupta, *India: Problems of Governance*, Konark Publishers Private Limited, Delhi, 1996, p. 40.
83. R.N. Prasad, Supra no. 45, p. 15.
84. Atul Kohli, Supra no. 2, p. 4.
85. Niraja Gopal Jayal and Sudha Pai, Supra No. 78, p. 12.
86. *Ibid.*, p. 14.
87. R.N. Prasad, Supra. No. 45, p. 15.
88. Rajni Kothari, *State Against Democracy: In Search of Humane Governance*. Ajanta Publications, Delhi, 1988, p. 2.
89. *Ibid.*, p. 3.
90. *Ibid.*, p. 3.

4

Political Parties, Perception of Governance

If parliamentary democracy has not functioned satisfactorily in India in recent times, it is not because of the defects in the system but due to the incompetence or inefficiency of those entrusted with the task of running it.[1] Most of the problems in the 1990s were primarily due to the nature of party politics. All these tend to reduce the effectiveness of democratic governance. The nature of party politics in this context reflects the response of political parties to the issues and problems of people. This also reflects the nature of governance in India.

The way in which political parties perceive governance indicates their concern and response to the problems and aspirations of people. In view of this, it is pertinent to understand how political parties perceive governance. The best available source to know about political parties perception is through their manifestos. This also helps in understanding whether there is a difference between political parties, perception of governance and what they actually practice.

The role of political parties in democratic governance is significantly influenced by their electoral strength and parliamentary strength. Electoral strength and parliamentary strength determine power position of parties in parliament. The party or parties with majority may have more responsibility and obviously, it or they can give final shape to the policy decision. The opposition parties contribute to the policy decision by offering their advice and criticism.

The process of finalizing the policy decision is greatly influenced by the position of political parties in terms of electoral and parliamentary strength. Obviously, the process of finalizing policy decisions involves interactions among various parties. In view of this, effective formulation and implementation of policies was mainly influenced by the nature of interactions among political parties.

Interactions among political parties are affected by the principles, policies and programmes which they pursue. Party election manifesto indicates its perception in terms of programmes and policies representing its position on governance of the country. An understanding of parties' manifestos is necessary to examine their policies and programmes on which they contest the elections. It is through the policies parties highlight their stand on governance. It will have certain effect on the formulation and implementation of policies indicating the effectiveness of governance.

The concern expressed by the political parties about governance in their election manifestos represent their position on democratic governance. In view of this, we assume that manifestos of political parties constitute an important part of their documents indicating their efforts of public interest formation and manifestation in the form of policies and programmes. The other documents of parties like resolutions passed in the party meetings, speeches of the office bearers, and statements on public affairs inside and outside parliament are based on the broader commitment or promise made through the election manifestos. Therefore, election manifestos as documents are adequate to understand the perception of parties on policies, programmes and democratic governance.

Effectiveness of governance is to be evaluated based on the extent of fulfilment of aspirations of people. This study is confined to the major Indian political parties, namely, the BJP, the Congress, the CPI (M) and the CPI mainly due to time consideration and lack of availability of all party documents. The election manifesto is a document indicating the perspective of that party on governance. In this context, we assume that the election manifesto represents other party documents and it expresses the perspective of party on public policy issues and governance.

The BJP popularized the concept of governance. It was the first to incorporate the word governance in its manifesto. In the era of coalitions it was the BJP which had provided stable coalition government for the first time in India. By looking at the unstable coalitions, the Congress party claimed that there is no other party equivalent to it in providing stable government. With the promise of providing honest, transparent and good governance the BJP came to power in 1999. Though it failed to acquire power in 2004 general elections, understanding its perception of governance is more relevant. An understanding of the Congress party's perception is equally important which after the gap of eight years has again come to power. The perception of two major left parties is pertinent as they constitute major partners of the present UPA coalition.

BJP's Perception of Governance

It is obvious that decline of Congress party led to the emergence of multi-party system, which resulted in hung parliament. Unstable coalitions were formed and toppled. The recent phase of Indian politics has thus been characterized by considerable governmental instability. "Underlying this instability there are two sets of forces. First, regional parties face the problem of collective action: they find it difficult to co-operate to form national governments on their own; and, second, the BJP has so far failed to garner sufficient support to form a national government."[2]

Table 4.1: BJP Party Position in Lok Sabha

Year	Seats Sought	Seats Won	Percentage Votes Secured
1952	94	3	3.0
1957	130	4	6.0
1962	196	14	6.4
1967	251	35	9.4
1971	157	22	7.4
1977	405	99	41.3
1980	432	31	19.0
1984	223	2	7.7
1989	226	86	11.5
1991	468	120	20.1
1996	471	161	20.3
1998	388	180	25.6
1999	339	180	23.8

Source: *The Hindu*, April 9, 2000.

Table 4.2: BJP and its Allies (in 2004 General Elections)

Party	*Won*	*Voteshare*
BJP	138	21.48
SHS	12	1.79
BJD	11	1.29
SAD	8	0.89
JD (U)	7	1.98
TDP	5	3.01
AITC	2	1.99
NPF	1	0.18
MNF	1	0.05
ADMK	0	2.17
Total	**185**	**34.83**

Source: http:// *www.indian* elections.com/resultsupdate/

Table 4.1 reveals that the BJP which started with just two members of parliament in 1984, has become the single largest party in Indian Parliament in 1998 and 1999 elections. However, in 2004 general elections it won 138 seats, while its voting share came down to 21.48 in 2004 as against 23.8 in 1999.

Prior to 1989, the BJP and its predecessors the Bharatiya Jana Sangh (BJS), the political arm of the Rashriya Swayamsevak Sangh (RSS), never exceeded 10 per cent of the vote or 35 seats nationally, except for 1977 when as a component of the Janata party won 99 of 295 seats won by the Janata party.[3] The position of the BJP in the parliament improved after 1989 elections.

In 1991 election BJP mainly highlighted on clean political system and economic development. In its 1996 election manifesto it stated that, "With the BJP at the centre, the next five years will be devoted to implementing our Manifesto based on the four concepts of *Suraksha, Suchita, Swadeshi* and *Samrasata. Hindhutva*, or cultural nationalism, shall be the rainbow which will bridge our present to our glorious past and pave the way for an equally glorious future; it will guide the transition from swrajya to *surajya*. Our Manifesto reflects the application of these four concepts in good governance and their role in moulding the nation we dreamt of on the dawn of Independence—a prosperous and strong India, a country where every citizen regards this land of ours, this *Bharatbhoomi*, that stretches from the Indus to the seas, as his sacred motherland."[4]

In the thirteenth Lok Sabha elections, the BJP leadership had shown more maturity in its responses to the party alliances than the Congress leadership. Vajpayee's categorical assertion that even if BJP secures majority by itself, it would take its allies into the government is bound to give great confidence to its partners in bonding together.[5]

The BJP encashed on *Hindutva*, captured power in some states and went on increasing tally in the Lok Sabha from 2 MPs in 1984 to 180 in 1998.[6] It has attempted to rouse emotions of majority community by using the symbol of Rama, and especially by appealing to them in the name of doing away with the alleged injustice perpetrated some centuries back by Babar, the Muslim invader, by demolishing a temple of Rama and constructing a mosque there.[7]

The BJP changed its strategy in 1998 elections and entered into alliances with a number of regional parties. This strategy helped the BJP to improve its own score as well as of its alliance. However, when party leaders perceived that return of extreme politics were declining, they engineered a centrist shift. More recently, therefore, the BJP has offered itself as a party of stability and good governance, a political position that has catapulted it to the position of India's ruling party.[8]

BJP popularized the concept of governance in mid-1990s. In 1998 assembly elections, it charged the Congress with unbridled corruption, widespread maladministration and deplorable anti-people policies. It claimed that, "Earlier this year, India voted comprehensively against the malgovernance of a morally bankrupt and politically decrepit Congress and the misgovernance of a disunited and inept alliance called the United Front. The nation reposed its faith in the BJP and its allies."[9]

BJP on the eve of assembly elections in November 1998, claimed: "BJP under the leadership of Atal Bihari Vajpayee, was entrusted with the task of ending the malgovernance and misrule of the past. It was given a chance by the people at the Centre to set the National Agenda for Governance. It also claimed that, the National Agenda for Governance, which seeks to chart a new course for India and open a new chapter of purposive governance, has been the guiding spirit in all our actions."[10]

BJP also stressed on:

- Ensuring India's external and internal security;

- Seeking consensus to secure national objectives;
- Boosting India's agricultural economy;
- Protecting Indian industry from multi-national predators;
- Making social progress truly meaningful;
- Mandating probity in public life; and
- Upholding the best traditions of secularism."[11]

It pledged that in its rule, people will see a qualitative change in the culture of governance. It also assured people that duties and responsibilities of those in government take precedence over their prerequisites. Along with this change, there should also be a change in the mindset and behaviour of the people.

It presented agenda for institutional rejuvenation social infrastructure, agriculture, foreign policy, social philosophy, *Nari shakti*, population policy, policy for India's youth, family and society, policy on environment, science and technology, information technology, media, Arts etc., were included in 1999 election manifesto of Congress.

In 1999 Election Manifesto, BJP under the banner of NDA party included agenda for governance. Agenda for good governance included its commitment to good governance. "Our first commitment to the people is to give a stable, honest, transparent, and efficient government capable of accomplishing all-round development. For this, the government shall introduce time-bound programmes of needed administrative reforms including those for the police and other Civil Services."[12] It also included, Economy, Trade and Commerce, Labour, Eradication of Unemployment, Food Security and Price Stability, Health and Drinking Water, Education for all, Housing for all, Empowerment of children, Population, Constitutional and Legal reform, Corruption, New States, National Security, Internal security, International Relations, Genuine Secularism, Scheduled Castes and Scheduled Tribes and Backward Classes, Environment, Prasar Bharati, Science and Technology and Information Technology. It also claimed: "This National Agenda is sincere and solemn covenant aimed at changing the content and culture of governance of this great nation, freeing it of the triple curses of hunger (*bhookh*), fear (*bhay*) and corruption (*bhrashtachar*), and transforming it into a New India that is prosperous, strong, self-confident and at peace within itself and the world we appeal for the co-operation of all parties and all sections of society in this great endeavour."[13]

Unfortunately, the BJP by highlighting on good governance brought a new wave in the election process, but failed to achieve much practically in the governance process. However, it attributed its failure to the coalition government. It claimed that if the party was in majority it might have brought some change in the governance. In 2004 general elections it asked the people to elect BJP with majority so that it can fulfil its promise of good governance.

The BJP as the leading partner of NDA released its manifesto in April-May 2004. It claimed that it had an agenda for development, good governance and peace. In its agenda for good governance it dedicated one section to Governance Reforms in which it is stated that, "The NDA Government will unveil, before the end of 2004, comprehensive Good Governance Reforms, which will focus on:

1. Administrative reforms to check corruption, promote transparency and accountability, remove delays in decision-making; and to make government employees treat the people as their masters.
2. Electoral reforms to check the unhealthy influence of money power and prevent criminalization of politics.
3. Judicial reforms for speedy and affordable justice.
4. Political reforms to raise the standards and efficacy of Parliament, State Legislatures, and other elected bodies.
5. Reform of ministries to speed up decision making and develop better capabilities for policy formulation and implementation.
6. Good Corporate Governance reforms to ensure lawful and ethical business practices, protection of shareholders' interests, and consumer protection.

Electoral Reforms

1. Consensus will be evolved to prevent entry of criminal elements into politics.
2. In cooperation with all political parties, the NDA will work towards raising the standards of Parliament and State Legislatures.

3. A National Institute for Training Elected Representatives will be established.

Civil Society Empowerment

1. The NDA recognizes that maximizing people's participation in the implementation of all policies and programmes of the government is the key to India's rapid and all-round development. Towards this end, a National Council of Voluntary Organizations will be set up. States will be encouraged to establish similar Councils.
2. Involvement of religious establishments of all denominations, which are active in the social field, will be encouraged in areas like mass-feeding for the poor, care of orphans and destitute, campaign against social evils like female foeticide, environmental protection, etc.
3. Civil Society will be suitably empowered to help in achieving dispute resolution ranging from local disputes over minor issues to major ones over contentious issues outside the realm of the judiciary and government. Its cooperation will be sought in strengthening civic discipline, adherence to law, tax compliance, and care for public property."[14]

The party claims that the two main issues of Elections 2004 are good governance and accelerated, all-round development. "There is a new type of hunger in India, the tremendous hunger for development. It is especially acute in rural areas and among the urban poor. They want to free themselves from poverty, backwardness and underdevelopment. They want to see an end to regional and social imbalances in development."[15]

Ever since the beginning of 2004, BJP was very much confident and feeling good about what it had achieved during its tenure. Whether people had the same feeling, was not its concern. The BJP mainly concentrated on "Feel Good" and "India Shining" campaigns. It was trying to attract middle class votes and their campaign was mainly targeting them. However, it is also true that this section of society does not mean the Indian masses. It claimed that, "Roads and telecommunications have improved across the country, an economy of shortage is now wallowing in surplus and the purchasing power of this section has increased substantially.[16] There was a cruel irony in the fact that all these claims of a strong, prosperous and technologically advanced India were made when thousands of farmers were committing suicide, farmers were suffering from the problems of inadequate supply of electricity, water supply, unemployment problem hit hard the younger generation, poverty alleviation programmes were not reaching the poor. And when such acute problems were confronting the country the claim of "Feel good" and "India Shining" may not have been relevant.

The BJP's second main campaign issue was Sonia Gandhi's foreign origin. Expert studies indicate that the "Feel Good" propaganda offensive launched by the BJP is not devoid of a substantive social basis.[17] The "Feel Good" and "India Shining" campaign had negative impact upon the people. It failed to attract the votes to the party. The BJP's calculations were going wrong which compelled it to switch to personality cult. They perceived that Vajpayee *versus* Sonia presidential style campaign may help the BJP. Though it would be excessive to claim that there was an Atal wave in the country. The NDA claimed in its manifesto to have given India "a stable and purposive government under an able leader."[18] Sonia Gandhi's foreign origin issue had been included in the NDA manifesto. The BJP and the rest of the NDA found that they had nothing else but the professed virtues of Vajpayee's leadership to use as their trump card.[19]

In 2004 general elections, the BJP was expecting less Muslim votes due to Gujrat carnage. In order to attract the Muslim votes, the NDA manifesto had "promised a minorities development agenda within six months of the combine's return to power, special developmental programmes for socially and economically backward Muslims, enhanced Muslim representation at various levels of government and in public sector enterprises, a "riot-free" India, continuation of the peace process with Pakistan, jobs for Urdu teachers, minority status for Hamdard University and so on."[20]

Though the BJP was talking about transparent governance and good governance in most of its election manifestos on the basis of which it also acquired largest number of seats in the Lok Sabha in 1999 general elections, its failure in the 2004 elections confirmed the fact that though it talked more about governance, in practice it was not successful in ensuring good governance.

Table 4.3: Elections to the Lok Sabha 1952–99

	1952	*1957*	*1962*	*1967*	*1971*	*1977*	*1980*	*1984*	*1989*	*1991*	*1996*	*1998*	*1999*
Total Seats	489	494	494	520	518	542	542	543	543	543	543	543	543
Contested	479	482	491	515	517	540	529	541	528	521	543	539	543
Uncontested	10	12	3	5	1	2	1	1	1				
Indian National	364	371	361	283	352	154	353	415	197	232	140	141	114
Congress (INC)	(479)	(490)	(488)	(516)	(441)	(492)	(492)	(517)	(510)	(492)	(529)	(474)	(453)
(INCI) in 1980	45.0	47.8	44.7	40.8	43.7	34.5	42.7	48.1	39.5	36.5	28.8	25.9	28.3
Bharatiya Janata	3	4	14	35	22	295		2	86	120	161	179	182
Party (BJP),	(94)	(130)	(196)	(251)	(160)	(405)		(229)	(226)	(468)	(471)	(384)	(339)
(BLD) in 1977,	3.1	5.9	6.4	9.4	7.4	41.3		7.4	11.5	20.1	20.3	25.5	23.8
(BJS) till 1971													
Janata Dal			18	44	8				142	59	46	6	21
(United) (JDU)			(173)	(178)	(56)				(243)	(307)	(196)	(190)	(60)
in 1999, (JD)			7.9	8.7	3.1				17.7	11.8	8.1	3.2	3.1
1989-98, (SWA)													
till 1971													
Communist Party of	16	27	29	23	23	7	11	6	12	14	12	9	4
India (CPI)	(49)	(110)	(137)	(106)	(87)	(91)	(48)	(66)	(50)	(42)	(43)	(58)	(54)
	3.3	8.9	9.9	5.0	4.7	2.8	2.6	2.7	2.6	2.5	2.0	1.8	1.5
Communist				19	25	22	36	22	33	35	32	32	33
Party of India				(62)	(85)	(53)	(63)	(64)	(64)	(60)	(75)	(71)	(72)
Marxist—CPI(M)				4.4	5.1	4.3	6.1	5.7	6.5	6.2	6.1	5.2	5.4

(Contd.)

(Contd.)

	1952	*1957*	*1962*	*1967*	*1971*	*1977*	*1980*	*1984*	*1989*	*1991*	*1996*	*1998*	*1999*
Lok Dal (LKD) (JPS) in 1980, (INCO) till 1989					16 (238) 10.4	3 (19) 1.7	41 (294) 9.4	3 (174) 5.6	0 (117) 0.2	0 (78) 0.1			
Samajwadi Party (SP) in 1991 (JP) till 1989							31 (432) 19.0	10 (219) 6.7	0 (156) 1.0	5 (156) 1.0	17 (111) 3.3	20 (164) 5.0	26 (151) 3.8
Bhahujan Samaj Party (BSP)											11 (117) 3.6	5 (249) 4.7	14 (225) 4.2
Praja Socialist Party (PSP), (KMPP) in 1952	9 (145) 5.8	19 (189) 10.4	12 (168) 6.8	13 (109) 3.1	2 (63) 1.0								
Samyukta Socialist Party (SSP), (SOC) till 1962	12 (254) 10.6		6 (107) 2.7	23 (122) 4.9	3 (93) 2.4								
Others	47 16.5	31 7.6	34 10.5	45 10.0	53 13.8	52 9.9	35 8.5	44 10.0	44 12.2	41 12.1	115 21.5	141 26.3	143 27.1
Independents	38	42	20	35	14	9	9	5	12	1	9	6	6
	15.9	19.4	11.1	13.7	8.4	5.5	6.4	8.1	5.2	3.9	6.3	2.4	2.8

Source: Zoya Hassan, *Parties and Party Politics in India,* Oxford University Press, New Delhi, 2002, pp. 477-478.

Congress Party's Perception of Governance

As per Table 4.3 it becomes clear that Congress popularity is on decline. It has secured 45 per cent of votes in 1952, which had reduced to 28.3 per cent in 1999. Its largest electoral victory in terms of seats and per centage of votes was in 1984 under the dynamic leadership of Rajiv Gandhi. It polled 415 seats and 48.1 per cent votes. Failure of the Congress party and its leaders to provide effective governance led to the decline of Congress. Policies, programmes, principles and issues on which it fought elections were not properly implemented. If the Congress party had carried out what their manifestos have been promising from election to election over the last 45 years, the country would never have had to face the enormous difficulties in which it is engrossed today; for it is the Congress which has ruled for the most part of this period.[21] But, acceptance of coalition politics and mistakes committed by the NDA government contributed to the victory of the UPA under the leadership of the Congress in 2004 general elections. It secured 145 seats in the 2004 general elections while its vote share is 26.21 per cent, which is evident from Table 4.4. Though it has not secured majority of votes, by making an alliance with other parties it formed the government (United Progressive Alliance). Slowly Congress has been increasing its hold over centre as well as in states.

Table 4.4: INC and its allies (in 2004 General Elections)

Party	*Won*	*Vote share*
INC	145	26.21
RJD	24	1.86
DMK	16	1.79
NCP	9	1.76
PMK	6	0.55
TRS	5	0.62
JMM	5	0.46
MDMK	4	0.43
LJNSP	3	0.51
JKPDP	1	0.07
RPI (A)	1	0.09
MUL	1	0.1
RPI	0	0.07
AC	0	0.02
KEC (M)	0	0.05
IUML	0	0
Total	**219**	**34.59**

Source: http:// www.indian elections.com/ resultsupdate/

In 1991 election manifesto the Congress party stated that it wanted to give power to the people by according constitutional status to Panchayati Raj institutions. It had stated that it would give priority to poverty alleviation, tackling the unemployment problem, increasing agricultural production, welfare of the Scheduled Castes and Scheduled Tribes, family welfare, education, etc.

On the question of electoral reforms, which is essential to ensure accountability of the representatives to the people, the Congress said that, "The issues that need resolution are:

1. Election-related violence;
2. Use of money power, and
3. Caste and Communal considerations."[22]

On the question of responsive administration it said that, "The Congress Party reaffirms its belief in a responsive, open and accountable administration at all levels." It also says that, "The Congress stands for full openness in developmental programmes. The Congress will ensure that every rupee spent on development reaches the intended beneficiaries without waste and leakage. This will be achieved through imaginative project planning and implementation, decentralization of decision making and performance monitoring, involving the people and their representatives."[23]

Though the party assured the people of leakage free development programmes, the involvement of P.V. Narasimha Rao, the Congress leader, in the corruption charges had put a question mark on the performance of the Congress party in accordance with the promises made in the manifesto. It brought down the image of the party in the eyes of the people.

Stability was the main issue in most of the election manifestos of Congress party since the days of Indira Gandhi. In 1996 election manifesto it retained its earlier stand on stability, but along with it also stressed anti-poverty programmes, agricultural development, tribal development, welfare of women and minorities, etc. It was stated in its manifesto: "The Congress government is committed to providing an open, accountable and responsive administration at all levels. The accountability of all to Parliament will remain supreme."[24]

In 1996 election manifesto Congress emphasized stability, national security, harmony and development. According to the manifesto the Congress remains true to certain unchanging values. "They are:

- Unity and integrity;
- Democracy based on the parliamentary system;
- Secularism;
- An independent judiciary;
- Freedom of speech and expression and freedom of the press;
- Stability, social harmony and development."[25]

The Congress gives prominence to the issue of stability in its manifestos. The issue of governance did not gain much prominence in the election manifestos of parties until BJP popularized it. The Congress was stressing more on providing accountable and responsive administration. In the 1998 Lok Sabha election manifesto the Congress gave priority for providing responsive administration. The Congress believes: "accountability of officials to local bodies where local bodies have constitutional responsibilities and functions will be ensured.

The Congress review the existing policy in regard to secrecy and confidentiality with a view to opening the doors of government to the wider public in a meaningful manner."[26]

However, nothing was mentioned about the responsibility and accountability of political leaders and transparency in the election manifesto of the Congress party. With Sonia Gandhi plunging into politics she became the new *avtar* of the party. The Congress campaign was centered on Sonia Gandhi. The "Sonia factor" was instrumental in putting an immediate stop to the haemorrhaging of Congress members to the BJP, reviving the party's sagging morale, and bringing the BJP electoral juggernaut to a halt.[27] "This time besides flaunting its ideological under-pinnings of secularism, socialism and a casteless society, the Congress made stability the bedrock of its campaign, signifying its outright rejection of coalition experiment. The other major issues were economic self-reliance, and socio-economic justice. The party's main agenda was '*arthik swaraj*' and '*garibon ka raj*' (economic self-reliance and governance by the poor)."[28]

This manifesto stressed on stability and development. But for the first time the Congress included the role of NGOs in national development programmes. No other party expressed its stand on the significance of NGOs in national development. It stated: "The Congress believes that NGOs, voluntary agencies and social action groups are very important elements of a civil society which need to be nurtured and given every support.

While a certain adverbial relationship between government and those organizations is inevitable and even desirable, the Congress will ensure its full involvement in social mobilization and in the implementation of all development programmes."[29]

Mentioning the role of NGOs in its manifesto, the party makes it clear that the Congress recognized the importance of NGOs in the development process. The failure of Congress to attain majority in 1996 elections made the party express its concern to the people's response. The inclusion of the role of NGOs in the manifesto is an indicator of its perceptible change in its attitude towards people. This changing nature of the Congress towards people is also highlighted in its 1999 election manifesto. It states: "The Congress sees public life not just in terms of politics but more importantly in terms of the exercise of power by the people themselves.

Ultimately, people themselves guide the government. The government derives its support from the people and the ultimate goal of development must be to build up the self-help capacities of people and communities."[30]

The 1999 election manifesto also stressed more on stability. The Congress pledged to provide to India stable government, an able government, and experienced government.[31] But, in the Conference of the Congress Chief Ministers held on 16th June, 2001, Sonia Gandhi asked them to provide responsive administration. She asked them to strive to become a model for good governance, growth-oriented and equity-based economic management.[32]

In the opening address of the Congress president at the Vichar Manthan Shivir on 7th July 2003, Sonia Gandhi charged the BJP with failure to provide development and governance and claimed that it is time once again for Congress party to come to power. She said: "We are the only party whose philosophy of governance combines economic growth with social cohesion, public investment with private initiative and meritocracy with equality of opportunity. Our governance philosophy is not captive to any dogma. Instead, it is anchored in a vision of an India that ensures each of its citizens a better quality of life and a life of dignity."[33]

Though the concept of governance had not got much relevance in election manifestos of Congress party, they got priority in the speeches of leaders. However, most of its manifestos throw light on open, transparent, accountable and responsive government in one or the other way.

In the 2004 election manifesto, "The Congress makes a solemn commitment to the people of India: to restore peace among all of its peoples, to strengthen the secular order through emphasis on social harmony, cultural pluralism and respect for the rule of law, and to ensure a bright and secure economic future for every family in our country."[34]

The Congress in its manifesto has given six basics for governance. They are as follows:

Six Basics for Governance

- *Samajik Sadbhavna*, to ensure social cohesion and harmony by taking the strictest possible action against those who promote bigotry and hatred;
- *Yuva Rozgar*, to accelerate growth of productive and secure employment opportunities increase by around one crore a year and ensure that each family has at least one job;
- *Grameen Vikas*, to improve the income and welfare of *kisans* and *khet mazdoors* across the country;
- *Arthik Navotthan* to unleash the creative energies of our professionals and entrepreneurs, the cutting edge of our middle class;
- *Mahila Sashaktikaran*, to provide for the political empowerment and full educational, economic and legal equality for women;
- *Saman Avsar*, to provide for equality of opportunity in every way for *dalits*, *adivasis*, OBCs and religious and linguistic minorities."[35]

Thus, we find gradual shift in the stand of Congress party from stability to governance. When the Congress realized that, the BJP's concept of governance is more attractive than of stability, it made a shift from its claim of stability to governance. However, what contributed to its victory in 2004 general elections was not only its shift to 'governance' but more importantly the failure of the BJP to implement its promise of good governance.

Before 1999 elections, "Even at the rhetorical level, the Congress refused to countenance the idea of coalition governance, equating it with instability. The party revealed itself to be out of tune with the aspirations of the new segments entering the political process."[36] Congress changed its stand in 2004 general elections and formed coalitions with regional parties. Its alliance in Maharashtra, Tamil Nadu, Jharkhand, Andhra Pradesh, Bihar paid more dividends to the party. As a result in 2004 general elections people of India once again have given a chance to Congress party to prove its governing ability. Only the future will decide how far the Congress party stands up to the expectations of the people.

Communist Party's Perception of Governance

Although the Left in India is not very strong both in terms of its electoral success and also in its area of influence, it has never been in the shadows since India achieved her Independence.[37] Tables 4.5 and 4.6 indicate the parliamentary strength and electoral strength of the party.

Table 4.5: Party Position of CPI and CPI (M) 1952–1999

Year	*CPI*			*CPI (M)*		
	Seats contested	Seats won	Percentage of Voting	Seats contested	Seats won	Percentage of voting
1952	49	16	3.3			
1957	110	27	8.9			
1962	137	29	9.9			
1967	106	23	5.0	62	19	4.4
1971	87	23	4.7	85	25	5.1
1977	91	7	2.8	53	22	4.3
1980	48	11	2.6	63	36	6.1
1984	66	6	2.7	64	22	5.7
1989	50	12	2.6	64	33	6.5
1991	42	14	2.5	60	35	6.2
1996	43	12	2.0	65	32	6.1
1998	58	9	1.8	71	32	5.2
1999	54	4	1.5	72	33	5.4

Source: Zoya Hassan, *Parties and Party Politics in India*, Oxford University Press, New Delhi, 2002, p. 477.

Table 4.5 reveals that CPI which got 16 seats in 1952 was reduced to 4 seats in 1999. But, it got 10 seats in 2004 general elections. The CPI (M) which emerged after the split earned 19 seats in 1967, which increased to 33 seats in 1999 and 44 seats in 2004. CPI's vote-share has increased from 1.5 per cent in 1999 elections to 1.38 per cent in 2004 general elections. While CPI (M) got 5.4 per cent votes in 1999, and 5.6 per cent votes in 2004 general elections. The above tables reveal that both the communist parties are slowly increasing their electoral as well as parliamentary strength.

Table 4.6: Seats Won and Vote-share of Political Parties in 2004 General Elections

Party	*Won*	*Vote share*
CPM	43	5.6
SP	36	4.06
BSP	19	5.08
CPI	10	1.38
IND	4	4.06
JD (S)	4	1.52
RSP	3	0.44
RLD	3	0.57
AIFB	3	0.35
AGP	2	0.53
JKN	2	0.11

Source: http://www.indian-elections.com/resultsupdate/

Right from the first general elections the Communist Party is trying to replace Congress party by forming United Front. "...its attitude towards Congress party had always been a thorny question and it became the central point of the inner party differences."[38] The communist party was split into CPI and CPI (M) mainly due to the divergent views and attitude of its members towards the Congress party.

Despite their continued ideological differences, a series of domestic and international events during the period from April 1978 to January 1980, particularly the disintegration of the Janata Government in the summer of 1979, eliminated a major source of conflict between the CPI and CPI (M). As a result the two Communist parties began to narrow down their differences and they untidily fought elections in 1980.[39]

Communist Party of India's Perception on Governance

In the 1991 election manifesto, the CPI stressed democratization of socio-economic structure. It claimed: "While firmly adhering to socialism as the goal, the Communist Party of India does not press it as the immediate objective in the present stage of our country's development. It calls for a thorough democratic restructuring of our entire socio-economic system."[40]

It also states: "It requires the speedy implementation of comprehensive measures of social justice, including job reservation for OBCs on the lines of Mandal Commission report, with 27 per cent reservation in central jobs for the OBCs and 10 per cent reservation for the economically weaker sections of the forward castes, and 30 per cent job reservation for women in all categories; land reforms in the interests of the landless and poor; provision of jobs and reasonable wages for urban and rural workers."[41]

The other features of 1991 election manifesto are: consistent federalism, independent foreign policy, economic measures, protection for minorities, uprooting corruption, etc.

In 1996 and 1998 election manifestos CPI mainly stressed on economic development, agricultural development, health, social security, defence of rights of SC, ST, women, minorities and other, special provisions for tribals, etc.

The 1999 election manifesto of CPI stressed more on land reforms, economic development, agriculture, rights of the working class, secularism, federalism, national security and for the rights of *dalits* and tribal people, minorities, etc.

The 2004 election manifesto of CPI stands for land reforms, health and education programmes, protecting agriculture and small scale sectors, privatization and disinvestments of PSUs, women and child welfare, rights of dalits and tribals and minorities, etc.

Governance is not the main issue in the election manifestos of CPI. It stressed more on the welfare of the people than on accountability, transparent and responsive government. Unless we improve the quality of governance, welfare measures are meaningless. Its stand on uprooting corruption can be a good move towards achieving effective governance because corruption is one of the important impediments in achieving democratic governance.

Communist Party of India (Marxist)'s Perception of Governance

The CPI(M) in its manifesto mainly highlights the issue of corruption, protection of rights of minorities and oppressed classes and social security etc. In 1991 election manifesto it stated that the CPI(M) has always tried to provide an alternative economic policy aimed at alleviating the miseries of our people.

The party states: "The CPI(M) and the mass organizations in which it is working have been constantly active in the defence of the rights of the working class, agricultural workers, peasantry, youth, students, women and various sections of employees. It has tirelessly worked for forging united struggles of different sections of the people."[42]

The CPI(M) while supporting reservation as a measure for advancing social justice, believes that the rural poor in the backward communities will find their basic problems addressed to only through radical land reforms and the elimination of feudal relations in the villages by speedy industrialization of the country.

In 1991 elections CPI(M)'s main stress was on protection of minority rights and social justice, which play very important role in democratic governance. The manifesto of the CPI(M) reveals that it wants to empower the people in the real sense. Only when all the people are made to actively participate in the political life, it ensures democratic governance.

There is no reference of governance in the 1996 election manifesto of CPI(M). Its main stress is mainly on corruption, economy, rights of the working people, improving living conditions of the people, agrarian sector, social justice, women, strengthen secularism, strengthen parliamentary democracy, federalism and decentralization, defend national unity, etc.

In the eleventh Lok Sabha election manifesto CPI(M) gave priority to the problems like unemployment, education, health, poverty, electoral reforms, corruption, etc. The words, governance and accountability for the first time figured in its 1998 election manifesto.

The 1998 election manifesto of CPI(M) was mainly in favour of

- "A strong secular-democratic system;

- A just socio-economic order for all oppressed sections;
- Economic growth with equity;
- Corruption free governance and accountability."[43]

The 1998 election manifesto of the CPI(M) was divided mainly into four parts:

I. *Secularism and Federalism*: Cornerstone of Indian Unity: It includes strengthen federalism, defend national unity and foreign policy.
II. *For an Alternative Economic Policy*: It included land reforms: key to progress, agriculture, agricultural workers, rights of the working class, industries and infrastructure, financial sector, adequate resource mobilization and public distribution system.
III. *For Betterment of Citizens' Lives*: It included education, health, water resources, housing, employment, women, population policy, for social justice, dalits and adivasis, rights of minorities, youth, media and culture, science and technology and environment.
IV. *Strengthening Democratic System*: It included electoral reforms, curb corruption and judicial reforms.

In 1999 election manifesto the CPI(M) appealed to the people to defeat the BJP and its allies and strengthen the CPI(M) and other left parties. In 1999 and 2004 election manifestos it was stated to strengthen secular foundations, federalism for national unity, foreign policy, national security, economic policies, women, child care, education, health, water resources, housing, employment, social justice for dalits and adivasis, rights of minorities, curb corruption and judicial reforms.

The CPI and CPI(M) are the two main left parties in India. The term governance had not been used by both CPI(M) and CPI in their election manifestos upto 1998. The CPI(M) claimed that it will try to attain corruption-free governance and accountability. But their claims for strengthening secular foundations, federalism for national unity, land reform, foreign policy, national security, economic policies, women, child care, education, health, water resources, housing, employment, social justice for dalits and adivasis, rights of minorities, curbing of corruption and judicial reforms have much relevance in the governance process.

Election manifestos are of great significance and purpose for the voters. The election manifestos of political parties are full of promises, for maximizing the electoral strength. They provide an opportunity for all political parties to articulate their loftiest hopes and noblest aspirations.

Though most of the parties are stressing mainly on good governance, in reality not much was achieved in this direction. The problems of poverty, illiteracy, unemployment, child labour, etc., remain unsolved problems. Apart from these, many new problems are cropping up, "...twin challenges of globalization and economic reforms, on the one hand, and a distinctively new phase of identity politics, on the other—have tended to exert contrary pressures on the state, pulling it in opposite directions."[44]

What is needed is that, the political parties after carefully preparing their manifestos should adhered to it. With the emergence of coalitions political parties mainly concentrated on getting power. To share power, most political parties have sidetracked the principles stated in their manifestos. Political parties concentrate more on party interest and give very little attention to the interest of the people. Failure of governance is seen most vividly in its poor performance and lack of implementation of adopted agenda.[45] Institutional reform by themselves will not achieve the desired results unless those who run political institutions should become people's representatives and reform themselves by observing a democratic code of conduct.

REFERENCES

1. C.V. Raghavalu, Indian Republic and Governance Concerns, *The Indian Journal of Political Science*, 62(1), March 2001, p. 14.
2. Atul Kohli (ed.), *The Success of India's Democracy*, Cambridge University Press, New Delhi, 2001, p. 10.
3. Zoya Hassan (ed.), *Parties and Party Politics in India,* Oxford University Press, New Delhi, 2002, p. 485.
4. *Election Manifesto 1996, Bharatiya Janata Party,* Kapoor Press, New Delhi, 1996, pp. 6-7.

5. Deccan Herald, September 6, 1999.
6. M.A. Rane, Political Parties and Preservation of Democracy, *The Radical Humanist*, 62(3), June 1998, pp. 7-8.
7. Editorial, Vote for Whom? *Janata*, 46(15), May 19, 1991, p. 5.
8. Atul Kohli (ed.), *The Success of India's Democracy*, Cambridge University Press, New Delhi, 2001, p. 13.
9. *A Statement of Choice Before the Electorate in the November Assembly Elections*, Bharatiya Janata Party Publication, New Delhi, 1998, p. 1.
10. *A Statement of Choice Before the Electorate in the November Assembly Elections*, Bharatiya Janata Party Publication, New Delhi, 1998, p. 1.
11. *Ibid*, p. 2.
12. Election Menifesto Lok Sabha Election 1999, Bharatiya Janata Party Bharatiya Janata Party Publication, New Delhi, 1999, p. 4.
13. *Ibid.*, p. 10.
14. *An Agenda for Development: Good Governance and Peace*, BJP Publication, New Delhi, April-May 2004, pp. 31-33.
15. V. Venkatesan and Siddharth Narrain, Unfounded Optimism, *Frontline*, 21(8), April 23.
16. Saba Naqvi Bhaumik, Fable of the Rooster, *Outlook*, 44(3), January 26, 2004, p. 32.
17. Sukumar Muralidharan, Bankrupt Campaign, *Frontline*, 21(9), May 7, 2004, p. 5.
18. V. Venkatesan, A Coalition's Woes, *Frontline*, 21(9), May 7, 2004, p. 6.
19. *Ibid.*, p. 7.
20. Purnima S. Tripathi, Strategic Voting, *Frontline*, 21(10), May 31, 2004, p. 12.
21. Editorial, Vote for Whom?, *Janata*, 46(15), May 19, 1991, p. 4.
22. Election Manifesto, General Election 1991, Indian National Congress (I), New Delhi, p. 49.
23. *Ibid.*, p. 51.
24. Election Manifesto, General Election 1996, Indian National Congress(I), New Delhi, p. 29.
25. *Ibid.*, p. 4.
26. Election Manifesto Lok Sabha 1998, Indian National Congress, New Delhi, p. 45.
27. Tamesh Thakur, A Changing of the Guard in India, *Asian Survey*, 38(6), June 1998, p. 607.
28. Meenu Roy, *Elections 1998: A Continuity in Coalition*, National Publishing House, New Delhi, 1999, pp. 50-51.
29. Election Manifesto General Election 1999, Indian National Congress, New Delhi, p. 54.
30. Election Manifesto Lok Sabha 1999, Indian National Congress, New

Congress (I) Publication, Delhi, p. 12.
31. *Ibid.*, p. 7.
32. Action Plan for State, *Congress Sandesh,* 3(10), June 2001, p. 7.
33. *This is Ideological Battle, Congress Sandesh,* 5(11), July 2003, p. 7.
34. Election Manifesto of Indian National Congress, Lok Sabha Election 2004, Congress (I) Publication, New Delhi, p. 13.
35. *Lok Sabha Elections 2004: Election Manifesto of the Indian National Congress*, Congress (I) Publication, New Delhi, 2004, p. 13.
36. Zoya Hassan, The New Power Centers, *Frontline,* 21(8), April 23, 2004, p. 8.
37. Anil Kumar Jana (ed.), *Indian Politics at the Crossroads,* Commonwealth Publishers, New Delhi, 1998, p. 49.
38. Anil Kumar Jana (ed.), *Indian Politics at the Crossroads,* Commonwealth Publishers, New Delhi, 1998, p. 61.
39. *Ibid.*,.p. 68.
40. *CPI Manifesto: Election 1991,* New Age Printing Press, New Delhi, 1991, p. 5.
41. CPI Manifesto; Elections 1991, CPI Publication, New Delhi, 1991, p. 6.
42. *Election Manifesto of CPI (M)*, CPI (M) Publications, Delhi, 1991, p. 10.
43. *Communist Party of India (Marxist) Manifesto*, CPI (M) Publication, Delhi, 1998, p. 1.
44. Niraja Gopal Jayal and Sudha Pai, *Democratic Governance in India: Challenges of Poverty, Development and Identity,* Sage Publications, New Delhi, 2001, p. 132.
45. Bhabani Sen Gupta, *India: Problems of Govemance,* Konark Publishers Private Limited, Delhi, 1996, p. 404.

5

Political Participation and Democratic Governance

Democratic governance stands for governance in the interest of the people and for their overall development. The nature and extent of political participation determines the effectiveness of democratic governance. In this respect political parties play a crucial role. Political parties are primarily responsible for democratizing the entire process of governance. Political parties constitute an institutional mechanism through which people express their views on public affairs for the consideration of government.

Political parties play an important role in formulating public policies. Politicians have preferences over policies if they reward from holding office or the probability of re-election depends on the policies they adopt.[1] Peoples' active participation in politics makes political parties responsive to the popular needs. Voters must be able to vote out of office parties responsible for bad performance, and the parties they select must be able to enter government.[2] Participation is simultaneously an assertion of control over governments by those who have elected them.[3] A democratic society allows those classes which formerly took a passive part in political life. It expects the participation of almost all people in the process of running the government. Popular participation should not be reduced only to taking part in elections, because quality of voting is ensured by continuous participation of the people in political affairs. To R.C. Dutt, participation "...involves the central notion of political accountability in two ways: as responsive political authority, and as limits on the exercise of power."[4] It enables men by giving them a sense of their own dignity and value, alerts both rulers and ruled to their duties and responsibilities, and broadens political understanding.[5]

The study of both the political parties participation and popular participation in the political process is crucial for a proper understanding of democratic governance. Popular participation and political parties participation are interlinked. We cannot study any one without the knowledge of the other.

Political parties' participation or popular participation is a complex phenomenon, which depends on a number of variables, responsible for increasing or decreasing their interest in political participation. Important among them are social, political and psychological variables. These variables also differ from country to country and from time to time. An attempt has been made here to analyze the effect of these variables on participation in the Indian context.

In the social variable, we can include education, occupation, income, age, race, religion, sex, mobility and residence which have an effect on participation. Obviously, it includes social and economic status of people. The theory of social environment emphasizes that race, religion, caste, sex, education, age, occupation, residence, mobility, etc., play an important role in the political participation and affect the political behaviour of individuals and groups.[6] In Indian politics, "age and influence, age and power and age and performance will go hand in hand. It could be hypothesized that "the older the age, the greater is their influence in the political process."[7]

Table 5.1: Age Group of Respondents

S. No.	*Age Group*	*No. of Respondents*	*Percentage*
1.	18-20	15	4.78
2.	21-30	88	28.03
3.	31-40	116	36.94
4.	41-50	59	18.79
5.	51 & Above	36	11.46
	Total	**314**	**100.00**

Source: G. Palanithurai, *People Perception of Politics: An Indian Perspective,* Kanishka Publishers, Delhi, 1995, p. 28.

Table 5.1 reveals that people in the age group of 31-40 participate more actively in political activities than the people from the age group of 18-20. While the percentage of respondents is 36.94 per cent in the case of the age group between 31 to 40, it is only 4.78 per cent in the case of the age groups between 18 to 20. Again with the increasing age active participation decreases. From Table 5.1 it is found that people actively participate in politics more in the middle ages than in youth and old age.

Apart from age, income, occupation, availability of leisure, education, etc., influence political participation. It may be participation as a leader or a follower. It is generally believed that participation tends to be higher among well educated, higher occupational and income groups. Men's participation in political activities is higher than women's. Dominant ethnic and religious groups and urban people take more interest in politics than the people of lower caste and those living in villages and tribes. This low participation among the villages and tribes and among the lower castes may be due to lack of proper communication and information facilities. Studies have revealed that not all people are equally interested in politics.

For a long time in India the people belonging to low castes were denied most of the facilities like good education, access to temple, and many such activities of social nature. They were also not allowed to mix-up with the higher caste groups. Such inhuman treatment made them detached form the mainstream of life. After independence special privileges were provided to them, which slowly increased their social status and interest in political matters. In practice, because of adult franchise many social groups have become aware of their numerical strength and bargaining power, and have realized that they are in a position to put considerable pressure.[8] Numerical strength of castes can be used to put pressure on government in order to achieve its sectarian interest which ultimately contributes to change the power structure. Hence, by using the relative numerical strength on the basis of caste, different groups have been able to maintain their own political identity, to overthrow the dominant and vital group or groups from seats of political power and to improve their own socio-economic position.[9] Individuals and groups which have lost their earlier social status under modernization and democratic process use the same democratic institutions as a means to reassert their historic positions in new forms.[10] The implementation of Mandal Commission report in 1989 seems to have brought some changes in their social, political and economic life. It also drastically affected the Indian political process. Individuals and groups which had been subjected to inequality and deprivation took active role in modern democratic politics in order to overcome inequalities and deprivation.[11]

Political environment has its own effect on political participation. Individual factors, like general interest, economic interest, psychological environment and a sense of competition affects political participation. Political environment that includes party system, elections, nature of campaign, issues of public importance, ideologies, etc., influence political participation. Wide spread participation is presumably further discouraged when the major parties are large, loosely knit brokerage agencies which lack enrolled membership, effective discipline, or vital centers for adopting party policy.[12] The presence of a large number of political parties perhaps confused the Indian electorate. There were totally 718 political parties in the 2004 general elections. Regional parties, which better represent the regional interests, are getting more prominence over national parties in their respective regions. As a result of this, the task of national parties to influence the voter has become difficult. The umbrella character of the Congress party held different factions together. But, with the decline of the Congress, no party was able to hold different factions together. In recent years the BJP has been struggling to be a party of common people. The party is mainly based on *Hindutva* ideology, it had realized the fact that *Hindutva* alone will not lead the party to power. The strategy of the BJP is to attract the votes of all sections of people like Muslim or women, scheduled castes and scheduled tribes, backward classes, etc.

The implementation of a policy may also have a different impact on different people. "It means that political participation cannot flourish until and unless a citizen by reason of his privileged position in society and effective relation to the polity, finds it advantageous to work within the existing socio-political set-up. Heinz Evlen defines this type of political participation as the 'politics of happiness'."[13] The people who are benefited by it may feel more interested in politics than those who are not benefited and *vice versa*.

If some segments in the society are benefited by government policies for a long time their interest in politics may diminish. The groups who feel continuously neglected may become more active and pressurize the government to fulfil their demands. This is what happened in Indian politics after 1989. The 1989 election was a landmark in Indian political history. Regional aspirations, which were so far neglected by the dominant Congress party, got their voice represented in the regional parties. As a result of this regional parties started getting more importance thereafter and the status of national parties started declining.

The implementation of the Mandal Commission report by V.P. Singh government brought about a number of changes in Indian politics. Subsequently, the backward class and caste groups got more representation in every walk of life and got a say more effectively in government decisions. The following table shows that in Indian polity, a major segment is represented by backward and most backward groups.

Table 5.2: Caste Respondents

S. No.	*Caste*	*No. of Respondents*	*Percentage*
1.	FC	6	1.91
2.	BC & MBC	238	75.80
3.	SC/ST	70	22.29
	Total	314	100.00

Source: G. Palanithurai, *People Perception of Politics: An Indian Perspective*, Kanishka Publishers, Delhi, 1995, p. 28.

Since 1989 no party can dream of getting elected without the support of the backward castes and classes. At present caste is not only a determinant of social status, but has also become a deciding factor in the electoral politics. Tribals, women and many such other groups are also demanding more and more share in power.

Beliefs of the people are changing very fast. Now, the upper caste or class cannot claim its dominance over the inferior castes or class. Women now are not confining themselves to the household activities. They are demanding equal power with men. Changes in the social and political environment may also be one of the reasons for the change in the psychology of these groups. These groups are becoming increasingly aware of their political rights and demanding more and more share in power. So, they can better represent their interest.

Political participation, therefore, will increase the extent to which a nation is democratic only in so far as such participation involves at some point influence by the participant over governmental decisions.[14]

In general psychological variables may be thought of as those stemming from individual personality trait (whether primarily constitutional—genetic or primarily learned) and from cognitive structure, which in this case prevent certain characteristic ways of conceptualizing the self and surrounding socio-political world.[15]

Political Parties' Participation

Political participation in order to be effective and integrative needs to be organized in political institutions. Political institutions, which are differentiated from social structures, can perform the task of organizing and integrating political participation and relating it to society-wide policy-making process.[16] A political party is one such important institution.

Most of the works on political participation deal with popular participation, while political parties' participation received scant attention of the scholars. Political parties, participation is significant in democratic governance because political parties provide major channels of linkage between citizens and policy makers. Opinion polls in India have repeatedly shown that people generally prefer to vote for party candidates than independent candidate. Table 5.3 highlights this fact.

Over the thirteen general elections to the Lok Sabha, the number of independent candidates*getting elected has declined considerably. Table 5.3 reveals that though the number of independent candidates contesting Lok Sabha elections is considerably increasing, the number of candidates who get elected is declining. The number of independent candidates who had contested elections in 1952 were 849 while that of candidates elected to Lok Sabha in 1952 were 36. While the number of independents contesting elections in 1999 increased to 1,945 but the number of candidates who got elected came down to 6. But, in the 2004 general election 137 independents got elected. The sudden increase in the number of independent candidates may be due to factional politics. Usually the candidates who do not get party tickets contest the elections as independent candidates. This

---

* The number is derived from http://www.indian.elections.com/resultsupdate/

Table 5.3: Independents: Fading Fortunes

Year	Total No. of Independent Candidates	Elected	Percentage Forfeiting Deposits
1952	849	36	59.25
1957	667	73	51.27
1962	480	20	78.96
1967	865	35	86.36
1971	1,134	14	94.00
1977	1,224	9	97.22
1980	2,821	8	98.94
1984	3,792	5	98.79
1989	3,712	12	98.90
1991	5,687	5	99.52
1996	10,635	9	99.70
1998	1,915	6	99.11
1999	1,945	6	99.33

Source: *The Navhind Times*, March 19, 2004, p. 7.

is also an important indicator of candidates, zeal for power. The leaders sidetrack ideologies, principles, policies and values. Their only aim is to attain power. Thus, though the effective participation of political parties is significant in the democratic governance of India, their functioning is not satisfactory. In some cases leaders and candidates are more influential than the party. By and large parties are more influential than the independent candidates. Parties are dominated by the leaders and get identified by leaders.

Contesting elections is an important form of political participation of parties. Political parties contact and register voters, select candidates, organize the campaign and tell supporters what to believe on issues and how to vote.[17] "Parties themselves are often non-democratic in their internal functioning, and even if they are democratic to some extent party bosses play unjustifiably predominant role."[18] Party bosses decide as to who should contest the election which tends to deprive the people of their right to choose those whom they believe to be their real representatives.

Political parties choose candidates for election. A sizable body of research has shown that participation is associated with political awareness, that is, actual knowledge of political affairs.[19] The candidate should be a person with character and wisdom and well aware of the problems of the people in his/her respective constituency. But, in reality, it is different. Caste, class, religion, language, money power and many other factors play a vital role in selecting the party candidate for election.

Campaigning is one of the regular modes of activity during elections. "The campaigners are the activists of the party and exercise greater influence in party politics than the ordinary voter. The outcome of the elections, to some extent, depends on the nature of the campaigners and campaigning."[20] Campaign activities of political parties may educate the voters about the problems confronting the country. They also promise solution to these various problems. Political leaders try to capture the minds of the people by attractive slogans and appealing speeches. "Slogans like "Gribi Hatao" in 1974, democracy itself in 1977, a government that promised to work in 1980, the slogan of taking the nation into twenty-first century in 1984, the promise of a revolution in 1989, stability in 1991, 1996."[21] For the BJP it was "corruption-free government" in 1989 when it was an ally of National Front government, the reality of coalition culture and promise of good governance in 1996, 1998, 1999 and 2004 elections.

Political parties educate the voters, nominate candidates for election and by helping to conduct elections they provide opportunities to the members of less favoured class for upward mobility. They make known to the people their 'policies and programmes on which it is contesting elections and assure them of their fulfilment after getting to power. Parties or candidates make policy proposals during campaigns and explain how these policies would affect citizens welfare…'.[22] In electoral campaigns parties propose policies and project the personality of candidates. The questions we need to examine are whether (a) electoral campaigns are informative, that is, voters can justifiably expect that parties would do what they proposed, and (b) pursuing the winning platform, the mandate, is always in the best interest of voters.[23] Politicians want to get elected and re-elected. Political parties expect that voters are vigilant about how they pursue the policies that they offered in their election campaign. If politicians know the preferences of the decisive voters, they offer a platform that coincides with these preferences. If they expect that voters' preferences will not change or that these preferences will be confirmed by observing the outcomes of implementing the mandate (Huntington, 1993a), then the incumbents pursue the announced policy in quest of re-election.[24]

Up to a point parties bring individuals and groups under their influence in their effort to create, coordinate and mobilize public opinion.[25] Political parties therefore are mainly engaged in propagating their programmes and policies, which are an important principal means of appealing to the masses. They organize public meetings, rallies, processions, *morchas* and *jathas*, *dharnas*, *gheraos*, signature campaigns, submit memorandums and pass resolutions, door to door canvassing, persuading voters to go to polling booths to vote for their candidates and organizing processions. "The activities of parties aimed at creating public opinion are always organized around their programme. The programme of a party is a collection of its views on topics of national and international importance, and a formal expression of the socio-politico-economic changes it proposes to introduce in conformity with its ideological tenets for the general well-being of society. The programme is mainly the product of its doctrine, the image of its socio-economic ideals, and provides a firm basis and justification for its actions, aimed at securing durable public confidence."[26]

Campaigners adopt various means to canvass for their parties and candidates. These means are used to mobilize people in their favour. The effectiveness of the means of campaign depends on social composition of society and the level of technological development.[27] Among all campaign techniques most effective is the face-to-face communication with voters. The popularity and the charisma of the candidate is a contributing factor in campaign. Campaign chiefly reaches the faithful, crystallizing partisanship and reinforcing the intention of committed party adherents to vote and to pursue others to vote.[28]

Interest articulation and aggregation functions of political parties are crucial for democratic governance. "Unless interests are aggregated how can a legislator articulate in the decision making forum? So, it is an imperative need to have contact with the constituents either through his representatives or by himself or through party nominee to aggregate their demands. Whether the people feel it or not, a legislator has to do it as he has to play a representative role in the legislative body".[29] Parties are institutions that seek to represent more than a single narrow interest in the society.[30] It is true that most of the parties attempt to aggregate a range of interests in society, but the experience with some of the regional parties in India is different. They represent the interest of some sections in their region and become popular in their respective regions.

Since the society remains stratified into the privileged and the under privileged and the power resources remain unequally distributive, a system of conflicting interests remains in the society. [31] It is believed that the under-privileged or the deprived sections of the society can best participate through their respective socio-political organizations, who work as vanguards of their interests. It is related to worldwide acceptance that political parties primarily represent interests of a particular class or classes.[32] The literature on the subject indicates that almost all the rightist parties, directly or indirectly, have been supported by different interest groups representing a mixture of racial, religious and class interest.[33] Historically, it can be proved that the rightist parties have been representing the vested interests of the classes they represent.[34] In India, political parties or groups like the RSS, the Hindu Mahasabha, the Jana Sangh, the Muslim League, etc., are known as the rightist groups or parties. They are supporting the aims and interests of particular communities in India.

On the other hand, the left oriented parties mostly represent the interests of the deprived people who constitute a major section of the society. They are supposed to be an instrument of social change. "These parties have been struggling for equality, democratization and mass-participation in all spheres of social action. They have been mobilizing the masses through their organizations and respective trade unions to fight for equality and justice and to demand for their legitimate upliftment."[35] In India, Forward Bloc, CPI and CPI (M) are the leftist parties struggling for the upliftment of the deprived people. Congress is considered as the centrist party.

Indian society is heterogeneous in character. Different classes and groups have their own interest. There is a tendency towards a 'catch-all' electoral strategy amongst parties.[36] They try to appeal to each and every section of the people. The party which wants to get elected has to give proper representation to each section and group of people. Party manifestos have to be carefully prepared by political parties, which highlight their position on different issues and policies. Promises made by parties in their manifestos are not binding on them. Usually, they get prominence at the time of elections.

Electoral Politics in India

The nature of electoral politics may be regarded as an indicator of political participation of parties. Electoral issues indicate how parties articulate and aggregate the interest of people. Performing the function of interest articulation and aggregation by parties demonstrate the nature of their political participation. Often political parties seek the support of the people by superficially explaining their ideologies, programmes and achievements and at the same time highlighting the failures and shortcomings of other parties. Peoples' opinion always take backseat in electoral politics. Thus they politicize citizens opinion and involve them in various political issues. They swing the opinion of people in favour of or against a particular issue.[37]

Political parties raise different issues at the time of election and convert them into electoral issues. In India caste, class, religion, language, communal tensions, foreign origin, Kargil war issue, were politicized by the political parties. Almost all the studies on political parties in the Indian context have at length discussed the role of religion, caste, linguistic ties and community orders, as the most important determining factors for influencing the electoral behaviour of person.[38] "Parties are framed and identified on basis of caste, communal and regional feelings instead of seeking identification with national problems and issues. The emergence of the BJP as a political force is largely accredited to the religious issues such as Ram Mandir and *Hindutva* awakening."[39] Similarly, the voting behavioural pattern of Muslims is greatly influenced by religious sentiments. Issues of national importance receive scant attention from people where communal tensions prevail. As a result of this, we come across communalization and regionalization of Indian politics.

In the Indian political history religion has been a very powerful tool for mobilizing large sections of the masses and such other communities that are prone to religious sentiments. Since independence the Sikh Party has been demanding 'Sikhistan', a separate state for the Sikhs. Since such a communal demand in the post-independence phase has been politically inopportune, the demand for a 'Sikhistan' found itself distinguished in one for a 'Punjabi' speaking state.[40] In an effort to encounter the Akali's demands, Hindu organizations like the Jana Sangha and the Hindu Mahasabha demanded the creation of Maha-Punjab so as to diminish the proportion of Sikhs.[41]

Sometimes national political parties are also using linguistic issues for their political gain. For example, "The local unit of the Congress in the Tamil-speaking district of Travancore-Cochin supported such a demand and broke away from the parent organization and formed the Tamil Congress in order to press for the merger of their area with the neighbouring Tamil-speaking State of Madras."[42]

However, the role played by casteism in Indian politics is not so simple, because caste under constitutional provisions can be organized to form formal associations to win benefits for themselves.[43] Any caste may support a single political party or it may play an independent political role as in the case of the Kammas in Andhra supporting overwhelmingly the Communist Party of India.[44] Sometimes two different castes become opposed to each other and act as political opponents to each other such as predominantly non-Brahmin, Dravid Munnetra Kazhagam (DMK) of Tamil Nadu and the Brahmin-dominated Congress Party in the state.[45] According to *The Times of India*: "Admittedly the Congress is the most caste-ridden of the Indian political parties, whose factions always revolve around personalities and caste. It selects its electoral candidates, ministers and even judges on the basis of castes, shows caste preference in almost all appointments. Its ministers show favours to their own caste men."[46]

"Since the boundaries of the caste system more or less overlap those of the class structure of India, we find that different castes of the same class status collaborate with each other and display mutual help in protecting their common interests. The main forces working in favour of this trend are: (a) increasing industrialization and urbanization, (b) increasing literacy and social mobility, (c) strong communication channels. All these factors have been found quite effective in developing interest oriented political consciousness among the masses."[47] "Paul Brass, in his study of the industrial Kanpur City, has pointed out that the Communist Party was able to increase its influence in all occupational categories cutting across the boundaries of different castes and communities. It reflects the increasing orientation of class interests among the voters. He further writes that the voters were influenced by anti-establishment slogans and they preferred a Communist supported candidate, a trade unionist against the Congress party."[48]

Religion can be used by the political parties for the political mobilization of citizens. Some groups or parties in India had mobilized the people for political participation in the name of Ram Janmabhoomi and Babri Masjid in India. Certain political parties in India are founded on the basis of religions and have mobilized their supporters for political participation.[49] Caste and religion have become powerful divisive forces in politics because all major democratic parties and leading social classes have fought their political battle of legitimacy on caste and religious basis.[50] Political parties have successfully exploited these sentiments of the people for gaining electoral support and for their political mobilization. "There is a regular and organized effort to politicize these feelings of the people. But, parties which avowedly stand for it have so far failed to achieve much success."[51] For instance, the BJP played its card more on *Hindutva*. For some time it succeeded in attracting large section of Hindu votes but to attain power at the centre it had to sidetrack its ideology. The party realized: "It is only by moving away from the *Hindutva* bogey that the party could realize its dream of emerging as a real alternative to both the Congress and NF-LF kind of coalition and assume power at the centre."[52]

Little efforts have been made to rule out political parties from gaining electoral advantages by indirectly appealing to voters on the ground of religion, castes and sub-castes etc. The goal of efficiency in the performance of the government and scope of open entry through merit is being consciously traded off with that of allocation and distribution of opportunities to various groups on a caste basis.[53]

During elections political parties are not throwing up far reaching debates on crucial issues of public importance. The political agenda charted out by parties set the term for debate; these terms are conceived either in trans-class terms viz., populism, or on the immediate issues—corruption, price-rise, national unity, etc.[54] In India political parties relegate policy issues to background and often adopt populist techniques to secure attention of masses.[55] For example, after the death of Nehru, Indira Gandhi used the populist method to attract the voters. In the beginning they yielded good results but in the long run they failed to provide the expected result. More stress on populism tends to the subordination of organizational base of the party. Persons near and dear to the party high command were given the ministerial berth. Rajiv Gandhi tried to strengthen the organization of Congress party but was not be successful. With the weak organizational base of the Congress party, its support base declined. The Congress party started losing its hold over the people. This is not the case only with the Congress party but most of the political parties in India lack effective organization base and are more inclined towards populist measures to attract the voters.

"Generally, political parties through their organizational and propaganda technique would transmit the issues of the society, polity, economy, culture and religion to the people periodically and keep the mass alive in political issues of political action. But it is a major perplexing question whether political parties are really highlighting the issues that are confronting the society?"[56]

When asked about whether political parties are really interested in bringing issues to the people? 71.34 per cent said that political parties were not bringing issues to the people. Table 5.4 explains such facts.

***Table 5.4:** Political parties bring issues to the people

Sl. No.	*Category*	*No. of Respondents*	*Percentage*
1.	Yes	90	28.66
2.	No	224	71.34
	Total	314	100.00

* The above table is drawn from the sample survey conducted by G. Palanithurai.

Source: G. Palanithurai, *People's Perception of Politics: An Indian Perspective,* Kanishka Publishers, Delhi, 1995, p. 28.

The above table indicates that only a small section of people, that is, 28.66 per cent believe that political parties bring the issues of public importance to the people. Political parties hardly provide knowledge about the major issues confronting the country. "As a consequence the common voter hardly knows anything about the major issues involved or the challenges before the nation when he casts his vote. For example, economic reforms for liberalization, privatization and globalization have been the most important issues influencing the fortune of the voters but they have never been issues in the several general elections held during the last decade. How can then the citizen understand the implications of economic reforms or extend their co-operation for making a success of economic reform?"[57]

All these adversely influence inter-party and intra-party competition. As a result of the nature of inter-party and intra-party competition, the political participation of parties as well as people has become mechanical/formal. The nature of party politics may have serious implications for the functioning of democratic governance in India. Politics played by parties in parliament has weakened the democratic spirit in the decision-making process and outside the parliament the nature of party politics is adversely affecting the participatory role of political parties.

Basically, party politics is nothing but the interaction among political parties. This interaction among political parties is affected by the policies, programmes, ideologies of different political parties. The nature of party politics has drastically changed since 1970s. Soon after independence Congress came to power in Centre as well as in almost all States and remained in power till 1967. The opposition parties were weak and the Congress was dominant party. Therefore, it was described as, One Party Dominant System. The dominance of Congress in Indian politics was so strong that it was not paving the way for any other party to gain strength. Its role in the freedom struggle, its umbrella character and presence of charismatic leaders made Congress more powerful. In the post-independence India, "In the case of the Congress, power served as a factor of unity because it had Nehru, a leader who could serve as the last court of appeal for intra-party disputes and who could evolve policies, domestic and foreign, which had a wide appeal, specially among the intelligentsia in his party."[58] After 1967 its control over some states declined considerably.

The 1977 elections put an end to One Party Dominant System. "Mrs. Indira Gandhi sought to centralize power by undermining the role of the Congress chief ministers. In place of excellence, competence and independence of the state level leaders, loyalty to the Prime Minister and control by the high command acquired prominence during her regime. In the post-Nehru era the organizational wing was totally subordinated to the governmental wing."[59] The whole period, starting with the emergency and ending in the erosion of the

Congress in the social sphere led to growing uncertainty in the arena of democratic politics.[60] Absence of charismatic leaders like Nehru, declaration of emergency in 1975, failure in economic field and other factors contributed to its decline. It started losing its hold over most of the states. As a result of this regional parties started becoming more powerful in their respective regions. At the Centre, Janata Party and BJP took advantage of this. Regional parties became so powerful that they started claiming more share in the national politics.

Coalitions or minority politics owing to the plurality of the Indian society and regional diversities resulting the multi-party system has come to stay in the political governance of India.[61] The installation of coalition governments marked the beginning of a new type of governance. As coalition governments became inescapable political parties started aligning themselves with one or the other party. "As a result, smaller parties and regional parties are getting a significant role in governance and policy formulation but it is more related to political exigency resulting in a process of adoption and accommodation in policies formulation. Ideologically divergent allies/ partners are bringing greater conflicts in governance."[62] Every party in a coalition has its own ideology, policies and progarammes. To attain power these different parties agree on some Common Minimum Programme. Though the parties in the coalition have agreed on Common Minimum Programme, they have not lost their separate identities. But, even when they evolve what they call a Common Minimum Programme, they are so self-centred that Common Minimum Programme is reduced to common personal programme and national agenda to personal agenda.[63] The political situation in the Centre does not hold any hope for even minimum good and coherent governance because artificially created majorities cannot conceal the prevailing real vacuum in political power.[64] Coalition politics requires a mechanism of conflict resolution of different interest groups; so that they presume that they would be better off as a part of the coalition rather than out of it.[65] But this is possible only when political parties' alignments are based on policy commitments and not on the whims and fancies of their leaders.

While formulating any public policy, the leader of a coalition has to take into confidence not only his coalition partners but also the opposition parties. In the coalition era both inter-party competition and intra-party conflicts pose a challenge not only to the existence of the government but also to the democratic governance in the country.

Since the resultant coalition alliances are neither 'ideological' nor have any common objective to cement them together, they are merely short term tactical arrangements established by ambitious politicians that are rooted in the exchange of mutual benefits and compulsion for power, the mobilization of electorate is done through a strategy of support to regional-*cum*-segmental or ethnic issues without giving overriding support either to national or primarily local issues.[66] Each party before joining a coalition, calculates the extent of gains, i.e., payoff. Political parties in parliamentary democracy always strive to form minimum winning coalitions. In such a coalition, even a small party can challenge the very existence of a coalition. That is what happened to the BJP-led coalition in 1998. The confidence motion moved by the BJP-led coalition government under the leadership of A.B. Vajpayee was defeated by just one vote. As Lord Bryce says, "An administration formed by a coalition of parties is usually weak, not merely because the combination is unstable, but because men whose professed principles differ, are likely to be entangled in inconsistencies or driven to unsatisfactory compromises. In multi-party parliaments, each party makes bargains with one another and by their combination, perhaps secretly and suddenly formed, successive ministries may be overturned with injury to the progress of legislation and to the continuity of national policy."[67] Political parties are concerned mainly with attaining and maintaining power. In the quest for power, political parties are neglecting their ethical and moral responsibilities towards the people.

The success and failure of the working of a coalition government depends on its partners. To make coalition experiment a success, there should be ideological and functional cohesiveness and their conscious efforts to be made to evolve a coalition culture.[68] Parties outside coalition desire to capture power. Parties within the coalition are usually unhappy about their ministerial payoff. Consequently, there is constant danger for the very survival of coalition from both parties within the coalition and outside the coalition. The governance under coalition arrangements will have to take the course of accommodation and reconciliation to moderate the conflict of interests rather than curb them.[69] The whole idea of coalition government is based on fair play. But in India, unfortunately, neither the dominant political party nor the minority groups acted on this basis.

"Parties are fast becoming a type basically because all of them are out to seek power and power they can acquire only after winning elections. Naturally then, the emphasis is not on winning the minds, it is on winning the votes. And now that electoral success has become something that can be achieved by a particular technique, parties appear to be concerned about just that, nothing more and nothing less."[70] Winning election has become their main aim. To win elections, political parties started using many cutthroat means. The use of money, muscle and mafia power vitiated the participatory process of Indian democratic governance.

To participate effectively in the political process, political parties require funds. Politicians are concerned only with winning elections, but to win they must raise resources.[71] Raising funds is one of the important participatory activities of political parties. Funds are essential for effective functioning of political parties. "This money is needed both for winning elections and therefore, for consolidating—or dislodging—the ruling group within the majority party."[72] Money is essential for the day-to-day running of the party organization. "In short, it is an essential element of electoral, legislative and party politics. As the money needed has kept rising (multiplied by the new assumptions on the importance of money in winning elections introduced by the fund collectors and dispersers whose position in the party depends on the need for big money), the system has had to rely increasingly on secret deals, and has become the source of corruption in public life and put a premium on black-money." [73]

These funds are collected from the companies, private bodies, institutions and individuals. But when these funds come from companies, private bodies, institutions, etc., they require some favour in exchange. It has placed disproportionate power in the hands of political financiers (largely from private industry) and of those who can manage to get money from such financieries.[74] "...politics being treated as private enterprise in which illegal and unauthorized money becomes the principal currency. As this happens, the manipulative aspect of politics gains further in proportion as the participant aspect loses".[75]

Criminalisation has drastically affected the participatory process of political parties. With criminal elements entering into politics political parties almost cease to be the representatives of the people. Politics has become a number game. To attain the required majority number politicians are using criminals. With the help of criminals politicians are "able to terrorise the voters and the polling and the presiding officers. As a result, in the states like Bihar and UP a number of dreaded criminals have entered the house."[76] The interests of the politicians and the criminals are complementary to each other. On the one hand the criminals need protection from the government and on the other, the politicians need criminals for money and mafia power for booth capturing, impersonation, rigging etc. Thus, the politician-criminal nexus in one party breeds similar nexus in other parties, because the parties holding clean chits also feel that criminal elements are indispensable for any party to survive in an election contest.[77]

Indian political parties have become mainly personality oriented. Unfortunately, they revolve round a particular person. "Where is the question then of democratic processes in that party? Where is the scope for participation of the people when everything is personality centred?"[78] They are running away from ideologies, principles and values. "It is seen that our democratic pattern allows the rule of a party and most of the parties are guided by and led by either a charismatic personality or small group of persons. In both these cases neither the will of the people nor the welfare of the people is reflected."[79] "A number of political parties emerge with the popularity of a particular leader and sink with his political career. We have observed emergence of several new political parties on the election eve; and most of them either disappear as soon as the election is over or are merged with some other dominant party. We still have to develop healthy democratic tradition of ideologically organized political parties, instead of leader centred parties, such as Lok Dal (Charan Singh), Congress (T) (N.D. Tiwari), Congress for Democracy (Jagjivan Ram) and Janata Dal (V.P. Singh)."[80] After Nehru, sycophancy became the order of the day and Congress men looked towards an individual leader (Mrs. Indira Gandhi) for retaining their electoral position.[81] It is not the case only with Congress but in other Indian political parties also, the high command or the leader became dominant in deciding the party affairs. In the functioning of the parties, personalized control has become more important than any other issue. It is generally agreed that powerful leaders are partly responsible for the deinstitutionalization of the Indian party system. "...that the inherent inadequacies have come to the surface and provided a framework in which a highly centralized and narrowly confined elite has established itself in power, lost touch with the people and become insensitive and non-productive."[82] Neither the opposition nor the government really cared for the people and all that gained importance was a game of power within a narrow elite which had lost all contacts with the people.

However, it is essential to emphasise that however distasteful the working of our political parties and politicians may have been, a conscientious citizen cannot afford to show indifference.[83]

Popular Political Participation

Much of the contemporary research in political behaviour revolves around the role of citizens' perception of politics and their participation in the political process of the society.[84] By popular participation we mean the participation of people in politics. One of the foremost concerns of contemporary political writers is the manner and the degree of citizens' participation in politics. The central focus of governance is on how a society through the nation state, handles the affairs of the state, which enables its people to lead a peaceful orderly and reasonably prosperous and participative life in running their affairs.[85]

Public participation is generally intended at direct participation of public in administrative decision-making and policy-formulation, its implementation and evaluation.[86] Direct participation of the people in the decision making process is not possible in modern democracy. The representatives of the people are formulating policies on behalf of people. Popular participation can make their representatives accountable and responsive to the fulfilment of their needs and aspirations. "Alex De Tocqueville, the French political thinker, was of the view that civic participation is a must for saving democracy. The very existence of democracy is endangered when the general public is unable to influence government decisions."[87]

It is pertinent to understand, why to participate and whether participation should be open to all or restricted to those who know how to use it wisely. In this regard a number of political philosophers and scientists have different views. Political participation is not a natural activity but can be learnt through socialization process. For learning one must have capacity, motivation and opportunity. As Bryce observed, only a small group gives constant attention to politics, a slightly larger group is interested but comparatively passive, while the masses of men are largely indifferent.[88]

With regard to popular participation, we can classify the thinkers mainly into two groups. Some thinkers believe that high participation of community is essential to preserve democratic spirit. On the other hand, there are some thinkers who believe that participation by all people in political affairs is dangerous to democracy.

The advocates of the higher participation hold the view: "A situation which results in high participation by members of a group normally has higher potential for democracy—that is, for the maintenance of an effective opposition—than one where few people show interest or participate in the political process."[90] "...Participation in politics provides groups with the opportunity to offset their social and economic disadvantages, at least to a degree, by giving them the means to reduce such disadvantages through the active exercise of political power."[91] "Greater participation may provide more effective checks on the power of sinister interests. It may also give increased assurance that no interests are excluded from the governmental process and left out of account."[92]

There are some observers who believe that non-participation may create some problems. It may tend to inadequate expression of the interest of some sections of society. As far as possible government attempts to give representation to various sections of society. In spite of this, some sections may not be adequately represented. Such sections of society have to raise their voice to get adequate representation in the government. In this respect political parties and NGOs presuppose to play an important role in promoting awareness among the neglected sections of society. Ultimately, this contributes to get adequate representation for the neglected sections of society.

"Widespread apathy increases the chances that government will be dominated by men who are unresponsive, self-aggrandizing and unscrupulous; participation, on the other hand, reminds those who govern that they must attend to their duties and serve the electorate."[93] Increased participation is required for "the most simple and obvious reason, whether or not sound, is to achieve improved governmental output—better policies more efficiently and fairly administered."[94]

According to some political philosophers universal participation is nor possible and neither desirable. "Rousseau, in a famous passage in *The Social Contract* links emancipation and sovereignty to direct involvement, arguing passionately that to be represented is to give up—to alienate—powers that individuals alone can rightfully exercise. Deputies are acceptable since they are merely the agents of the people. Representation, on the other hand, an odious modern idea, involves a form of slavery—a negation of will."[95] It was believed that little would be gained by making the citizens participate in politics who are politically uninformed and uninterested. "Such people are likely to misperceive their own and societies best interest. They are likely to have the poorest understanding of the requirements of a democratic system (civil liberties, tolerance of non-conformity, etc.) and are more susceptible to misleading inappropriate leader."[96]

There are different arguments of the scholars on political participation of citizens but whatever may be the arguments of the scholars, "the founding fathers of India's republic built the entire edifice of her constitution and democratic polity on the quintessential principle of sovereignty vesting in the people. Democratic governance can be ensured only when citizens can stand up for their rights."[97] Alertness, vigilance and active and continuous participation of the citizens in the affairs of governance are vital to the sound functioning of democratic system. A constitution alone may not suffice to ensure good government, unless the citizens continuously take interest in the proper working of the constitutional provisions.[98] In representative democracy, the citizens have to remain active. It is made meaningless by the complacent citizen who avoids participation or declines to accept responsibilities for what the government does, thinking of politics in terms of "we" who are governed and "they" who govern.[99] "Governments are "accountable" to the people only when voters can have the ability and capacity to decide whether governments are acting in their interest or not. So that, those incumbents who act in the best interest of citizens win re-election and those who do not lose them. Accountability representation occurs when, (1) voters vote to retain the incumbent only when the incumbent acts in their best interest, and (2) the incumbent chooses policies necessary to get reelected."[100]

People should organize themselves and fight for their rights. There is a need to make all citizens aware about their fundamental rights. The knowledge of political affairs and awareness affects both the amount and the quality of participation. If people become actively involved in the process of government, so the argument runs, they will be motivated to obtain more, better, and more coherent information on public affairs.[101] Men without a sense of involvement become apathetic or sometimes turn rebellious.

"Citizens contribute something to the public good through participation in political process and such participation increases their creative energy. Political participation makes a government responsible to people and responsive to their demands and aspirations."[102] "It is the people who are the best judges of their pleasures and pains. They can maximize their pleasures and minimize their pains by actively participating in the political process."[103] In the words of Saul David Alinsky: "There can be no democracy unless it is a dynamic democracy. When our people cease to participate, to have a place in the sun then all of us will wither in the darkness of decadence. All of us will become mute, demoralized lost souls."[104]

According to Almond and Verba, the citizen of a democratic polity is expected to:

"Engage in political discussion;
Take interest in politics;
Vote;
Knowledge of politics;
Express a general sense of competence to influence the government; and
Participation in civic affairs."[105]

Among all the citizens, the democratic citizens have ample opportunities to participate in political process in several ways, with different degrees of involvement and at various levels of political systems.[106] But, because of differences in standard of living, level of education, social environment, political culture, etc., we find variations in citizens' participation in the political process.

Operation of democratic institutions and expression of people's desires are facilitated through political participation like voting, campaigning, contesting, holding elective offices, etc.[107] Most popular participation includes voting, seeking information, discussing and proselytizing, attending meetings, contributing financially and communicating with representatives.[108] Citizen can participate in political activities in a variety of ways. But, most of the studies mainly focus on voting. Voting indicates citizen's choice, but it communicates little information about the preferences or interests. The scope of the outcome is very broad and it affects every citizen.

The nature of party politics affects election turnout. Where parties are competitive, participation tends to increase; whereas single party consistently wins elections, turnout tends to be lower.[109] In India during the Congress rule election turnout was less. With the emergence of competitive parties, which have the ability to challenge the Congress party election turnout is slowly increasing. Table 5.5 highlights this point.

Table 5.5: Voter Turnout

Year	*Duration of Holding Elections*	*Voter Turnout*
1991	26 days	56.73 %
1996	11	57.94%
1998	13	62.00%
1999	29	61.00 %
2004	20	*56.00 %

* From websitehttp: // www.indian-elections.com/resultsupdate/

Source: Meenu Roy, *Electoral Politics in India*, Deep and Deep Publications, New Delhi, 2000, p. 270.

The voter turnout was high in 1998, that is 62.00 per cent. After 1998 again we can find slow decrease in the voter turnout, that is 61.00 per cent in 1999 and 56.00 per cent in 2004. Coalition politics and unstable governments can be one of the factors for the low percentage of voting in 2004 elections. So, we can say that competitive parties alone are not responsible for increasing election turnout. There are other factors, which are equally important such as dissatisfaction, distrust and desire for radical change as was seen in Indian electoral politics. During the last decade of twentieth century voting turnout increased. People were fed up with the Congress rule. Their desire for a change in party was reflected in the voting turnout. The problem is that during normal time the citizens are somewhat unenthusiastic and indifferent to exercise their voting rights.[110] The emergence of regional parties and with them the emergence of coalition governments aroused new hopes in the minds of electorate. People of India want to lead the nation in a different direction, the direction in which welfare of the people should be the main motto of the government. But, the experience with coalition governments made it clear that with the change in government style there is no change in its governance. All political parties were concerned more about their welfare and not much worried about the welfare of the people. With this again there was considerable decline in the voting turnout in 2004 general elections.

Genevieve Knupfer believes that: "the economic and educational limitations accompanying low status produce a lack of interest in and lack of self-confidence in dealing with certain important areas of our culture; as a result, there is reduced participation."[111]

Most people believe that right to vote is a sacred right. Yet, it is not clear that high turnout is in itself desirable. Increased turnout most of the time brings those who generally do not vote. Habitual voters vote in part because they believe that they should participate—that participation is essential to democracy.[112] Critics believe that even this kind of participation is very low. They believe that the decline reflects "alienation" a feeling on the part of the non-voters that voting is futile because they don't like any of the realistic options or because they feel powerless to affect the result in any significant way.[113]

The primary means by which citizens control their government is voting in free and fair elections. "For the healthy functioning of democracy, it is essential that the voter must not only be free to vote as per the dictates of his conscience but also that he should be aware of the philosophy and ideals of the political parties and candidates in the fray. It is only then that his vote will be an informed one, cast after due consideration."[114]

The fuller and whole hearted participation of citizens is further discouraged by:

"(a) incorrect and incomplete voters list;
(b) intimidation of voters to prevent them from voting;
(c) exercise of money and muscle power to get votes;
(d) winning elections with minority of votes;
(e) defections after elections."[115]

The elections are manipulated right from the time of enlisting the voters whereby some people are debarred from voting and fictitious names are included as voters thereby frustrating the very basic concept of 'adult franchise."[116] The voters list, which is the first prerequisite in any election, is manipulated in various forms. False, non-existent persons' name find place in voters' list by deliberate manipulation.

The candidates are chosen by political parties and do not have much to say.[117] It appears that candidates are not genuine representatives of the people. The making and unmaking of the ministers is in the hands of the party high command. Thus everything is controlled by party high command.

Yet, elections have also been marked increasingly by use of violence on an unprecedented level, rigging, booth-capturing, threatening of polling staff, use of big money, legitimization of criminals as granting of party tickets to people with criminal records.[118]

For the democratic polity to function properly it is important that all citizens exercise their right to vote and that they cast their vote rationally, i.e., make their choice among the candidates after proper consideration.[119]

Peoples' participation in political process generally comes once in five years. "After voting once, for five years they have nothing to do with the process. What is necessary is not merely participation in the electoral process but participatory democracy. Participation in democracy has to be a continuous process.[120] To ensure people's continuous and active participation it is most important to create awareness among the people. Electoral results have a vital impact on the lives of all the people and also on the future of the country. Therefore, a choice has to be made and made as carefully as possible because at the moment it is only from among the existing contenders that the future government of the county will be formed.[121] Voters' awareness and their active participation in the election process from selection of the candidates by the political parties to election campaign and actual voting can definitely make a difference. "...it does not suffice for the government as a whole to be accountable to the electorate; but rather the voter should be able to identify the responsible authorities and hold them accountable as a group for their deeds and misdeeds."[122] Political participation therefore, will increase the extent to which a nation is a democratic only in-so-far as such participation involves at some point influence by the participant over governmental decisions.[123]

Some NGOs and group of people make efforts to make the people aware about their political rights. "We do have some NGOs and group of people in many places in the country doing some work in the area of political awareness. But, these activities and programmes are *adhoc* in nature and they are seasonal and their purpose is very limited in scope."[124] The programmes of such group are informal and unorganized but their impact is not felt to the extent it should. Much had been talked about Voters' Council to minimize the evils in the election process but we do not have any such model.[125]

The electoral process has brought an increasingly politicized voter into the participatory process. Voting provides an opportunity to the people to elect a government which can be responsible to the people and responsive to their needs. But, at the time of elections, electoral behaviour is more influenced by the factors like money power, muscle power, liquor, caste, language, community, religion, etc. They may prefer the candidate of their own caste, religion, or language while electing them.

In India religion, language, caste and class are powerful tools for mobilizing various sections of people. They have become the part and parcel of individuals life and so emotional is its hold that a person is prepared to make supreme sacrifice to uphold its prestige and sanctity. "The last decade of 20th century saw a sharp rise in political mobilization on the basis of social cleavages based on inscriptive identities, in particular of religion and caste. Casteism, communalism and personality domination have been the main planks around which the fragmentation of political parties has taken place, which has resulted in more caste and class-based political violence in the society.[126] "Citizens' participation in the voting process has degenerated as it is being promoted to be more on communal and caste lines rather than on the basis of merits of individual candidates. In many instances of voting candidates with criminal backgrounds of one's own caste or religion were found to have been preferred and elected instead of good, well qualified and meritorious candidates of other castes or religions."[127]

Campaign activity is the second mode of participation available to the citizens. Campaigning requires a group of people having similar interests. It can communicate more information about the participants, preferences because campaign activists are a more clearly identifiable group with whom candidates may be in close contact.[128] This activity requires lot of co-operation among citizens. "Political campaigns are episodic, but working in them requires a considerable amount of time. Self-confidence and a feeling of social ease are important prerequisites to participation in the socially interactive phase of campaigning."[129]

Communal activity is the third kind of popular participation available to the citizens. It involves two types of activities. It may be a contact by an individual with government official or it may be a contact by group or organization with the government official for some general social purpose. These kinds of activities provide more information to government about their preferences. The amount of pressure depends on the influence of the participating individual or group.

The next mode of popular political participation is particularized contact. Here, an individual contacts a government official to solve his own problem.

"Contributing money is also an important indicator of an individual's interest in politics. Money is a powerful weapon to influence policy-makers, and rich and busy persons who are not able to take time off to attend rallies and meetings look upon monetary contributions as a substitute for their personal participation in 'gladiatorial' activity. This is more so in the Indian case where money is scarce."[130]

The more active form of popular participation includes formal enrollment in a party, canvassing and registering voters, speech writing and speechmaking, working in campaign and competing for public and party office.[131] Popular political participation "enables men by giving them a sense of their own dignity and value, alerts both rulers and ruled to their duties and responsibilities and broadens political understanding."[132]

As Saenger points out, political activity is not merely a matter of awareness of what is going on but is also affected by the "amount of time and energy specific activities require."[133] Political participation is closely associated with the leisure available to the citizens. Political participation has little relevance to a person who hardly gets any leisure. Table 5.6 portrays the details of leisure available to the individual per day.

***Table 5.6:** Hours of Leisure Per Day

S. No.	*Hours*	*No. of Respondents*	*Percentage*
1.	0-3	144	68.57
2.	4-7	49	23.33
3.	8-10	7	3.33
4.	11 & above	10	4.76
	Total	210	100.00

* The above table is drawn from sample survey conducted by G. Palanithurai.

Source: G. Palanithurai, *People Perception of Politics: An Indian Perspective*, Kanishka Publishers, Delhi, 1995, p. 41.

Out of 210 respondents only 10 people get more than 11 hours leisure per day i.e., 4.76 per cent only. Even if an individual gets leisure time, there is no guarantee that he/she spends it in political discussion. Table 5.6 highlights this fact.

From Table 5.7 it is inferred that, out of 210 respondents 136 respondents that is 64.76 per cent citizens were interested in discussing cinema. Only 37 people that is 17.62 per cent were interested in political discussion.

***Table 5.7:** Subject of Discussion During Leisure

S. No.	*Subjects*	*No. of Respondents*	*Percentage*
1.	Talk about others	58	27.62
2.	Self-Development	26	12.38
3.	Politics	37	17.62
4.	Cinema	136	64.76
5.	Family	73	34.76
6.	Country	10	4.76
	Total	**210**	**100.00**

* The above table is drawn from sample survey conducted by G. Palanithurai.

Source: G. Palanithurai, *People Perception of Politics: An Indian Perspective*, Kanishka Publishers, Delhi, 1995, p. 41.

With such a low percentage how can we expect qualitative participation by the citizens? It is true that the popular political participation increases awareness about politics. However, to increase awareness citizens should have interest to participate. Political interest and awareness are related variables that are even more difficult to assess than participation, because their manifestations are less overt.[134]

"Political participation is not "natural", but must be learned and for learning to occur, one must have capacity, motivation, and opportunity. In some strata of the society, all three are preconditions are missing."[135]

It is a pity that the elite class which is supposed to be the backbone of citizens participation in political awareness programmes, not only participates in party politics but directly and indirectly supports and many a time encourages and initiate the process of corrupt practices in politics. Political leaders of courage placing national interests above group/partisan interests, who are prepared to face the wrath of their narrow populist supporters in the interest of the nation, are becoming scarce.[136] This is a class of citizens if they collectively decide to assert themselves for upholding the democratic values in society can certainly make a difference.

REFERENCES

1. Adam Przeworski, Susan C. Stokes and Bernard Manin, *Democracy, Accountability and Representation*, Cambridge University Press, Cambridge, 1999, p. 31.
2. *Ibid.*, p. 48.
3. R.C. Dutt, *People and Politics: The Indian Experience*, Lancer Publishers Private Limited, New Delhi, 1992, p. 144.
4. *Ibid.*, p. 144.
5. David L. Sills (ed.), *International Encyclopedia of Social Sciences*, Vol. 12, The MacMillan Company and The Free Press, America, 1968, p. 253.
6. R.T. Jangam, S.H. Patil and S.S. Patagundi, *Political Analysis*, Oxford and IBH Publishing Company, New Delhi, 1997, p. 116.
7. G. Palanithurai, *People's Perception of Politics: An Indian Perspective*, Kanishka Publishers, Delhi, 1995, p. 28.
8. A.P. Barnabas, Caste in Transition, *Religion and Society*, 5(3), September 1958, p. 14.
9. R.P. Verma, *Peoples' Participation in Indian Politics*, Rajat Publications, New Delhi, 2002, p. 9.
10. R.T. Jangam, S.H. Patil and S.S. Patagundi, Supra no. 6, p. 116.

11. *Ibid.*, p. 6.
12. David L. Sills (ed.), Supra no. 5, p. 259.
13. R.P. Verma, Supra no. 9, p. 3.
14. Kurt L. Shell, *The Democratic Political Process*, Blaisdell Publishing Company, London, 1969, p. 60.
15. David L. Sills (ed.), Supra no. 5, p. 258.
16. Thomas Pantham, *Political Parties and Democratic Consensus*, The MacMillan Company of India Limited, Delhi, 1976, p. 11.
17. David L.Sills (ed.), Supra no. 5, p. 258.
18. Keerat Joshi, in Subhash C. Kashyap (ed.), Supra no. 18, p. 123.
19. David L.Sills (ed.), Supra no. 5, p. 261.
20. R.T. Jangam, S.H. Patil and S.S. Patagundi, Supra no. 6, p. 125.
21. Dr. Meenu Roy, *Elections 1998: A Continuing in Coalition*, National Publishing House, New Delhi, 1999, p. 50.
22. Adam Przeworski, Susan C. Stokes and Bernard Manin, Supra no. 1, pp. 32-33.
23. *Ibid.*, p. 30.
24. *Ibid.*, pp. 32-33.
25. S.N. Sadasivan, *Party and Democracy in India*, Tata McGraw-Hill Publishing Company Limited, New Delhi, 1977, p. 320.
26. *Ibid.*, p. 320.
27. R.T. Jangam, S.H. Patil and S.S. Patagundi, Supra no. 6, p. 125.
28. David L. Sills (ed.), Supra no. 5, p. 258
29. G. Palanithurai, Supra no. 7, p. 76.
30. Alan Ware, *Political Parties and Party Systems*, Oxford University Press, New York, 1996, p. 4.
31. R.P. Verma, Supra no. 9, p. 4.
32. V.O. Key, *Politics, Parties and Pressure Groups*, Thomas Y. Crowell, New York, 1958, p 274-75.
33. A.G.Harold, Religion and Politics in U.P. Constituency, in B.E. Smith (ed.), *In South Asian Politics and Religion*, Princeton University Press, Princeton, 1969, pp. 51-52.
34. R.P. Verma, Supra no. 9, p. 5.
35. *Ibid.*, p. 5.
36. Alan Ware, Supra no. 30, p. 267.
37. R.T. Jangam, S.H. Patil and S.S. Patagundi, Supra no. 6, p. 119.
38. R.P. Verma, Supra no. 9, p. 12.
39. Suprabha V. Sahai, in Subhash C. Kashyap (ed.), Supra no. 18, p. 33.
40. R.P. Verma, Supra no. 9, p. 7.
41. Myron Weiner, *Politics of Scarcity: Public Pressures and Political Response in India*, Asia Publishing House, New Delhi, 1963, pp. 53-54.
42. *Ibid.*, pp. 61-62.

43. R.P. Verma, Supra no. 9, p. 10.
44. Selig S. Harison, *India the Most Dangerous Decade,* Princeton University Press, Princeton, 1960, pp. 211-212.
45. R.P. Verma, Supra no. 9, p. 10.
46. *Ibid.*, p. 9.
47. *Ibid.*, p. 11.
48. *Ibid.*, pp. 11-12.
49. R.T. Jangam, S.H. Patil and S.S. Patagundi, Supra no. 6, p. 118.
50. R.N. Prasad, *Governance of India: Issues and Perspectives,* Concept Publishing Company, New Delhi, 2002, p. 26.
51. Surendranath Dwivedy, Indian Political Scenario, *Janata,* 51(21), October 13, 1996, p. 5.
52. Rajni Kothari, Interpreting 1996-II, *Janata,* 51(15), August 18, 1996, p. 11.
53. R.C. Dutt, Supra no. 3, p. 161.
54. *Ibid.*, p. 149.
55. P.R. Dubhashi, in Subhash C. Kashyap (ed.), Supra no. 18, p. 88.
56. G. Palanithurai, Supra no. 7, p. 48.
57. P.R. Dubhashi, in Subhash C. Kashyap (ed.), Supra no. 18, p. 89.
58. S.S. Patagundi in Subhash C. Kashyap (ed.), Supra no. 18, p. 156.
59. *Ibid.*, p. 157.
60. Rajni Kothari, "*Memoirs: Uneasy is the Life of Mind*", Rupa Company, New Delhi, 2002, pp. 195-196.
61. R.N. Prasad, Supra no. 50, p. 23.
62. *Ibid.*, p. 23.
63. Ram Ranbir Singh and Jagjit Kaur, Coalition Politics in India: Problems and Prospects, *Review of Politics*, 7(1-2), January-June and June-December 1999, p. 87.
64. Attar Chand, *Prime Minister: H.D. Deve Gowda,* Gyan Publishing House, New Delhi, 1997, p. 27.
65. *The Times of India,* June 4, 1999.
66. www.ncrwc.nic.in
67. Lord Bryce, Modern Democracies, Vol. I, The MacMillan Company, New York, 1921, pp. 121-122.
68. Ram Ranbir Singh and Jagjit Kaur, Supra no. 63, p. 87.
69. Trimph of Coalition Politics, *Monthly Commentary,* October 1999, p. 6.
70. Vinay Sahasrabuddhe, in Subhash C. Kashya, (ed.), Supra no. 18, p. 163.
71. Adam Przeworski, Susan C. Stokes and Bernard Manin, Supra no. 7, p. 34.
72. Rajni Kothari, *Democratic Polity and Social Change in India,* Allied Publishers, New Delhi, 1976, p. 29.

73. *Ibid.*, pp. 29-30.
74. *Ibid.*, p. 29.
75. *Ibid.*, p. 31.
76. G.S. Rajhans, in Subhash C. Kashyap (ed.), Supra no. 18, p. 227.
77. Subrabha V. Sahai, in Subhash C. Kashyap (ed.), Supra no. 18, p. 31.
78. P.A. Sagma, in Subhash C. Kashyap (ed.), Supra no. 18, p. 158.
79. Bharat Jhunjunwala, *Governance and Human Rights*, Kalpaz Publications, Delhi, 2002, p. 128.
80. Subrabha V. Sahai, in Subhash C. Kashyap (ed.), Supra no. 18, p. 32.
81. S.S. Patagundi in Subhash C. Kashyap (ed.), Supra no. 18, p. 158.
82. Rajni Kothari, *Politics and The People: In Search of a Humane india*, Vol. I, Ajanta Publications, 1989, p. 243.
83. Editorial, Vote for Whom, *Janata*, 46(15), May, 1991, p. 4.
84. G. Palanithurai, Supra no. 7, p. 20.
85. S.K. Chopra (ed.), *Towards Good Governance*, Konark Publishers Private Limited, Delhi, 1997, p. 2.
86. C.P. Barthwal, *Good Governance in India*, Deep and Deep Publications Private Limited, New Delhi, 2003, p. 189.
87. *Ibid.*, p. 189.
88. David L. Sills (ed.), Supra no. 5, p. 256.
90. David V.J. Bell, Karl W. Deutch, Seymour Martin Lipset, *Issues in Politics and Government*, Houghton Mufflin Company, NewYork, 1970, p. 59.
91. R.P. Verma, Supra no. 9, p. 315.
92. J. Roland Pennock, *Democratic Political Theory*, Princeton University Press, New Jersey, 1979, p. 441.
93. David L. Sills (ed), Supra no. 5, p. 263.
94. J. Roland Pennock, Supra no. 92, p. 441.
95. John Hoffman, "*Citizenship: beyond the state*", Sage Publications, London, 2004, p. 150.
96. David L. Sills (ed.), Supra no. 5, p. 262.
97. V.A. Pai Panandikar, Subhash C. Kashyap (ed.), *Political Reforms: Asserting Civic Sovereignty*, Konark Publishers Private Limited, New Delhi, 2001, p. 1.
98. Subhash C. Kashyap (ed.), Supra no. 18, p. 81.
99. V.A. Paipanandikar and Subhash C. Kashyap (ed.), Supra no. 92, p. 6.
100. Adam Przeworski, Susan C. Stokes and Bernard Manin, Supra no. 1, p. 40.
101. J. Rolland Pennock, Supra no. 92, p. 442.
102. R.T. Jangam, S.H. Patil and S.S. Patagundi, Supra no. 6, p. 113.
103. *Ibid.*, p. 115.

104. M.G. Chitkara and B.R. Sharma, *Indian Republic: Issues and Perspective*, A.P.H. Publishing Corporation, New Delhi, 1997, p. 44.
105. Dhirendra K. Vajpey, *Modernization and Social Change in India*, Manohar Publications, 1979, New Delhi, pp. 73-74.
106. R.T. Jangam, S.H. Patil and S.S. Patagundi, Supra no. 6, p. 113.
107. *Ibid.*, p. 115.
108. David L. Sills (ed.), Supra no. 5, p. 252.
109. Seymour Martin Lipset, *The Encyclopedia of Democracy*, Routledge, London, 1995, p. 917.
110. U.C. Agarwal, in Subhash C. Kashyap (ed.), Supra no. 18, p. 87.
111. R.P. Verma (ed.), Supra no. 9, p. 43.
112. Seymour Martin Lipset, Supra no. 109, p. 919.
113. J. Rolland Pennock, Supra no. 92, p. 438.
114. M.G. Chitkara and B.R. Sharma, Supra no. 104, p. 42.
115. U.C. Agarwal, in Subhash C. Kashyap (ed.), Supra no. 18, p. 83.
116. Robin Mukherjee, *Democracy-a failure, Theocracy-the solution for human welfare*, Indian Research Press, New Delhi, 2001, p. 40.
117. M.G. Chitkara, B.R. Sharma, Supra no. 104, p. 40.
118. R.C. Dutt, Supra no. 3, p. 148.
119. P.R. Dubhashi in Subhash C. Kashyap (ed.), Supra no. 18, p. 88.
120. P.A. Sagma in Subhash C. Kashyap (ed.), Supra no. 18, pp. 17-18.
121. Vote for Whom, Editorial, Janata, 46(15), May 19, 1991, p. 4.
122. J. Roland Pennock, Supra no. 92, p. 267.
123. Kurt L. Shell, Supra no. 14, p. 60.
124. Himmat Bhai Patel and Shantibai, in Subhash C. Kashyap (ed.), Supra no. 18, pp. 103.
125. *Ibid.*, pp. 106.
126. www.ncrwc.nic.in.
127. U.C. Agarwal, in Subhash C. Kashyap (ed.), Supra no. 18, pp. 17-18.
128. Sidney Verba, Norman H. Nie, and Jae-on Kim, *Participation and Political Equality*, Cambridge University Press, Cambridge, 1978, p. 53.
129. Dhirendra K. Vajpeyi, Supra no. 105, p. 77.
130. *Ibid.*, p. 78.
131. David L. Sills (ed.), Supra No 5, pp. 252-253.
132. *Ibid.*, p. 253.
133. R.P. Verma (ed:), Supra no. 9, p. 39.
134. David L. Sills (ed.), Supra no. 5, p. 254.
135. *Ibid.*, p. 254.
136. R.C. Dutt, Supra no. 3, p. 161.

6

Popular and Political Parties' Responsiveness in Democratic Governance

Responsiveness has become one of the important characteristics of good governance. C.P. Bharathwal points out the characteristics of good governance as, "participatory, consensus oriented, accountable, transparent, responsive, effective and efficient, equitable and inclusive, and follows the rule of law."[1]

Responsiveness is one of the important features of democratic governance. A democratic government should respond to, reflect and give expression to the will of the people.[2] In a representative democracy political parties are the important channels between interest of people and government. They should give adequate representation to the interest of the people in formulating public policies. However, there is no guarantee that political parties always work in the interest of the people. "In elections, parties or candidates present themselves to voters, informing them about their policy intentions. Specifically, they tell voters which policies they intend to pursue, for what purposes, and with what consequences. Once elected, the victorious candidates choose policies, not necessarily the same as announced."[3] They may want to pursue some goals or objectives which may be different from those of the citizens. Of course, there should be politicians and civil servants who accept political and administrative responsibility for the conduct of the affairs of government. Since they are supposed to be irresponsive to public opinion and pressure, the ultimate responsibility is that of the citizens.[4] People are responsible to make political parties responsive towards their needs. Popular responsiveness determines political parties' responsiveness. Citizens are to be alert and vigilant. Policies formulated by political parties are supposed to give adequate representation to all sections of people. Here, popular responsiveness of the people towards the policies is the feedback available to the political parties to analyze their policies. In the light of the available feedback political parties make necessary changes in their policies. Thus for democratic governance responsiveness of both political parties and people is very crucial. In this regard party politics plays a crucial role.

Responsiveness of Political Parties

The main purpose of democracy is to establish government by representation, to provide a mechanism of political set-up to make policy decisions for welfare of the people and also to take measures for its implementation.[5] In other words, democratic government requires institutional mechanisms—established procedures and organizations—to translate public opinion into government policy to be responsive.[6] Elections, political parties, legislatures and interest groups and many others provide such institutional mechanism in politics. The political party is one of the most important institutional mechanisms available for expressing public opinion. Political parties in India are able to exercise this influence because in the absence of associational life they provide a key link between state and society.[7] Thus, political parties have become the very soul of Indian democracy. They have proved to be a bulwark against the tyranny of the government. Grievances of the people are easily ventilated when the parties concerned keep their representatives in legislature fully informed of peoples' problems. As political parties are responsible for the conduct of public affairs, their responsiveness in terms of representing aspirations of the people is crucial for democratic governance.

Democratic governance is not an independent variable. Political parties determine the extent of democratization of governance. They should be able and willing to chalk out the directions of economic development and translate their policies into action through an accountable, transparent and responsive administration.

How political parties respond to the expectations of the people is very crucial. The word responsiveness obviously denotes responding or answering. After articulating and aggregating the interests and aspirations of the people, political parties have to respond through working out the public policies and programmes. Therefore, political parties play a vital role in formulating and implementing public policies. Governance means the process of decision-making and the process by which decisions are implemented (or not implemented).[8] Democratic governance involves the study of how process of public policy decision making takes place. Public policy has a direct bearing on the life of the people. Public interest is at the core of public policy.[9] "Public policy is something which the government does or chooses not to do. It is the total of all governmental activities that has an impact on society."[10] Policy is based on demands made by a large number of individuals with a common problem that is beyond their ability to resolve.[11]

The crisis of governance in India can be attributed mainly to lack of responsiveness of political parties towards the aspirations and needs of the people. Atul Kohli attributes the crisis of governability to the decline of the Congress party. The Indian model of development did quite well during the Nehru period, but after him the new operators of the system showed scant understanding of its nature and began to operate in ways that put the complex balance of the system out of gear and produced a number of distortions in its operations.[12] Thus the leadership that immediately followed Nehru and Shastri (the latter did not have enough time to tide over the transition after Nehru), namely, the agglomerate of state leaders who operated without the presence of a dominant national figure, lost touch with the people, made the party more important than the government (under Nehru there was a fine balance between the two) and simultaneously subjected national politics to the pressure of state politics to such an extent that the power and the position of Prime Minister and the central government began to be undermined.[13]

The Congress served as a federation of interest groups, allowing it to accommodate the legitimate socio-cultural and regional aspirations of the people within its organizations and in the national policy framework which checked the growth of regional parties.[14] In the post-Nehru era, the Congress party started getting deinstitutionalized due to a number of factors. The support base of the Congress party considerably declined in the 1980s.

Steady decline in intra-party democracy tended to lack of responsiveness of political parties. "The contributions of political parties and party system to the public policy and law making primarily depend on the intra-party democracy. The intra-party democracy enables political parties to debate the issue of public policy and law extensively which ultimately contribute to refine the dimensions of public policies and various provisions of law."[15] The interaction among political parties presupposes to contribute to interest articulation and interest aggregation. In this regard organization wing of political party plays a vital role. For, it provides linkage between people and government and works out broad policy guidelines in accordance with the aspirations of the people. They provide the base for formulating public policies and their implementation by governmental wing of the party. "The governmental wing has the responsibility of formulating policies and implementing them based on guidelines of the organizational wing. The guidelines provided by the organizational wing are to be based on the electoral promises made in the election manifesto."[16]

However, it is unfortunate that most of the political parties in India have no strong organizational wing. Party high command or leader controls everything within the party. "It is generally agreed that powerful leaders are partly responsible for the deinstitutionalization of the Indian party system. Differences with party leader are regarded as anti-party activity and there is no scope for dissent, which is an integral part of the democratic process. Therefore, powerful leaders in India have often proved to be enemies of institutions such as political parties."[17] These developments were responsible for the decline of party organization at the local level, which kept the party close to the people. With the decline of party organization the medium through which the wishes and opinion are transformed into the party was lost. This in turn made the political parties less responsive to the aspiration of the people. Indifferent performance led to voter dissatisfaction and large scale erosion of electoral support.[18] This type of functioning of parties may not lead to democratic governance.

The viable means of making political parties responsive to the peoples' hopes and aspirations and responsive for the objective of providing good governance consists in regrounding them in the associational matrix of active community life.[19] Democratic governance is possible when friendly relationship between people and political parties prevail. In India, personality of leaders gets more prominence than their parties. Party leaders have become so important that political parties are trying to capture votes not on the basis of performance but on their leader's personality. India during the Congress rule is dominated by leaders like Nehru, Indira Gandhi, Rajiv Gandhi and Sonia Gandhi. In the absence of Nehru and Gandhi family members the Congress party faced many problems until Sonia Gandhi entered politics. "In the thirteenth general election (1999) to the Lok Sabha and some of the State Assemblies, for example, there were hardly any issues of policy or even programmes before the electorate. All the campaigning and the contests were personality and power oriented. Parties were only vaguely talking about development, national pride, security, secularism, etc."[20] But, thanks to the 'feel good' factor and 'India shining campaign' by the BJP, in the 2004 general elections more prominence was given to performance by political parties. Whether BJP succeeded in making people feel good or not, or whether India is shining or not that is a different matter. The positive side of this is that, it made possible a large number of debates on performance of political parties.

A certain degree of resilience and dynamism has entered the political process and determining variable of any party's fortune in the electoral battle revolves around its performance and sensitivity to the art of governance.[21] While assessing the performance of parliamentary democracy it needs to be emphasized that its functional validity is dependent to a great extent on the maturity of political parties and the responsible behaviour of political leaders.[22] It is argued that the conditions of political parties' responsiveness are satisfied when political parties give enough attention to the needs, problems and preferences of citizens. But, there is a gradual decline in the capacity of political parties to respond rationally, creatively or even adequately to pressures from society. Political parties have become more concerned about attaining power than to respond to the aspirations of the people. The issue of whether or not the aspirations of the people are satisfied has always been secondary to the leaders. "Leaders have mobilized socio-economic groups more as power resources in inter-elite struggle and less to satisfy group aspirations. Thus, Indira Gandhi discovered India's poor when she was pressed politically by other members of the Congress elite."[23] Thus most often populism was used by the political parties to mobilize the support of electorates.

Responsiveness of political parties can be ensured by making politicians responsible for their actions and overall government policies and avoiding to acquire power by narrow interest. Since the mid 1980s big scandals like Bofors and the bank and the security scam, touching incumbent Prime Ministers (though not proving charges against them) and involving other ministers have reduced public confidence in political leaders.[24] One can hardly cite an example that a politician is punished for the offence in recent times. The unending series of scams for which not one person has been actually convicted so far, the hawala scandal which effectively removed the thin mask of respectability from the face of any politicians, the fodder scam which proved that the so-called poor and backward classes could also take to looting of public funds with gusto, and, to top them all, the exposure of the criminalization of politics and the nexus between highly placed politicians and ruthless criminals, have all added to the disillusionment of the common man with the general run of politics and politicians in the country.[25] These facts make the people lose confidence in political parties being responsive.

It is only at the time of elections that every party attempts through spending a lot of money on posters and advertisements to attract the voters. Catchy slogans and promises confuse the electorates.[26] A number of promises are made by the political parties to win election and there is a little performance in the government in accordance with the promises.[27] When asked whether they believe that political parties are keen in keeping their promises 67.52 per cent of people responded negatively, while only 32.48 per cent of people believed that they kept their promises. The table given below confirms this fact.

Table 6.1*: Do you agree that political parties are keen in keeping their promises?

S. No.	Category	No. of Respondents	Percentage
1.	Yes	102	32.48
2.	No	212	67.52
	Total	**314**	**100.00**

* This table is drawn from the result of sample survey conducted by G. Palanithurai.

Source: G. Palanithurai, *Peoples' Participation in Politics: An Indian Perspective*, Kanishka Publishers, Delhi, 1995, p. 69.

In order to get more votes the candidates formulate attractive programmes. Most of the time to make the programmes and promises attractive to the voters, in a competitive situation, the feasibility of the programme and the practicability of promises are ignored by the campaigners, reducing quite often, their status to false promises.[28] After coming to power by fair or foul means they are mainly concerned with feathering their own nest. They behave as if they are not at all accountable to the people. If at all accountability exists, it is to the party high command and not to the people.

While assessing the performance of political parties it can be said that its functional validity is mainly dependent to a great extent on the maturity and the responsible behaviour of political leaders. The primary goal of elite-led mobilization in India has been power for elite. The issue of whether or not the aspirations of the mobilized groups can be satisfied has always been secondary in the minds of the mobilizers.[29] India's democracy has been democracy from above: for most of its existence, it has been more of a gift from the elite to the masses than something the masses have secured for themselves.[30] In India since independence governance has been mainly in the hands of elites. This elite class mostly consists of rich class and upper castes. As a result of this, most of the policy decisions of the government are mainly in favour of these higher class and caste groups. And the interest of the minority groups are neglected. Party tickets are given only to those who can contribute to the party fund.

The process of formulating public policy can further be made ineffective by party politics. Evolving consensus on public policies is essential. But the nature of party politics weakens the process of evolving consensus. Emergence of coalition politics further aggravated this problem. Changing nature of party politics has direct bearing on the implementation of economic and social policy in India. With the emergence of unstable coalition governments, policy issues are marginalized by most of the parties and their immediate concern is to acquire and maintain power. Several parties came together and formed government. With hung parliaments such alliances have become inevitable. "This alliance brought together under one broad umbrella numerous disparate, ideologically and pragmatically incompatible-frequently unmixable-political parties signifying a marriage of convenience. But no sooner was it formed, it developed cracks under the pressure of contrary demands and expectations of coalition partners and the coalition government fell leaving behind a bitter trail of animosity, bickering and frustration."[31] According to Rajni Kothari, "the country had entered a phase of transition which was full of confusion and instability, out of which had emerged a framework of power but not an alternative framework of governance."[32]

With such coalition governments coming to power, public policy making process becomes ineffective. Every party within and outside the coalitions is after power. Slight difference of opinion among the coalition partners will lead to the downfall of government. And to remain in power the party or group of parties has to satisfy the demands of all its partner and have to act according to their expectation. Bringing consensus among the coalition partners has become a difficult task. The political parties are so preoccupied with the struggle for survival in power that they have no time to pay attention to the problems of the people. If coalition partners have agreed on some policy the opposition may disagree on the same. As no single party enjoys majority support in the Lok Sabha, policy making becomes a difficult task. We can quote here the examples of Lokpal and Lokayukta Bill and Women's Reservation Bill. Since 1968, the Lokpal Bill was introduced in the Lok Sabha several times (in 1968, 1971, 1977, 1985, 1989, 1996) but it lapsed as the governments dissolved before it was sanctioned. The Lokpal and Lokayukta Bill was introduced for the first time in 1968 and was passed by the Lok Sabha and sent to the Rajya Sabha. Since, the house was dissolved, the Bill could not be passed. The same bill was introduced in 1971 but remained pending until the house was dissolved. It was again introduced in 1977, 1985 1989, 1996 and 1998 but again met with the same fate. Very recently in the month of February, 2004 Karnataka had the privilege to have Lokayukta. It was mentioned in the *Sunday Vjay Times*: "The State of Karnataka holds the privilege of having been the first to enact a state legislation enforcing the institution of Lokayukta."

With regard to Women's Reservation Bill, it was argued that, "if 50 per cent of the citizens are women and if we have only 10 or 12 per cent of women members sitting in the Parliament or less than 10 or 12 per cent sitting in the State Legislature, this is not conducive for the democracy. This is why we shall have to invent some device which will really help a reasonable number, if not 50 per cent to enter Parliament."[33] Tables 6.2 and 6.3 highlights the strength of women members in the Lok Sabha.

Table 6.2: Women Contestants in Lok Sabha Elections 1952–1999

Years	*Seats*	*Lok Sabha Women MPs*	*% of Women MPs*
1952	499	22	4.41
1957	500	27	5.40
1962	503	34	6.76
1967	523	31	5.93
1971	521	22	4.22
1977	544	19	3.49
1980	544	28	5.15
1984	544	44	8.09
1989	517	27	5.22
1991	544	39	7.17
1996	543	39	7.18
1998	543	43	7.92
1999	543	49	9.02
Average	**528**	**33**	**6.15**

Source: Jayaprakash Narayan, Representational Legitimacy and Electoral Reforms, *Seminar*, 539, July 2004, p. 50.

Table 6.2 reveals that the percentage of women members in Lok Sabha remains under 10 per cent. In 1962 the percentage of women members in the Lok Sabha was 4.41 while it is 8.09 in 1984 and 9.02 in 1999. In recent parliamentary elections the number of

Table 6.3: Percentage of Women Members in Lok Sabha

Lok Sabha	*Women Contestants*	*Elected Women MPs*	*% of Representation*
13th Lok Sabha	247	49	9.02
14th Lok Sabha	177	44	8.10

Source: Jayaprakash Narayan, Representational Legitimacy and Electoral Reforms, *Seminar*, 539, July 2004, p. 51.

women MPs elected to the Lok Sabha came down from 49 to 44 which is 9.02 per cent in the 13th Lok Sabha to 8.10 per cent in 14th Lok Sabha. Looking at the percentage of women members in the Lok Sabha we can say that our Parliament is male dominated. While women candidates are being elected more often than their male counterparts, the actual proportion of women candidates nominated by parties and elected remains under 10 per cent.[34] What has contributed to the gradual decline in the number of women representatives is not yet clear. Growing criminalization of politics can be one of the major reasons for the decline in the women representatives. Due to growing muscle and mafia power in election the parties are reluctant to give tickets to the women members. For winning election one does need lots of money; that also can be one of the reasons for declining number of women representatives.

In 1996, the Women Reservation Bill was first introduced by the then Deve Gowda ministry. Due to the internal problems of the UF government the Bill could not be passed. Once again UF government in 1997 under the leadership of I.K. Gujral introduced it. This time the Janata Dal, the Indian Union Muslim League, the Samata Party and some from the Samajwadi Party prevented the Prime Minister from moving the Bill for discussion. They insisted on a quota for Other Backward Castes within Women's quota and also insisted on quota for Muslims. In 1998 elections, "almost all the political parties in their respective election manifestos blared loudly on women upliftment by promising to give one-third reservation to them but actual position was horrifying which speaks of hypocrisy that has struck firm roots in Indian politics over the past 50 years."[35] Out of 4756 candidates in the election, only 267 were women. "Out of 267 women contestants, there were 115 party nominees with Congress heading the list with 39 followed by 30 of BJP. The number of women nominees of other parties were JD 11, MCP and SP 8 each, CPI 6, TDP, RJP, SP (Samata Party) 3 each and SAD, AIADMK, HLD(R), TC one each."[36] In 1998 once again the issue of women's reservation was raised. Opposition members and some of BJP's allies like MDMK's Vaiko and AIADMK's S.R. Muthaia opposed the Bill.[37] Though BJP was able to get the support of the Congress, it failed to pass the Bill. "Bringing legislation for granting 33 per cent reservation for women in Parliament and State Legislatures is burning question with the Union Government and all the political parties. Practically, nothing is being done. Surprisingly none of the political parties have cared to grant this reservation to women in their parties."[38]

Though 13 urgent Bills were pending before the Lok Sabha during the winter session in 1998, the House could not pass a single one of them.[39] All these clearly indicate how party politics hampers the public policy making which ultimately adversely affects governance in India.

Policy preferences are not the only things a political party brings to parliament. It also brings a weight, the proportion of seats in parliament it controls.[40] To pass any policy it requires the sanction of majority members. If a single party gets required majority in the Parliament, it becomes easier for the party to get policies passed. With the emergence of small regional parties at the centre political parties have lost their weight in the Parliament. Regional parties are the common features of a federal system and their main purpose is to stand for social and economic justice for the particular region. However, when these regional parties started contesting national elections they send a handful of representatives to parliament. As the seats in the parliament are divided among the national and regional parties no party is in a position to form the majority. Even the party with the largest number of seats does not have required strength in the parliament and depends on its allies not only for strength but, for its continuance in the parliament. Any disagreement with its ally may lead to loss of power. Inclusion of regional parties in the national government brought greater conflicts in governance. The fact of inclusion of regional parties in national government for attaining majority improved their bargaining power. If coalition governments succeed in holding on to power for considerable time this does not ensure that parties evolve appropriate policies and take effective steps for dealing with emergent difficult socio-economic and political problems. The reason is that owing to the difficult ideological and pragmatic commitments and continuous pressures, it becomes difficult to forge a consensus on what should be the most effective way of handling an emergent situation.[41] When there are too many partners, the personal ambitions, intrigues and bargains abound; even combinations are secretly and suddenly formed, successive ministers are overturned, with injury to the progress of legislation and to the continuity at national policy.[42]

Both intra and inter-party politics will affect the public policy making process. Opposition parties are always in search of an opportunity to bring down the government. The role of opposition is crucial in making the government responsive to meet the aspirations of people. "The opposition is an agent of citizens because it wants to win office and, in order to win office, it must also anticipate the retrospective judgements that the voters will make about the incumbents at election time. Anticipating these judgements, the opposition has incentives to monitor the government and to inform (truthfully or not) voters about the performance of the incumbents."[43] It was generally found that opposition parties oppose the actions of the ruling parties. As a result they cannot contribute to public policy making in terms of policy alternatives.

In the parliamentary democracy the usual practice is discussion, argument, persuasion and ultimate decision and acceptance of that decision. Thus it means tolerance and signifies the willingness to recognize the existence of different points of view and to allow the strongest view to prevail.[44] However, it is sad to record that the tolerance, logical argument and creative thought is disappearing or sinking fast in our deliberative chambers.[45] The lack of interest, poor attendance, floor crossing, obstructive methods, waste of time, ignorance of technicalities and procedures, are commonly found in the working of parliament. Decline of legislature is a serious threat to democracy. S.K. Jain observes that, "the malaise of non-functioning of legislatures as exemplified by Parliament and the state legislatures are indeed a matter of grave concern for it affects the very foundations of democracy and the credibility of democratic institutions as the custodian and guardian of the trust of the people."[46] The behaviour of legislators makes the Speaker switch off TV reporting. Too common now-a-days are stalling of the proceedings, motion of pandemonium, shouting over a fellow M.P. when the Speaker is asked to speak, rushing into the well of the House, sitting in a '*dharna*'—some members even snatch away papers from the hands of the speaker—all these practically making the Speaker to adjourn so frequently.[47]

One of the important responsibilities of leaders is to reflect public opinion in the deliberations of Parliament. They are supposed to debate matters of vital public importance. It is deplorable to note that serious debate usually does not take place in the legislature. Thus, resulting in waste of time. "Over 10.5 per cent of the time of the Tenth Lok Sabha was wasted in such hold-ups of business. Full eight days time of both houses of Parliament was mostly wasted, except for the presentation of the Railway and General Budgets, in the Budget session of 2000 on the issue of the Gujarat Government permitting its employees to become members of the *Rashtriya Swayamsevak Sangh.* From 1992 onwards, the Lok Sabha has been adjourned for 111 hours on Ayodhya controversy (excluding the number of hours lost in December 2001), while only about 40 hours have been utilized for discussion on the issue. In 2001, the working of Parliament has been similarly disrupted for days together."[48] The same story was repeated in the budget and monsoon session of 2002. A Code of Conduct was adopted on 25 November 2001 on discipline and decorum in Parliament and state legislatures but it has not made any difference to the functioning of these bodies even thereafter.[49] Little effort has been made to improve qualities of discipline, character, high sense of public morality and willingness to hear and accommodate minority views, which are the essential prerequisites for the success of parliamentary democracy.

One should not neglect the money spent on such proceedings. Time management is the biggest problem faced by the Parliament. For the conduct of parliamentary proceedings elaborate rules and procedures are laid down, but, politicians rarely observe these rules. Unless all parties agree to obey the rules of the Parliament no change can be expected. Some solution to this crucial problem has to be identified otherwise the responsiveness of political parties is likely to become totally ineffective. "The budgetary allocation for Parliament has gone up steeply from Rs. 12.49 crore in 1983-84 to Rs. 173.09 crore in 2000-01. It is estimated that each minute that Parliament fails to conduct business costs the exchequer Rs. 17,000; a full day Rs. 55 lakh."[50]

The essential prerequisites for quality governance are that the system should be good and suited to the needs, aspirations, background and ethos of the people concerned and that those selected for operating the system should be endowed with character and competence and motivated by the spirit of service.[51] In recent times the acts of omissions and commissions by the legislatures are hurting the interest of the people. The government that has to run through discussion and debate in democracy is subjected to the influence of powerful drive to maintain power at the centre.

A large number of criminals and mafia powers have entered the Parliament. The criminals have started entering the Parliament in recent times. The scenes inside Assemblies are hardly conducive for an efficient working of parliamentary democracy.[52] Criminalization of politics adversely affects the responsiveness of the political parties. Sometimes criminals are selected as party candidates. They also get elected as they have money power. Hence, they do not give much importance to their accountability to the people. Accountability is a prerequisite for ensuring responsiveness. Unless political parties are accountable to the people they cannot be responsive. Lack of accountability affects political parties responsiveness. In 1996, Lok Sabha elections (the situation was no better in 1998 and 1999), in UP there was as many as 35 "history sheeters" against whom dozens of cases of murder, arson, loot and rape were pending in courts. BJP had 9 such history sheeter candidates, the Congress (Tiwari) had 3, Bahujan Samaj Party had 6, Samajwadi Party had 10. One candidate was a convicted person. He was sentenced to life imprisonment in a murder case by the Supreme Court, but was given the Presidential Pardon under political pressure."[53] When such persons enter Parliament it will affect the quality of debate. In 1997, the then Speaker of the Lok Sabha, Mr. P.A. Sagma got a resolution passed in the House in which genuine concern was expressed about the criminalization of politics.[54] It was hoped that political parties would take some steps to reduce the criminal elements in the elections and parliament but, unfortunately not much was achieved in this direction. Criminalization of politics is growing in India. "Earlier, the criminal sought the protection of the politician, now it is the politician who needs the protection of the *dadas* or the two have become one and the same person. Governments have lost their credibility, legitimacy and even their representative credentials."[55]

Some people do believe and protagonists of democracy make it a strategy to make people believe that all powers of formation of government are in the hands of voters. But the above example and reality are that they are made to behave as puppets in the hands of such manipulators.[56] The biggest damage to good governance today has been caused by the leaders, who have lost credibility by their moral misdemeanour, particularly theft of public property by corrupt practice.[57]

Defections have further put a question on the responsiveness of the political parties. If the voters succeeded in voting without any fear and favour to the person of their choice after analyzing their proposed policies there is no guarantee that the chosen representative will work for the fulfiiment of the same policies. There is always a danger of defection and the candidate may change his party and he may also change his policy position. Presently it is seen that one who is elected on the ticket of say party 'A' is able to change over to party 'B' on promises like a ministerial berth or other temptations.[58] Laws have been passed to arrest defections. The enactment of the anti-defection law or the Tenth Schedule of the Constitution greatly conditioned and changed the behaviour of the legislators and the functioning of the opposition but failed to control the evil of unprincipled defections.[59] Anti-defection law is not so effective in preventing defections. According to this law, if 1/3rd members of the party agree to quit the party, it is not considered as defections but a split in the party. For small parties it is not a difficult task to get the support of 1/3rd members of the party. Sometimes taking advantage of the defects in the provision of the Act the art of pulling down the governments by encouraging defections has been practiced. With such practices the representative character of legislatures loses its significance.

It was considered that the democratic way of governance was best suited for contemporary times. Indian democracy is lacking in the basic requirement of real representation of the people. Most of the parties which get elected do not have majority support. Obviously by majority we mean fifty plus one. Even the ruling parties failed to get the support of the majority. With such parties forming the government how can we expect democratic governance? Always governance to be responsive should be in the interest of the majority of people. With parties not having majority support in terms of percentage of votes secured how could we expect that they are able to represent the interest of all sections in the society. "The largest party often needs only 30-40 per cent of the votes polled to obtain a majority of seats in the legislature under our present system. Considering that only about 60 per cent of the votes are polled, the actual voter support to obtain a majority of seats could be as low as 20 per cent."[60] Thus the will of 70 per cent of the electorate remains unrepresented. That is the main reason for all-round dissatisfaction about Government performance prevailing amongst the people as a whole.[61]

The winning candidate becomes still less representative of the area if account is taken of those citizens who did not or could not vote due to the inaccuracy of the electoral rolls or due to their own indifferences.[62] False voting is rampant and one is likely to see that his vote has already been cast and many a time the genuine voter is taken to the prison for insisting that he has right to vote.[63] Voters list are incomplete and most of the voters do not find their names in the voters list. In recent elections most of the important and well known persons do not find their names in the voters list. Many such persons have protested for demanding proper voters list.

Since democracy is about expressing views and willingness of the majority to accommodate minority requirements, the fact that the problems and views of smaller groups are vocalized and brought on record, seems a good reason that every identifiable segment of society should find representation in the Parliament.[64] Indian society is stratified into a number of castes, classes, creeds, religions, education, etc. It also consists of a large segments of tribal population and many backward regions in the country. In this background, the electoral mechanism has to be so designed that it takes care of the needs and aspirations of all the segments of the society.[65]

It is a general belief that the policies and decisions are the outcome of the articulation of legislators. In reality it is not so.[66] Most of the time the representative is not aware of some of the pressing problems of his/her constituency. The tables given below highlight on this fact.

Common welfare which should be one of the important duties of political parties is being replaced by personal welfare. When the respondents were asked: "Can you state a single problem repeatedly

Table 6.4*: Do you agree that legislators know more about the problems and priorities than the people?

S. No.	*Category*	*No. of Respondents*	*Percentage*
1.	Yes	105	33.44
2.	No	209	66.56
	Total	**314**	**100.00**

* This table is the result of sample survey conducted by G. Palanithurai.
Source: G. Palanithurai, *People's Perception of Politics: An Indian Perspective,* Kanishka Publishers, Delhi, 1995, p. 80.

Table 6.5*: Is the Legislator aware of your constituency's problems?

S. No.	*Category*	*No. of Respondents*	*Percentage*
1.	Yes	75	23.89
2.	No	239	76.11
	Total	314	100.00

* This table is the result of sample survey conducted by G. Palanithurai.
Source: G. Palanithurai, *People's Perception of Politics: An Indian Perspective,* Kanishka Publishers, Delhi, 1995, p. 80.

highlighted by your representative? And can you state a single step taken by your representative for your common welfare? Answers are not affirmative. They openly answered that representatives never had the habit of registering their mark by doing services to the public.[67] The table given below reveals the response of the people towards the performance of their representative.

Table 6.6*: Is their (Legislator) success decided by their performance?

S. No.	*Category*	*No. of Respondents*	*Percentage*
1.	Yes	77	24.52
2.	No	237	75.48
	Total	**314**	**100.00**

* This table is the result of sample survey conducted by G. Palanithurai.
Source: G. Palanithurai, *People's Perception of Politics: An Indian Perspective,* Kanishka Publishers, Delhi, 1995, p. 81.

It is evident from Table 6.61 that the respondents have a very poor opinion about the functioning of their representatives in the political process. What we need first of all is to get the basic needs of our people fulfiled. How can we talk about good governance if we cannot fulfil the basic needs of life, like drinking water, adequate nutrition, adequate energy, clothing, housing, health and education facilities. What is actually happening is not only wants are shaped by the government but they are satisfied by their very expression. Thus as one writer puts it, "responsiveness to the will of the people means rather less than meets the eye". When asked about whether they feel that the politicians are responsible, for the socio-economic crisis? "...63.06 per cent of the respondents have confusion in locating the segment which is responsible for the ills in the society. But, 36.94 per cent of them categorically said that the politicians are responsible."[68] The verdict of 2004 election is very crucial in this regard. It makes it clear that no amount of reform can be tolerated unless it addresses basic issues such as employment, reduction of poverty and provision of basic services.[69] The verdict also supports the contention that, irrespective of the performance of the economy, the crucial concerns today are the above mentioned basic issues rather than the much hyped "would be India" factor.[70]

Some parties have strong support base in a few large states, in that case how they can represent the entire country? It is enough if it captures a few large states, and certain small states remain unrepresented in terms of power configuration.[71] Table 6.7 highlights this fact.

The political parties try to attract the voters of large states which have more seats and most of the policies were directed in their interest. This may lead to the neglect of the aspiration of smaller states. Politics is a number game. Political parties try to get majority seats enough to form comfortable government. In India a party which secured 272 seats can form the government, political parties, calculations are mainly directed towards securing 272 seats and not towards 300 or 350 seats. In the wake of coalition government, attaining 272 mark itself has become difficult. National parties have to ally themselves with regional parties to win 272 seats. In this number game sufferers were the small states with only 1 or 2 seats. In order to draw the attention of the government about the interests of small states their representatives should have to work hard.

Table 6.7: All India Seats— 543

The North *126 Seats*		*The South* *132 Seats*		*The East* *142 Seats*		*The West* *142 Seats*	
Haryana	10	Andhra Pradesh	42	Arunachal Pradesh	2	Daman Diu	1
Himachal Pradesh	4	Karnataka	28	Assam	14	Goa	2
Jammu & Kashmir	6	Kerala	20	Bihar	37*	Gujarat	26
Punjab	13	Tamil Nadu	39	Manipur	2	Madhya Pradesh	29
Uttar Pradesh	80*	A.N. Islands	1	Meghalaya	2	Maharashtra	48
Chandigarh	1	Lakshadweep	1	Mizoram	1	Rajasthan	25
Delhi	7	Pondichery	1	Nagaland	1	Dadar & Nagar Haveli	1
Uttarakhand	5*			Orissa	21	Chhattisgarh*	11
				Sikkim	1		
				Tripura	2		
				West Bengal	42		
				Jharkhand	17*		

* After the creation of Uttarakhand, Jharkhand and Chhattisgarh the seats were divided between Uttar Pradesh (80) and Uttarakhand (5), Bihar (37) and Jharkhand (17) and Madhya Pradesh (29) and Chhattisghar (11).

Source: Meenu Roy, *Elections 1998: A Continuity in Coalition*, Deep and Deep Publication, New Delhi, 1999, p.70.

India needs to define a national vision including the right of the populace relating in the first place to the human development index delineating the minimum basic needs of the people and at the second level it needs to inject public accountability into the political and administrative spheres leading to a largely transparent and honest administration.[72] With respect to policy reform, accountability refers to the design of development—enhancing reform programmes, making these congruent with their implementation and enforcement and eventually ensuring an efficient use, stewardship and allocation of resources. This requires, on the one hand, competent policy making, that is adequate government capacities and capabilities to take and implement decisions at the right time and to manage public service delivery, and on the other hand the establishment of agencies of restraint (such as anti-corruption offices and ombudsmen) and monitoring devices both for overall economic policies as well as public procurement and investment.[73]

Thus, it is not unreasonable to conclude that the organizational vacuum in Indian politics is the root cause of the growing gap in that country between how power is won and how power is used, or between personalization of power, on the one hand, and the inability to use that power to solve pressing problems, on the other.[74] Today, most parties are identified in terms of style of functioning, marked with manipulation, personal ambition, corruption, populism etc. A former CPI (M). M.P., A.K. Roy, pointed out that "The differences between the parties have decreased and those between the parties and the people have increased."[75] As explained by Hugh Gaitskell, "The differences between the parties must not be so great that one party prefer to destroy democracy rather than allow the other party to come to power. Nor must they be so slight as to make nonsense of the idea of free choice for the electorate."[76] Political parties are not expected to be always busy with power struggle. They should provide proper channel between the people and the government. Unless they provide this channel they cannot come close to the people. For ensuring this, effective control of the people over the political parties is essential. Thus the basic question is how to establish peoples' control over the government in true sense.

Popular Responsiveness

Popular responsiveness is crucial for democratic governance. People in democratic government not only enjoy rights but they also have certain duties. In the unforgettable words of Felix Frankfuter, "democracy involves hardship—the hardship of the unceasing responsibility of every citizen. Where the entire people do not take a continuous and considered part in public life there can be no democracy in any meaningful sense of the term."[77] Some democratic thinkers, particularly in United States, are inclined to believe that the destiny of any given society depends on the "will of the people" or, to put it in current American idiom, on "group thinking" or "group dynamics".[78]

Responsiveness of people plays a significant role in democracy. In modern democracy people are not directly taking part in the public policy making. They "participate in government by electing officials to make government decisions for them."[79] The representatives of the people are the agents of the people, who are expected to represent voters' interests. "...it does not suffice for the government as a whole to be accountable to the electorate; but rather the voter should be able to identify the responsible authorities and hold them accountable as a group for their deeds and misdeeds."[80] Each generation has to try hard to defend its interests and see to it that it is passed on to the next generation. For this citizens have to be alert, active, vigilant and well informed. For most of the citizens, democracy means voting in elections. They think "politics in terms of "we" who are governed and "they" who govern."[81] But who has given them the right to govern? It is the people who are the makers of the government. If they wish they can call back the government. Most of the time people are reluctant to accept their responsibilities as citizens. One of the greatest problems of democratic governance is to ensure continuous participation of the people in the political process. Democracy as a method of government is not whatever the people at a given moment may happen to decide, but a set of arrangements for securing their control over the public decision-making process on an ongoing basis.[82] Participation of the people therefore, "will increase the extent to which a nation is democratic only in so far as such participation involves at some point influence by the participant over governmental decisions."[83]

The responsiveness of people towards governmental decision is crucial for effective functioning of democracy. As democratic government presupposes peoples rule, the involvement of people cannot be confined to the elections. Government should be people oriented. In India, "the people who are the true sovereign are mostly forgotten after they have exercised their franchise and regain importance only in next election year. Thereafter once a new government is elected for the next five years is characterized by little regard for the need of the people, particularly the poor."[84] In such a situation it is the responsibility of the citizens to make the representatives responsive towards the needs of people. In this regard Key was motivated by an ethical or at least a practical concern: if politicians "see voters as most certainly responsive to nonsense, they will give them nonsense. If they see voters susceptible to delusion, they will delude them."[85] "Democracy is thus characterized by the fact that power over significant authoritative decisions in a society is distributed among the population. The ordinary man is expected to take an active part in governmental affairs, to be aware of how decisions are made, and to make his own views known."[86] In democracy the role of a citizen as respondent is significant. Responsiveness of citizens towards governmental decisions makes policies more responsive to the needs of the beneficiaries.

For the individuals or for particular groups of citizens the most important political activities may be those in-between election period, when citizens try to influence government decisions in relation to specific problems that concern them.[87] The emergence of coalitions tended to the rise of serious impediments in the process of public policy making. Most of the time political parties are interested in their privileges and means of acquiring power. In the context of such state of affairs, participation of people plays a crucial role in public policy making. While public policy formulation and their implementation constitute a major factor determining the effectiveness of good governance, to influence the policies, people need some strongly organized channels between the people and government. This enables the people to influence the proceedings of the parliament or outcome of the policy in question. In this regard collective efforts of the people to influence government carries more weight. People need some outside support for organizing themselves so that they could also become active participants in good governance.[88] The NGOs, self-help groups, pressure groups and other voluntary organizations are the important means available to the people through which they can influence public policy decisions. Social mobilization, enabling and empowering the people to receive fully and fruitfully what is intended for them, is the central issue in good governance.[89] The NGOs have a crucial role to play in this task. In the governance process the responsibility for development and welfare is shared by government and civil society.

In independent India, dependence of people on government considerably increased. NGOs, self help groups, etc. contribute to reduce the dependence of people on government. Through them people attempts to influence public policy decisions. The people's responsiveness towards public policies is considered as oxygen to democracy.

There should be some mechanism for formal or informal interaction between people and government. "By definition, the "average" man's influence over the government must be small. Compared with the forces of the government and the state, he is a frail creature indeed, and this would apply to local as well as national government. If the ordinary man is to have any influence vis-à-vis the government, it must be in concert with his fellows."[90]

Civil society is one such group or association which has gained a significant role in government in recent years. "Civil society in the present context is being increasingly relied upon by people for a responsive and performing democratic governance, but it always functions within the state and has a certain degree of autonomy."[91] Where a citizen or group of citizens is too weak and needs protection, it is the duty of civil society to defend its interests through positive social, political, economic and legal action.[92] Common welfare is the main aim of civil society. In recent years the use of informal groups as a means of influencing the government has become an important means of protesting against the government. By and large people are slowly getting political awareness. Popular awareness enables people to exert pressure on government to promote their interest. Since people are politically mobilized, for their socio-economic problems, they began to exert pressure on the government through various organizations to demand more in the resource allocation of the government.[93] Civil society enables the people to raise their voice to pressurize the government.

People cannot be responsive unless they are educated. Unfortunately, most of the citizens of India are illiterate, ill-informed, poor and destitute, and living in areas bereft of all facilities of communication and interaction.[94] It is the primary responsibility of the political parties to educate the voters about the policies, which they pursue after getting elected. They also have to inform the people about the policies and programmes discussed and implemented in the Parliament. However, political parties do not pay adequate attention for educating the people. Perhaps people have realized their importance in governance. "They may analyze the manifestos issued by different political parties and help the citizens to make a choice between them. They may also on behalf of the citizens monitor the elections, identify malpractices if any and take steps to see that they are eliminated and those indulging in such malpractices are punished under the law."[95] "This education would be effective to the extent it is imparted in the voters' idiom, in the language they easily understand. One of the most important reasons for the fast deteriorating standards of our parliamentary system borrowed from the West is that the masses do not understand the values, rules, operations and purposes that underlie the system precisely because they are not explained to them in the language they understand and linked with the values they cherish."[96]

"If the electorate tries to select good types, then bad types may moderate their policy choices in the direction of what the electorate wants, as in the classical theory of electoral accountability. But, then in-so-far as bad types become harder to distinguish from good types, selection is rendered problematic."[97] People have to be educated in terms of getting information about the functioning of the government. From this perspective peoples' involvement in the process of governance plays an important role. By involving people in politics, they can respond better.

People play a significant role in making the government accountable and transparent. Transparency basically arises out of the citizens' right to information-the right to know what decisions public institutions take and for what valid reasons.[98] "The greater the transparency, the greater the accountability, the greater the accountability, the greater the responsiveness of government. The need for transparency to ensure more accountable governance is therefore obvious."[99] Political parties are accountable to the people not only at the time of election, but they are also answerable to the people for the day to day activities of the government. People can make their representatives accountable only when they are well informed. Peoples right to information also increases transparency. Thus, information can be the main source of peoples' power. Through this power they can ensure the political parties responsiveness. The concern of the representatives for people is primarily by votes. How much well informed and enlightened they are determines how responsibly they vote.[100]

In turn, citizens do not have sufficient information to evaluate the incumbent governments. The threat of not being re-elected is insufficient to induce governments to act in the best interest of the public.[101] There is also a necessity to inform the people about the criminal record of the candidates. The criminal elements in the Parliament may affect the quality of debate in Parliament. If the people are informed about the criminal records of the candidates, it is hoped that they can elect a responsible and efficient person as their representative. As regards criminalization of politics the Delhi High Court in Association of Democratic Reform *vs.* Union of India, gave the verdict: if voters are made aware of the criminal propensities and activities of a candidate, it will help in eliminating criminalization of politics. Further, the court has also directed that the Election Commission should provide the information to the voters regarding (i) a candidate having been accused of any offence punishable with imprisonment, (ii) assets possessed by a candidate, or his/her spouse and dependent persons, (iii) a candidates competence, capacity and suitability including educational qualifications and (iv) capacity and ability of the political party fielding the candidate.[101] In a major judgement to curb criminalization of politics the Supreme Court on May 2002 asked the candidates for Lok Sabha and State Legislative Assemblies to disclose their antecedents, assets and educational qualifications, if any, to help the voters to make the right choice. "The little man may think over before making his choice of electing law-breakers as law-makers," said the Bench.[102] Such judgements could boost the morale of the public spirited people who can make use of the opportunities given to them and can drive away criminals from the political life of this country. Such actions of the people may pressurize the candidates to live up to the expectations of the people.

For the first time in the fourteenth general elections the Election Commission implemented the Supreme Court's directions on affidavits to be submitted by candidates along with their nomination papers. "The affidavits will carry information on a candidates' criminal antecedents if any, property, liabilities and educational qualifications. The Election Commission, as per the directive of the Delhi High Court on March 1, will also seek affidavits from candidates regarding their dues to the government in respect of water and electricity consumption, telephone calls and hotel bills, and give them due publicity".[103]

It is not only the job of Election Commission and Supreme Court to ensure free and fair elections but people can also contribute in this regard. Citizens now have the fundamental right to know the antecedents of the candidates—an important input in the process of making an informed choice.[104] The Delhi Watch Groups, a coalition of civil society organizations, committed to the cause of transparency in the electoral system, did a commendable job in compiling and analyzing the affidavits filed by the candidates for the recent Delhi assembly elections.[105] There is need for organizing such groups in every state.

"Peoples United for Better Living in Calcutta, popularly known as PUBLIC, mobilized their members to keep watch on whether political parties observe the code of conduct required as per Election Commission norms during the 1998 election. The members of PUBLIC also took up the job of removing undesirable and abusive slogans and other political writings from the walls of private and public building."[106] Thus people have to come forward and take up their responsibilities, then only democratic governance is ensured. The Maha Gujarat and Navnirman Movement in Gujarat are the glaring examples of what differences the people make if they come forward to work.[107]

Making people aware of their duties and responsibilities is very vital in ensuring good governance. The glaring example for this is, "in the winter of 1989 the Citizens' for Democracy (CFD) and the Sampoorna Kranti Manch (SKM) supported by the Indian Radical Humanist Association (IRHA) and the People's Union for Civil Liberties (PUCL) presented to all the contesting political parties a Charter of Peoples' 14 Demands for acceptance with a promise to implement them within 18 months of their assuming power."[108] National Front was the only party which had accepted the demands and promised to implement them. But, unfortunately, it did not last long in office to fulfil its promise, primarily due to the kind of party politics.

To give a person a share of the responsibility for governing the society of which he is a part was, Mill argued, the most effective way of contributing to his moral and intellectual development; while on the contrary, to deny a man power over his government was sure of discouraging his interest in it and his concern for it.[109] Of course, there have to be politicians and civil servants who accept political and professional responsibility for the conduct of the affairs of the government. But, since they are supposed to be irresponsive to public opinion and pressure, the ultimate responsibility is that of the citizens.[110]

People should also realize that the way the political parties are collecting their funds, formulate their policies and their internal organization and interactions among them vitally affect the Parliamentary proceeding. Ultimately it affects the people. The people should be vigilant about the party activities and should not hesitate to criticize and oppose their move whenever the parties encroach upon peoples' rights and liberties. Downs correctly assumes that, "parties formulate policies in order to win elections, rather than win elections in order to formulate policies."[111] Thus people have to take the responsibility to make the parties formulate such policies which are in the interest of the people. Much of democratic control rests not only on voters' ability to make meaningful electoral choices predictive of policy performance, but also on the ability of voters to inflict retrospective electoral punishment for party failure.[112]

Party politics presupposes to refine the public policy making. This study indicates that the issues influencing the popular and political parties' responsiveness have adversely affected the party politics. As a result of this, governance becomes less effective in terms of serving the purpose of fulfilling the aspirations of people.

REFERENCES

1. C.P. Bharthwal, *Good Governance in India,* Deep and Deep Publications Private Limited, New Delhi, 2003, p. 8.
2. J. Roland Pennock, *Democratic Political Theory,* Princeton University Press, New Jersey, 1979, p. 261.
3. Adam Przeworski, Susan C. Stokes and Bernard Menin, *Democracy, Accountability and Representation,* Cambridge University Press, Cambridge, 1999, pp. 30-31.
4. V.A. Paipanandikar and Subhash C. Kashyap (ed.), *Political Reforms: Asserting Civic Sovereignty,* Konark Publishers Private Limited, New Delhi, 2001, pp. 6-7.
5. S.S. Patagundi in Subhash C. Kashyap (ed.), *National Resurgence Through Electoral Reforms,* Shipra Publications, Delhi, 2002, p. 155.
6. Rabin Mukharjee, *Democracy- a failure, Shefocracy-the solution, for human welfare,* Indian Research Press, New Delhi, 2001, p. 44.
7. Pradeep K. Chibber, *Democracy Without Associations, Transforming of the Party System and Social Cleavages in India,* Vistar Publications, New Delhi, 1999, p. 177.
8. C.P. Bharthwal, Supra no. 1, p. 8.
9. *Ibid.*, p. 88.

10. *The Hindu*, May 17, 2004.
11. *The Hindu*, May 17, 2004
12. Rajni Kothari, *Democratic Polity and Social Change in India*, Allied Publishers, New Delhi, 1976, p. 13.
13. *Ibid.*, p. 13.
14. Ajay Kumar Singh, Regionalization Process and the Changing Party System of India, *The Radical Humanist*, May 1998, p. 12.
15. S.S. Patagundi in, Subhash C. Kashyap (ed.), Supra no. 5, p. 154.
16. *Ibid.*, p. 154.
17. *Ibid.*, p. 158.
18. V.A. Paipanandikar and Subhash C. Kashyap (ed.), Supra no. 4, p. 281.
19. *Ibid.*, p. 288.
20. *Ibid.*, p. 26.
21. S.K. Chopra (ed.), *Towards Good Governance*, Konark Publishers Private Limited, Delhi, 1997, p. 39.
22. *Ibid.*, p. 40.
23. Atul Kohli, *Democracy and Discontent: India's Growing Crisis of Governability*, Cambridge University Press, Cambridge, 1991, pp. 390-391.
24. Babani Sen Gupta, *Problems of Governance*, Konark Publishers, Delhi, 1996, p. 185.
25. M.G. Chitkara and B.R. Sharma, *Indian Republic: Issues and Perspective*, APH Publishing Corporations, New Delhi, 1997, p. 37.
26. *Ibid.*, p. 37
27. G. Palanithurai, *Peoples' Participation in Politics: An Indian Perspective*, Kanishka Publishers, Delhi, 1995, p. 19.
28. Dilip Halder, Democratic Governance No Penacea, *Indian Journal of Public Administration*, 50(1), January–March 2004, p. 209.
29. Atul Kohli, Supra no. 23, p. 391.
30. *Ibid.*, p. 390.
31. V.A. Paipanandikar and Subhash C. Kashyap (ed.), Supra no. 4, p. 272.
32. S.K. Chopra (ed.), Supra no. 21, p. 22.
33. Shivrah Patil in Subhash C. Kashyap (ed.), Supra no. 5, p. 12.
34. Jayaprakash Narayan, Representational Legitimacy and Electoral Reforms, *Seminar*, 539, July 2004, p. 50.
35. Subhash C. Arora, Women Empowerment in India, *Indian Journal of Politics*, 36(3-4), July-December 2002, p. 128.
36. *Ibid.*, p. 128.
37. Editorial, *Indian Recorder*, 5(32), August 6–12, 1998, p. 3826.
38. Rajinder Sachar in Subhash C. Kashyap (ed.), Supra no. 5, p. 187.
39. Ajay K. Mehra and Gert W. Kueck (ed.), *The Indian Parliament: A Comparative Perspective*, Konarch Publishers, Delhi, 2003, p. 141.

40. Adam Prseworski, Susan C. Stokes and Bernard Menin, Supra no. 3, p. 284.
41. V. A. Paipanandikar and S.C. Kashyap (ed.), Supra no. 4, p. 283.
42. L.S. Lathore, *Major Trends in Indian Politics*, C.P. Bharthwal (ed.), *Indian Administration Since Independence*, Bharat Book Centre, Lucknow, 2003, p. 13.
43. H.A. Gani, Political Parties and Degeneration of Democratic and Moral Values, *The Radical Humanist*, 62(2), May 1998, pp. 27-28.
44. P.I. Devraj, Party System-The Bedrock of Indian Democracy, *The Radical Humanist*, 62(2), May 1998, p. 43.
45. L.S. Lathore, *Major Trends in Indian Politics*, C.P. Bharthwal (ed.), Supra no. 42, pp. 9-10.
46. Sisir K. Dhar, Demoralized Politics Feudalising Democracy in India, *Janata*, 56(26), September 9, 2001, p. 29.
47. Sisir K. Dhar, The Ailing Political Life of India, *Janata*, 53(23), September 13, 1998, p. 17.
48. Ajay K. Mehra and Gert W. Kueck (ed.), Supra no. 39, p. 139.
49. *Ibid*., p. 140.
50. *Ibid*., pp. 140-141.
51. S.K. Chopra (ed.), Supra no. 21, p. 48.
52. Shivraj Patil in Subhash C. Kashyap (ed.), Supra no. 5, p. 13.
53. K.D. Sharma in Subhash C. Kashyap (ed.), Supra no. 5, p. 209.
54. G.S. Rajhans in Subhash C. Kashyap (ed.), Supra no. 5, p. 228.
55. S.K. Chopra (ed.), Supra no. 21, p. 49.
56. Rabin Mukharji, Supra no. 6, pp. 45-46.
57. S.K. Chopra (ed.), Supra no. 21, p. 26.
58. U.C. Agarwal in, Subhash C. Kashyap (ed.), Supra no. 5, p. 85.
59. V.A. Paipanandikar and Subhash C. Kashyap (ed.), Supra no. 4, p. 25.
60. Jayaprakash Narayan, Supra no. 34, p. 50.
61. S.D. Bali in, Subhash C. Kashyap (ed.), Supra no. 5, p. 185
62. U.C. Agarwal in Subhash C. Kashyap (ed.), Supra no. 5, p. 85,
63. Rabin Mukharjee, Supra no. 6, p. 46.
64. P.A. Sagma in Subhash C. Kashyap (ed.), Supra no. 5, p. 20.
65. P.A. Sagma in Subhash C. Kashyap (ed.), Supra no. 5, p. 19.
66. G. Palanithurai, Supra no. 27, p. 80.
67. *Ibid*., p. 81.
68. *Ibid*., p. 86.
69. *The Hindu*, May 17, 2004.
70. *Ibid.*
71. R.C. Dutt, *People and Politics: The Indian Experience*, Lancer Publishers Private Limited, New Delhi, 1992, p. 153.
72. S.K. Chopra (ed.), Supra no. 21, p. 33.

73. Joachim Ahrens, *Governance and Economic Development: A Comparative Institutional Approach,* Edward Elgar Publishing Limited., U.K., 2002, p. 135.
74. Rabin Mukharjee, Supra no. 6, p. 48.
75. Sisir K. Dhar, Supra no. 46, p. 37.
76. *Ibid.*, p. 38.
77. Navin Chandra Joshi (ed.), *Democracy and Human Values,* Sterling Publishers Private Limited, New Delhi, 1979, p. 23.
78. Vera Michels, *New Patterns of Democracy in India,* Harvard University Press, Cambridge, 1959, p. 24.
79. Kenneth Janda, Jefferty M. Berry and Jerry Goldman, *The Challenges of Democracy: Government in America,* Houghton Mufflin Company, Boston, 1992, p. 39.
80. J. Roland Pennock, *Democratic Political Theory,* Princeton University Press, New Jersey, 1979, p. 267.
81. V.A. Paipanandikar and Subhash C. Kashyap (ed.), Supra no. 4, p. 6.
82. David Held (ed.), *Prospects for Democracy,* Stanford University Press, California, 1993, p. 58.
83. Kurt L. Shell, *The Democratic Political Process,* Blaisdell Publishing Company, London, 1969, p. 60.
84. Richard Hofferbert (ed.), Supra no. 16, p. 13.
85. Giovanni Sartori, *Parties and Party System: A Framework for Analyses,* Cambridge University Press, Cambridge, 1976, p. 331.
86. Gabriel Almond, *The Civic Culture: Political Attitude and Democracy in Five Nations,* Princeton University Press, New Jersey, p. 162.
87. Sydney Verba, Norman H. Nie and Jae-on Kim, *Participation and Political Equality,* Cambridge University Press, Cambridge, 1978, p. 47.
88. Shivraj Patil in Subhash C. Kashyap (ed.) Supra no. 5, p. 15.
89. P.A. Sangma in Subhash C. Kashyap (ed.) Supra no. 5, p. 16.
90. Kurt L. Shell, Supra no. 86, pp. 68-69.
91. Satya Prakash Dash, The State, Civil Society and Democracy: A Note, *The Indian Journal of Political Science*, 62(2), June 2001, p. 241.
92. V.A. Paipanandikar and Subhash C. Kashyap (ed.), Supra no. 4, p. 5.
93. G. Palanithurai, Supra no. 27, p. 18.
94. Sumit Bhattacharya, Democracy and Election, *The Radical Humanist,* 55(2), May 1991, p. 1.
95. P.R. Dubhashi in, Subhash C. Kashyap (ed.), Supra no. 5, p. 90.
96. S.G. Kashikar in Subhash C. Kashyap (ed.), Supra no. 5, p. 199.
97. Adam Przeworski, Susan C. Stokes and Bernard Menin, Supra no. 3, p. 57.
98. Jayaprakash Narayan Supra no. 34, p. 4.

99. K. Kishore, *Governance for Citizens,* in C.P. Bharthwal (ed.), Supra no. 1, p. 24.
100. S.G. Kashikar in, Subhash C. Kashyap (ed.), Supra no. 5, p. 199.
101. Adam Przeworski, Susan C. Stokes and Bernard Menin, Supra no. 3, p. 30.
106. Shivraj B. Nakade in Subhash C. Kashyap (ed.), Supra no. 5, p. 146.
102. *The Navhind Times*, May 2002.
103. V. Venkateshan, Now the Countdown, *Frontline,* March 26, 2004, p. 27.
104. *The Hindu*, May 2, 2004.
105. *Ibid.*
106. Himmatbhai Patel and Shantibhai Patel in Subhash C. Kashyap (ed.), Supra no. 5,p. 105.
107. *Ibid.*, p. 104.
108. M.A. Rane, Peoples' Manifest: An Agenda for the Next Government, *The Radical Humanist*, 55(3), June 1991, p. 8.
109. J. Roland Pennock, Supra no. 82, p. 443.
110. V.A. Paipanandikar and Subhash C. Kashyap (ed.), Supra no. 4, pp. 6-7.
111. Giovanni Sartori, *Parties and Party System: A Framework for Analysis,* Cambridge University Press, Cambridge, p. 325.
112. Richard Hofferbert (ed.), Supra no. 16, p. 3.

7

Conclusions

Democratic governance is to promote the interest of the people. Due to large size in terms of population and territory indirect democracy has been accepted by modern Nation-States. Political parties and people play a significant role in democratizing the process of governance. Political parties are regarded as the most important institutional mechanism available to the people through which they can best represent their interests and aspirations. The interest and aspiration of the people are best articulated and aggregated by the political parties. In the Indian context, in the absence of associational life, political parties play a crucial role. No doubt, in recent years civil society is playing an important role. However, in civil society in which the role of voluntary organizations of the people like NGOs, Self-help groups, etc. is important in democratic governance, it is difficult for these organizations to keep in touch with each and every problem of the people who live in different areas under different conditions. One more problem faced by the civil society is that they can only influence and pressurize the government but the ultimate responsibility of formulating public policies is with the elected representatives, who are the members of one or the other political parties. Thus governance of our country is very much affected by the functioning of political parties.

At the time of elections political parties promise a number of policies and programmes, on which they contest elections. Based on these policies and programmes of various political parties, people may prefer to elect their representatives. Political parties are expected to formulate public policies after getting elected as per their electoral promises. The contribution of political parties to the formulation of public policies indicates their responsiveness in terms of fulfilment of the aspirations of people. For the effective formulation of public policies an active participation of political parties is essential. They should have adequate and correct knowledge about the problems of the people while formulating the policies. For this, they should be in close contact with the people, since parties are channels between the people and government. They cannot be responsive to the needs of the people unless they are in contact with the people. Thus, both participation and responsiveness of political parties are crucial in the functioning of democratic governance.

To what extent political parties represent the interests of the people is a matter of great significance for democratic governance. Participation and responsiveness of political parties indicate the extent of representation of interest of the people. To make the political parties responsive to the needs of the people, popular responsiveness plays a crucial role. As the political parties are regarded as the institutions of representing the people, it is the right as well as the duty of every citizen to make them responsive. One of the important and most popular means through which people can control their representatives is through elections. In elections people are given an opportunity to judge and evaluate the performance of their representatives belonging to various parties. But, peoples' role in political process should not be confined to only to electoral politics. They have to be more alert and vigilant in between elections. There is no guarantee that political parties always work in the interest of the people. There may be some personal interest or party interest which may overshadow the peoples' interest. Hence, active participation of the people can ensure responsiveness and accountability of the political parties. Responsiveness of people can make political parties accountable and answerable. It contributes to democratic public policy making.

India after attaining independence adopted parliamentary democracy. Political parties have been playing a significant role in Indian democracy though they are not mentioned in the Constitution of India. Indian One-Party-Dominant System provided stability and consistency of policies. Governance under the leadership of Nehru was satisfactory to a greater extent. Inter-party and intra-party democracy helped to develop consensus on major policy decisions. In the post-Nehru era, the emergence of leadership of Indira Gandhi with her populist politics weakened the Congress party as an institution. This made other parties not only to follow the populist politics but also compete with the Congress party. Organizational wing of the Congress party was weakened when the leader became very dominant. Elections were not held within the party. Everything was decided by a leader in the name of the party high command. The leader of the party became more important. Consequently, the Congressmen became answerable to the leader and not to the people. Though initially Rajiv Gandhi was able to revive intra-party democracy of the Congress party, subsequently nothing materialized with regard to revival of intra-party democracy in the Congress party.

In 1989, One-Party-Dominant system was replaced by multi-party system. With the emergence of domination of regional parties, government formation started to become a difficult task. This led to the emergence of coalition era in India. Democratic governance was further made difficult with the emergence of coalition government primarily due to the problem of evolving consensus on basic issues and problems of the country. Unstable coalitions have affected the policy formulation process of the government. Parties within the coalitions have their own ideologies, policies and principles. With so many differences arriving at consensus on policy decisions has become very difficult. Any small difference of opinion among the members may lead to the downfall of the government. Regional parties have become more significant because national parties are dependent on them in the formation of government as well as working of government. The party or parties to continue in power have to enjoy the confidence of its allies. The Indian experience of coalition governments has shown that one or the other ally of the coalition always gives priority to control or dictate the terms to the government. On the other hand opposition parties are waiting for an opportunity to break the coalition and to attract its allies on its side to form the government. Such politics has reduced government to a number game. Rarely do we find people who really want to serve the nation. Opposition parties are always obstructing the functioning of ruling party or parties with a view to make them unresponsive. If at all it comes to power it also meets the same fate because the party which forms opposition repeats the same to it. It is often said that in a coalition it is difficult to determine where government ends and opposition begins. The opposition of today may be a partner in the coalition government of tomorrow.

Political parties which are to be responsive to the interest of the people are becoming captives of sinister interest. Attaining power have become the main objective of most of the parties. To get power political parties are using all sorts of illegitimate means. Such unlawful acts of political parties make mockery of elections. It is through the elections the representatives are held accountable, answerable and responsive to the people. But, when the election process itself is vitiated and the leaders are elected by unlawful means, then how can we expect a responsive government from such leaders? Use of money, muscle and mafia power in elections, booth capturing, rigging, false voting, unfinished electoral rolls, etc., adversely affect the responsiveness of the political parties to fulfill the aspirations of the people.

The findings of the present study are as follows:

1. Power politics has affected the participation of political parties. For getting power political parties do not hesitate to adopt any illegitimate means. Politics has become a number game reducing the importance of performance by political parties. With the emergence of coalitions every party gives priority to forming alliance and maintaining that alliance with a view of getting power for it. Personal interests and party interests have become so important that interest of the people is subordinated.

The use of money, mafia and muscle power has devalued the accountability of political parties to the people. With the help of money and mafia power, some candidates get themselves elected. In many places some criminals themselves are entering politics. Some parties take the help of criminals to win elections. As a result of this, political parties give less importance for reforming their functioning to promote the wellbeing of the people.

2. The nature of party politics affected democratic governance in India. Different issues, policies, programmes, personal factors and style of functioning of parties affect party politics. Party politics has

not only affected the electoral process but also has affected the functioning of parliamentary democracy. Most issues of public importance are being politicized in India.

Both intra-party politics and inter-party politics are affecting democratic governance adversely. With the emergence of coalition governments there is also a change in the nature of party politics. The party which forms the government takes the support of a number of regional parties. Obviously, every party in the coalition is attempting to promote its party interest. These parties come together and agree for Common Minimum Programme not to serve the nation but to share power. The ruling party or parties are compelled to take its allies into confidence. With the decline of national parties, regional parties have become strong. Regional parties are pressing for the fulfilment of their demands. If their demands are not fulfilled they may bring down the government. This is what happened to the NDA government in 1998. If at all small regional parties within the coalition get united, the party giving support from outside may become a threat to the survival of the coalition. Here, we can mention the examples of National Front in1989 and United Front government in 1996.

Parties outside the coalition are always waiting for an opportunity to bring down the government. Often the opposition parties have negative approach to the policies introduced by the coalition government. Their main motive is to make the government ineffective.

3. Intra-party democracy also has some effect on democratic governance. We cannot strengthen the organizational wing of political parties unless and until democracy within the political parties is revived. It is the organizational wing of the party which keeps the party in touch with the needs and aspirations of the people. The leaders of the party should not be chosen by the party high command but should be elected by the members of the party. But, in India what we generally find is that, most of the time, the leaders are chosen by party high command. As a result, they feel responsible not to the people but to the party leader. A large number of people are mainly dependent upon the leader for party tickets. Such a state of affairs has weakened the political parties in India. So the revival of intra-party democracy is very essential.

4. Lack of strong coalition culture adversely affects democratic governance. When consensus is built among the political parties policy

making not only becomes democratic but also effective. But, with the differences in ideologies, programmes, policies, etc. it is difficult to arrive at consensus. There is need to strengthen coalition culture which ultimately contributes to evolve consensus. This will strengthen democratic governance in India. Cooperation, coordination and accommodative spirit are the prerequisites for strengthening democratic coalition governments.

5. Democratic governance is further affected by the nature of debate and discussion that take place within the Parliament. Parliamentary proceeding are mainly affected by the power struggle, party politics and disruptive elements. Poor attendance, floor crossing, shouting slogans, etc., not only disrupt the policy formulation process but also result in waste of time and money. The scenes inside the Parliament are not conducive for the effective formulation of public policies. There is need to improve the quality of debate in the Parliament. Proper training of the leaders is required to maintain the standard of debates and discussions. The members who are assigned with the great responsibility of representing the aspirations of people are expected to behave responsibly. There should be some norms for proper controlling of the behaviour of leaders in the Parliament. Unless and until we improve the quality of debate in the Parliament, we cannot hope for effective democratic good governance.

6. There is wide gap between what political parties pursue about governance and what they practice. This is especially found in the era of coalition governance. Since 1998 NDA had been talking about good governance mainly based on transparent, accountable and responsive government but in practice its efforts were very little in this regard. Not only NDA and its partners but almost all parties in one or the other way are talking about good governance. But, in practice how responsibly they talk in the Parliament is very vital. If political parties are concerned with the good governance and about the welfare of the people, it is not only when they get power but also when they are in the opposition they have to function responsively to promote good governance. Therefore, good governance should be above party politics. Good governance has become the concept to be included in the parties' manifestos for mobilizing the electorate. Every party has to internalize it in its actions. What is needed is practice by

political parties according to their promises in the election manifesto.

7. Lastly and most importantly, we should not neglect the role of people in democratic governance. The important responsibility of ensuring democratic governance rests on the shoulders of the people. But, the studies have revealed that by and large popular participation is not very satisfactory in India. Civil Society in India is not very much active. Some NGOs, pressure groups, self-help groups, etc., are playing an important role in giving education and information to the people about their rights and responsibilities. But, their scope is very limited in nature.

People have to come forward and organize themselves and be vigilant, informative and active in politics. They should make political parties responsible for their performance. But, if popular participation in the democratic governance is not satisfactory it is primarily due to the kind of party politics that prevails in India. As a result of this, people are losing confidence in the political parties and some times developing political apathy. People should realize that unless they are active participants and evaluate the deeds and misdeeds of government periodically, democratic governance cannot be strengthened. Ineffective popular responsiveness results in the dilution of democratic governance.

This study is not conclusive but it points to the need for extensive and intensive understanding of the role of parliament in the democratic governance in India.

Bibliography

Party Documents

Bharatiya Janata Party

1. Assembly Elections 1998, Bharatiya Janata Party, BJP Publication, 1998.
2. *BJP Today*, BJP Publication, 1997.
3. *BJS to BJP: Two Essays on Ideology In Action*, Bharatiya Janata Party, BJP Publication, 1997.
4. Election Manifesto 1991, Bharatiya Janata Party, BJP Publication, 1991.
5. Election Manifesto 1996, Bharatiya Janata Party, BJP Publication, 1996.
6. Election Manifesto 1998, Bharatiya Janata Party, BJP Publication, 1998.
7. Election Manifesto 1999, Bharatiya Janata Party, BJP Publication, 1999.
8. Election Manifesto 2004, Bharatiya Janata Party, BJP Publication, 2004.

Indian National Congress (I)

1. BJPs Crisis of Governance, *Congress Sandesh*, 1 (5), February 1999.
2. Congress Ready for Elections, *Congress Sandesh*, 5 (11), 2003.
3. Electoral Change, *Congress Sandesh*, 1 (2), October 1998.

4. General Election Manifesto 1991: Indian National Congress (I), Congress (I) Publication, 1991.
5. General Election Manifesto 1996: Indian National Congress (I), Congress (I) Publication, 1996.
6. General Election Manifesto 1998: Indian National Congress (I), Congress (I) Publication, 1998.
7. General Election Manifesto 1999: Indian National Congress (I), Congress (I) Publication, 1999.
8. Good Governance, *Congress Sandesh*, 3 (10), June 2001.
9. Manifesto Vidhan Sabha Elections 2002 (Uttaranchal), Indian National Congress (I), Congress (I) Publication, 2002.
10. *Speech of Leader of Opposition Smt. Sonia Gandhi In Parliament on Motion of No-Confidence*, 18th August 2003, Congress (I) Publication, 2003.

Communist Party of India

1. Election Manifesto 1991, Communist Party of India, CPI Publication, 1991.
2. Election Manifesto 1996, Communist Party of India, CPI Publication, 1996.
3. Election Manifesto 1999, Communist Party of India, CPI Publication, 1999.
4. Election Manifesto 2004, Communist Party of India, CPI Publication, 2004.

Communist Party of India (Marxist)

1. Election Manifesto 1991, Communist Party of India (Marxist), CPI (M) Publication, 1991.
2. Election Manifesto 1996, Communist Party of India (Marxist), CPI (M) Publication, 1996.
3. Election Manifesto 1998, Communist Party of India (Marxist), CPI (M) Publication, 1998.
4. Election Manifesto 2004, Communist Party of India (Marxist), CPI (M) Publication, 2004.

Books

Ahmed, Aijaz, *Lineage of the Present: Political Essays*, Tulika Publishers, New Delhi, 1996.

Ahren, Joachim, *Governance and Economic Development*, Edward Elgar Publishing Limited, U.K., 2002.

Ahuja, M.L. and Paul, Sharada, *1989–1991 General Elections in India*, Associated Publishing House, New Delhi, 1992.

Ahuja, M.L., *Electoral Politics and General Elections in India*, Mittal Publication, New Delhi, 1999.

Almond, Gabriel A. and Coleman, James S. (ed.), *The Politics of the Developing Areas*, Princeton University Press, New Jersey, 1970.

Banu, Gisela, *The Indian Challenge*, Allied Publishers, Delhi, 1992.

Baxi, Upendra and Parekh Bhikhu, *Crisis and Change in Contemporary India*, Sage Publication, New Delhi, 1994.

Bedi, Kiran, Jeet, Parminder and Srivastava, Sandeep, *Government@net: New Governance Opportunities for India*, Sage Publications, New Delhi, 2001.

Beteille, Andre, *Society and Politics in India: Essays in Comparative Perspective*, Oxford University Press, New Delhi, 1997.

Bharthwal, D.P. (ed.), *Indian Administration Since Independence*, Bharat Book Centre, Lucknow, 2003.

Binder, Leonard and Other (Contributors), *Crisis and Sequences in Political Development*, Addison Wesley Publishing Company, London, 1975.

Bishop, Hillman M. and HedeL Samuel, *Basic Issues of American Democracy*, Appleton-Century Crofts Inc., New York, 1951.

Bonner, Arthur et al., *Democracy in India: A Hollow Shell*, The American University Press, Washington, 1994.

Brass, Paul R., *The Politics of India Since Independence*, Cambridge University Press, Cambridge, 1990.

Breduuold, Louis L. and Ross, Ralph G. (ed.), *The Philosophy of Edmund Burke*, University of Michigan Press, Ann Arbor, 1960.

Chakravarthy, Paul, *Democratic Government and Electoral Process*, Kanishka Publishers, New Delhi, 1997.

Chatterjee, Parth, *A Possible India: Essays in Political Criticism*, Oxford University Press, Delhi, 1997.

Chatterjee, Parth, *State and Politics in India*, Oxford University Press, Delhi, 1997.

Chibber, Pradeep K., *Democracy Without Associations: Transforming the Party System and Social Change*, Vikas Publications, New Delhi, 1999.

Chopra, S.K. (ed.), *Toward Good Governance*, Konark Publishers Private Limited, Delhi, 1997.

Dhal, Robert A. and Dean, E. Neubauer, *Reading in Modern Political Analysis*, Printice-Hall, New Jersey, 1968.

Dodd, Lowrence C., *Coalitions in Parliamentary Government*, Princeton University Press, Princeton, 1976.

Duverger, Maurice, *Political Parties*, Methuen and Company Limited, London, 1954.

Frankel, Francine R., Hassan Zoya, Bhargava Rajeev and Arora Balveer (ed.), *Transforming India: Social and Political Dynamics of Democracy*, Oxford University Press, New Delhi, 2000.

Gauba, O.P., *An Introduction to Political Theory*, MacMillan, Delhi, 1995.

Gehlot, N.S., *Current Trends in Indian Politics*, Deep and Deep Publication, New Delhi, 1998.

Gupta, Bhabani Sen, *India: Problems of Governance*, Konark Publishers, Delhi, 1996.

Hasen, Thomas Blom and Jafferelot Christopher (eds.), *The BJP and The Compulsion of Politics in India*, Oxford University Press, Oxford, 1998.

Hassan, Zoya (ed.), *Parties and Party Politics in India*, Oxford University Press, New Delhi, 2002.

Held, David (ed.), *Prospects for Democracy*, Stanford University Press, California, 1993.

Jana, Anil Kumar (ed.), *Indian Politics at Crossroads*, Commonwealth Publisher, New Delhi, 1998.

Janda, Kenneth, Berry Jeffery M. and Goldman Jerry, *The Challenges of Democracy: Government in America*, Houghton Mufflin Company, Boston, 1992.

Jangam, R.T., Patil, S.H. and Patagundi, S.S., *Political Analysis*, Oxford and IBH Publishing Company Private Limited, New Delhi, 1997.

Jayal, Niraja Gopal and Pai, Sudha, *Democratic Governance in India: Challenges of Poverty, Development and Identity*, Sage Publications, New Delhi, 2001.

Jhunjunwala, Bharat, *Governance and Human Rights*, Kalpaz Publications, Delhi, 2002.

Kagalkar, Pratibha, *A Comparative Study of Socialism and Democracy*, Himalaya Publishing House, 1996.

Karunakaran, K.P. (ed.), *Coalition Governments in India: Problems and Prospects*, Indian Institute of Advanced Study, Shimla, 1975.

Kashyap, Subhash C.(ed.), *Coalition Government and Politics in India*, Uppal Publication, New Delhi, 1997.

Kashyap, Subhash C.(ed.), *National Resurgence Through Electoral Reforms*, Shipra Publications, Delhi, 2002.

Kashyap, Subhash C., *Nation and Policy Under Strain: The Indian Experience*, Uppal Publication, New Delhi, 1996.

Kaviraj, Sudipta, *Politics in India*, Oxford University Press, Oxford, 1997.

Khanna, D.D. and Wreck Gert, *Principles, Powers and Politics*, MacMillan, Delhi, 1999.

Khanna, S.K., *Contemporary Indian Politics*, Discovery Publishing House, Delhi, 1999.

Khanna, S.K., *Seasoned Diplomat to Scholar Prime Minister: Profile of I.K. Gujral*, Mittal Publication, New Delhi, 1997.

Khilani, Sunil, *The Idea of India,* Hamish Hamiltion, London, 1997.

Kohli, Atul (ed.), *India's Democracy: An Analysis of Changing State-Society Relation*, Princeton University Press, New Jersey, 1998.

Kohli, Atul (ed.), *The Success of India's Democracy,* Cambridge University Press, New Delhi, 2001.

Kohli, Atul, *The State and Poverty in India: The Politics of Reform*, Cambridge University Press, Cambridge, 1987.

Kohli, Atul, *Democracy and Discontent: India's Growing Crisis of Governability*, Cambridge University Press, Cambridge, 1991.

Kothari, Rajni, *Communalism in Indian Politics*, Rainbow Publishers, New Delhi, 1998.

Kothari, Rajni, *Democratic Political and Social Change in India,* Allied Publishers, New Delhi, 1976.

Kothari, Rajni, *Memoirs: Uneasy is the Life of Mind,* Roop and Company, New Delhi, 2002.

Kothari, Rajni, *Politics and People: In Search of Humane India,* Vol. I, Ajanta Publications, Delhi, 1989.

Kothari, Rajni, *State Against Democracy: In Search of Humane Governance,* Ajanta Publications, Delhi, 1988.

Leiserson, Avert, *Parties and Politics,* Alfred K. Knopf Inc., New York, 1958.

Limaye, Madhu, *Decline of Political System: Indian Politics at Crossroads*, Wheeler Publication, Allahabad, 1992.

Limaye, Madhu, *Indian Polity in Transition*, Radiant Publication, New Delhi, 1990

Lipson, Leslie, *The Democratic Civilization*, Oxford University Press, New York, 1964.

Meehan, E.J., Roche J.P. and Stedman M.S. Jr., *The Dynamics of Modern Government,* McGraw Hill Book Company, New York, 1966.

Merkl, Peter H., *Modern Comparative Politics,* Holsp., Rhinehart and Winston Inc., USA, 1970.

Mitra, Subrata K. and Chiriyankandath James (ed.), *Changing Landscape*, Segment Books, New Delhi, 1992.

Mitra, Subrata K. and Singh V.B., *Democracy and Social Change in India,* Sage Publications, New Delhi, 1999.

Pai, Sudha, *Understanding Indian Politics*, Sage Publication, New Delhi, 1990.

Paipanandiker, V.A. and Kashyap Subhash C. (ed.), *Political Reforms: Asserting Civic Sovereignty*, Konark Publishers Private Limited. New Delhi, 2001.

Palanithurai, G., *Peoples' Perception of Politics,* Kanishka Publishers, Delhi, 1995.

Pandit, Vajaylaxmi, *Elites and Urban Politics: A Case Study of Delhi,* Inter India Publication, New Delhi, 1984.

Pantham, Thomas, *Political Parties and Democratic Consensus*, The MacMillan Company of India Limited, Delhi, 1976.

Pateman, Carole, *Participation and Democratic Theory,* Cambridge University Press, Cambridge, 1970.

Pennock, J.R., *Democratic Political Theory,* Princeton University Press, Princeton, 1979.

Pennock, J.R., *Liberal Democracy: Its Merits and Prospects,* Rinehart Company, Inc., New York, 1950.

Prasad, Mahendra and Saxena Rekha, *India's Political Agenda*, Kalinga Publishers, New Delhi, 1996.

Prasad, R.N., *Governance of India: Issues and Perspectives,* Concept Publishing Company, New Delhi, 2002.

Puspa, Asthana, *Party System in India Development or Decay*, Criterion Publications, New Delhi, 1998.

Raj, Hans, *Indian Political System*, Surjeet Publications, Delhi, 1990.

Ramu, P.S., *Eleventh Lok Sabha Elections: Dangerous Portents-Prospects of Parliamentary Democracy in India,* ISE, New Delhi, 1993.

Roy, Meenu, *Elections 1998: A Continuity in Coalition,* National Publishing House, New Delhi, 1999.

Roy, Meenu, *Election Politics in India: Issues and Perspectives,* Concept Publishing Company, New Delhi, 2000.

Roy, Ramashray and Wallace Paul (ed.), *Indian Politics and the 1998 Elections,* Sage Publications, New Delhi, 1999.

Sahani, N.C., *Coalition Politics in India,* New Academic Publishing Company, Jallundur, 1971.

Salvadorai, Massimo, *Liberal Democracy,* Pallmall Press, London, 1958.

Sartori, Giovanni, *An Inquiry Into Structures, Incentives and Outcomes,* MacMillan, London, 1994.

Sartori, Giovanni, *Parties and Party System: A Framework for Analysis,* Cambridge University Press, Cambridge, 1976.

Satyanarayan, J., *e-Governance—The Science of the Possible,* Prentice Hall India, New Delhi, 2004.

Saxena, N.S., *India Towards Anarchy 1967-1992*, Abhinas Publication, New Delhi, 1993

Singh, M.P. and Saxena Rekha, *India at the Polls,* Orient Longman, New Delhi, 2003.

Thakur, Ramesh, *The Government and Politics of India*, MacMillan, London, 1995.

Tiwari, Murli Dhar, *Education and e-Governance,* MacMillan, Delhi, 2001.

Utley, T.F. and Maclure J.S. Stuart (ed.), *Documents of Modern Political Thought,* Cambridge University Press, New York, 1957.

Vajpey, Dhirendra K., *Modernization and Social Change in India*, Manohar Publications, New Delhi, 1979.

Verba, Sidney, Nie Norman H. and Kim Jae-on, *Participation and Political Equality*, Cambridge University Press, Cambridge, 1978.

Verma, R.P. (ed.), *Peoples' Participation in Politics*, Rajat Publications, New Delhi, 2002.

Ware, Alan, *Political Parties and Party System*, Oxford University Press, New York, 1996.

Weiner, Myron, *Party Politics in India*, Princeton University Press, Princeton, New Jersey, 1957.

Weiner, Myron, *State Politics in India*, Princeton University Press, Princeton, 1968.

Weiner, Myron, *The Indian Paradox*, Sage Publications, New Delhi, 1989.

Articles

Mainstream

Agarwal, Anuradha and Kumar Pankaj, The Election Scene, *Mainstream*, 27 (53), 30th September 1989.

Chakravarti, Nikhil, New Strings of Democracy Assertion, *Mainstream*, 34 (7), 20th January 1996.

Chakravarti, Nikhil, Coalition What Next?, *Mainstream*, 35 (20), 26th April 1997.

Dandavate, Madhu, In Search of Stability, *Mainstream*, 34 (25), 25th May 1996.

Dang, Satyapal, New for a Left Center Coalition With a Strong Left, *Mainstream*, 36 (19), 2nd May 1998.

Dasgupta, Gurudas, *Ram Rajya:* The Dirty Reality of BJP in Power, *Mainstream*, 36 (49), 28th November 1998.

Editorial, Aya Ram Comes to Parliament, *Mainstream*, 31 (38), 15th August 1993, p.3.

Editorial, Challenge of the Fractured Mandate, *Mainstream*, 34 (25), 25th May 1996.

Editorial, National Agenda for Governance, *Mainstream*, 36 (15), 4th April 1998.

Gujral, I.K., India—Fifty Years On: Promise for the Next Millennium, *Mainstream*, 35 (45), 18th October 1997.

Gujral, I.K., Challenge Before Our Polity, *Mainstream*, 31 (25), 1st May 1993.

Gupta, Indrajit, Growing Mal-Functioning of Parliament in Present Setting, *Mainstream*, 31 (23), 17th April 1993.

Jain, S.K., Article 356 and the Congress, *Mainstream*, 37 (16), 10th April 1999.

Kothari, Rajni, Implications of Left and Left on Centre Consolidation, *Mainstream*, 31 (37), 24 July 1993.

Kothari, Rajni, Towards Real People's Power, *Mainstream*, 34 (7), 20th January 1996.

Kumar, Anand, From Negative Coalitions to Dominant Caste Democracy, *Mainstream*, October 1999.

Majumdar, Madhumita, Party Wrecking, *Mainstream*, 29 (8), 15th December 1990.

Metthew, George, Democracy Discriminated, *Mainstream*, 34 (19), 13th April 1996.

Mehta, Balraj, On Post Election Party Alignment, *Mainstream*, 34 (25), 25th May 1996.

Mehta, Chimanbhai, Legislation Needed to Ensure Inner Party Democracy, *Mainstream*, 27th October 1990.

Mohan, Surendra, A New Beginning Amidst Confusion, *Mainstream*, 34 (19), 13th April 1996.

Muthamma, C.B., Chasing the Legislative Majority, *Mainstream*, 35, 20th December 1997.

Prasad, Kamala, BJP and the Nations Governance, *Mainstream*, 36 (52), 19th December 1998.

Prasad, Kamala, Confidence Vote, Parliament and the New Politics, *Mainstream*, 35 (21), 3rd May 1997.

Prasad, Kamala, Indian Leadership and Governance, *Mainstream*, 34 (42), 21 September 1996.

Puri, Yogesh, Evolution of Party System and Centricism in India, *Mainstream*, 29 (12), 12th January 1991.

Rajinwale, Anil, Secular Coalition Politics: A Negation of Anti-Congressism, *Mainstream*, 34 (36), 10th August 1996.

Sachar, Rajindar, Thoughts on Mystery Making at the Center, *Mainstream*, 36 (13), 21st March 1998.

Saxena, Rekha, Coalition Experiment: Problem and Prospects, *Mainstream*, 36 (18), 25th April 1998.

Sharma, R.N., Erosion of Parliamentary Democracy, *Mainstream*, 27 (50), 9th September 1989.

Shukla, I.K., Post-Congress India: A Prospect, *Mainstream*, 34 (24), 15th June 1996.

Shukla, I.K., Secularism and Future of Indian Democracy, *Mainstream*, 34 (23), 11 May 1996.

Verghese, B.G., Shedding Stability for Peace, *Mainstream*, 34 (28), 15th September 1996.

Organiser

100 Days of Good Governance, *Organiser*, 49 (49), 5th July 1998.

Batura, R.C., in Search cf Charisma, *Organiser*, 49 (21), 21st December 1997.

Beyond the Polls, *Organiser*, 42 (42), 26th May 1991.

Chari, Seshadri, Stability at Last, *Organiser*, 49 (36), 5th April 1998.

Chari, Seshadri, Towards a Mid-Term Poll, *Organiser*, 50 (29), 14th February 1999.

Chari, Seshadri, Whose Hidden Agenda?, *Organiser*, 12th April 1998.

Dichotomy of Mandate and Arithmetic of Numbers, *Organiser*, 47 (45), 9th June 1996.

Gupta, S.D., Indian Polity Needs Challenge of System, *Organiser*, 46 (3), 21st August 1994.

Kamat, M.V., Is this the Demise of National Parties?, *Organiser*, 47 (43), 26th May 1996.

Khosla, Shyam, A Compromise Cabinet, *Organiser*, 47 (46), 16th June 1996.

Khosla, Shyam, Alliance Must Follow Coalition Dharma, *Organiser*, 50 (29), 14th September 1999.

Khosla, Shyam, Alternatives to Instability, *Organiser*, 48 (17), 24th November 1996.

Khosla, Shyam, Face Mid-Term Elections, *Organiser*, 50 (40), 2nd May 1999.

Khosla, Shyam, Gowda Going Down?, *Organiser*, 48 (19), 8th December 1996.

Khosla, Shyam, Hard Choice for the President, *Organiser*, 50 (39), 25th April 1999.

Khosla, Shyam, No Alternative to Vajpayee Government, *Organiser*, 50 (38), 18th April 1999.

Khosla, Shyam, Old Turk Having A Pipe-Dream of Topping The Government, *Organiser*, 49 (49), 5th July 1998.

Khosla, Shyam, The Nation Looks Up With Hope, *Organiser*, 49 (35), 29th March 1998.

National Agenda for Governance, *Organiser*, 49 (35), 25th March 1998.

Patange, Ramesh, Meaning of 1996 Mandate, *Organiser*, 47 (45), 9th June 1996.

Singhal, Ashok, Nationalist will Come to Power, *Organiser*, 49 (25), 18th January 1998.

Srivastava, Baleshwari P., Morality, Politics and India, *Organiser*, 49 (15), 9th November 1997.

Vajpayee, A.B., Challenges to Democracy in India, *Organiser*, 48 (17), 24th November 1996.

Economic and Political Weekly

Bageshi, Amiya Kumar, Politics of Mass Democracy in India, *Economic and Political Weekly*, 33 (12), 21 March 1998.

Chakravarti, Uma, Saffroning the Past of Myths, Histories and Right-Wing Agendas, *Economic and Political Weekly*, 33 (5), 31st January 1998.

Chousalkar, Ashok, Party Elections: Long Road to Inner-Party Democracy. *Economical and Political Weekly*, 32 (37), 13th September 1997.

Kantha, Pramod K., General Elections 1996: BJP Politics: Looking Beyond the Impasse, *Economic and Political Weekly*, 32 (48), 29th November 1997.

Kothari, Rajni, Elections Without Party System, *Economic and Political Weekly*, 31 (16-17), 20th April 1996.

Kothari, Rajni, Interpreting 1996: Where do we Go from Here?, *Economic and Political Weekly*, 31 (24), 15th June 1996.

Kumar B. Venkatesh, Criminalisation of Politics and Election Commission, *Economic and Political Weekly*, 16th June 2001.

Mishra, Amresh, Political Alignment in the Making, *Economic and Political Weekly*, 27 (41), October 1992.

Mukharji, Nirmal, Strengthening Indian Democracy, *Economic and Political Weekly*, 31 (19), 11th May 1996.

Navlakha, Gautam, Politics: Fear of Freedom, *Economic and Political Weekly*, 32 (44-45), 8th November 1997.

Nayar, Deepak, Interaction of Economics and Politics in Independent India, *Economic and Political Weekly*, 33 (49), 5th December 1998.

Quick Decline of UF Government, *Economic and Political Weekly*, 31 (38), 21st September 1996.

Roy, A.K., Hung or Hanged: State of 11th Lok Sabha, *Economic and Political Weekly*, 31 (28), 13th July 1996.

Roy, Ashwini, Domestic Politics and National Security, *Economic and Political Weekly*, 33 (26), 27th June 1998.

Sathe, Dhanmanjiri, Economic Development and Political Democracy, *Economic and Political Weekly*, 34 (14), 3rd April 1999.

Sathe, S.P., Review of the Constitution, *Economic and Political Weekly*, 16th September 2000.

Yadav, Yogendra, Towards an Indian Agenda for the Indian Left, *Economic and Political Weekly*, 28 (41), 9th October 1993.

New Age

Banarjee, Subrata, Method in BJP's Failure in Governance, *New Age*, 46 (47), 22nd November 1998.

Banarjee, Subrata, Splits and Transformation of Indian National Congress, *New Age*, 37 (47), 19th November 1989.

Bardhan, A.B., Mobilise to Defeat BJP: Vote UF to Power, *New Age*, 46 (2), 11th January 1998.

Bardhan, A.B., 1998 Challenges and Hopes, *New Age*, 46 (1), January 1998.

Bardhan, A.B., Era of Coalition, *New Age*, 44 (21), 26th May 1996.

Bardhan, A.B., Main Issues Before Voters, *New Age*, 46 (7), 15th February 1998.

Bardhan, A.B., Over to the People, *New Age*, 14 (18), 23rd August 1998.

Bardhan, A.B., Some Questions and their Answers-A Catechism on the Present Situation, *New Age*, 45 (49), 7th December 1997.

Bardhan, A.B., The Exercise in Forming: A New Government, *New Age*, 44 (20), 19th May 1996.

Bardhan, A.B., This Government and Supporting Party, *New Age*, 39 (9), 3rd March 1991.

Bardhan, A.B., UF Guarantees Stability and Progress, *New Age*, 46 (9), 1st March 1998.

Dang, Sathyapal, Coalition Politics and Stability, *New Age*, 46 (17), 26th April 1998, p.3.

Dang, Sathyapal, Money-Muscle Power in Elections, *New Age*, 38 (3), 21st January 1999.

Faizee, Shameem, "Public Demonstration by BJP Government of its Incompetence", *New Age*, 47 (1), 3rd January 1999.

Faizee, Shameem, Defeat of BJP Game Plan, *New Age*, 44 (20), 19 May 1996.

Faizee, Shameem, Era of Coalition Government at Center, *New Age*, 44 (19), 12th May 1996.

Gupta, Indrajit, The Government has No-Confidence in Itself, *New Age*, 46 (14), 6th April 1998.

Lahiri, Pratap, BJP Going from Vote Division, *New Age*, 39 (24-25), 23 June 1991.

Mishra, Chaturanan, Instability is Today's Reality, *New Age*, 39 (14), 7th April 1991.

Mishra, U.N., Whither Indian Democracy?, *New Age*, 46 (19), 10th May 1998.

Prasad, Giri, On Emerging Political Scenario, *New Age*, 44 (33), 18th August 1996.

Singh, Mulayam, Why Nation has No-Confidence in Vajpayee Government, *New Age*, 46 (14), 6th April 1998.

Singh, Pardhuman, Wither Indian Parliamentary Democracy?, *New Age*, 44 (4), 28th January 1996.

Indian Journal of Public Administration

Bhambri, C.P., Elections and Political Change, *Indian Journal of Public Administration*, 37 (3), July-September 1991.

Dey, Bata K., E-Governance in India: Problems, Challenges and Opportunities—A Futures Vision, *The Indian Journal of Public Administration*, 46 (3), pp. 301–310.

Dhameja, Alka and Medury, Uma, ICT and Governance: The Socio-Economic Concern, *The Indian Journal of Public Administration*, 50 (1), January–March, 2004.

Farooqi, A.A., Advent of Vajpayee Government: Expectations and Prospects, *Indian Journal of Public Administration*, 32 (1-2), January–June 1998.

Gaur, M.K., Political Stability and Good Governance, *Indian Journal of Public Administration*, 44 (3), July–September 1998.

Kashyap, Subhash, Towards Good Governance: Need for Political Reforms, *Indian Journal of Public Administration*, 44 (3), July–September 1998.

Kogekarm, S.V. The Changing Pattern of Politics, *Journal of Indian School of Political Economy*, 6 (3), July–September 1994.

Maheshwari, Shriram, Political Reforms for True Governance, *Indian Journal of Public Administration*, 44 (3), July–September 1998.

Maheshwari, Sriram, The Conscience Keeper for Indian Democracy, *Indian Journal of Public Administration*", 37 (3), July–September 1991.

Narain, Iqbal, Future of Democracy in Some Reflections in the Context of the Tenth Lok Sabha Poll Verdict, *Indian Journal of Public Administration*, 37 (3), July–September 1991.

Pachauri, S.K., Election Administration in India—Reflections of Aspects of 1998 Elections, *Indian Journal of Public Administration*, 44 (20), April–June 1998.

Raghavalu, C.V., Indian Republic and Governance Concern, *The Indian Journal of Political Science, 62 (1)*, March, 2001.

Tripathi, R.C., Functioning of Parliament in India, *Indian Journal of Public Administration*, 43 (3), July–September 1997.

Frontline

Muralidharan, Sukumar, Bankrupt Campaign, *Frontline*, 21 (9), May 7, 2004.

Tripathi, Poornima S., On the Defensive, *Frontline*, 21 (9), May 7, 2004.

Tripathi, Poornima S., Strategic Voting, *Frontline*, 21 (10), May 31, 2004.

Tripathi, Poornima S., With Dogged Determination, *Frontline*, 21 (8), April 23, 2004.

Venkateshan, V. and Narrain, Siddharth, Unfounded Optimism, *Frontline*, 21 (8), April 23, 2004.

People's Democracy

Engineer, Asghar Ali, One Year of BJP Government, *People's Democracy*, 23 (15), 11th April 1999.

Surjeet, Harkishan Singh, A Month-Long Stability, *People's Democracy*, 22(18), 3rd May 1998.

Surjeet, Harkishan Singh, Day of Reckoning Zeroes in on BJP Government, *People's Democracy*, 23 (15), 11th April 1999.

Surjeet, Harkishan Singh, Meeting Political and Ideological Threat of BJP, *People's Democracy*, 22 (12), 22nd March 1998.

Surjeet, Harkishan Singh, What the BJP Government is Aiming at? *People's Democracy*, 22 (14), 5th April 1998.

Manthan

Jaitely, Arun, When Democracy Was Under Seige, *Manthan*, 17 (3), July-September 1996.

Vajpayee, A.B., Democracy will Prevail, *Manthan*, 17 (3), July-September 1996.

Vajpayee, A.B., Indian Democracy Being Worm-eaten, *Manthan*, 17 (3), July-September 1996.

International Social Science Journal

Apter, David, Institutionalism Reconsidered, *International Social Science Journal*, 43 (3), August 1991.

Hermet, Guy, The Age of Democracy, *International Social Science Journal*, 43 (3), May 1991.

Joseph, Bob, The Rise of Governance and Risks of Failure: The Case of Economic Development, *International Social Science Journal*, 11(5), March 1998.

Kazancigil, Ali, Governance and Science: Market like modes of Managing Society and Producing Knowledge, *International Social Science Journal*, 11(5), March 1998.

Merrian, Francois-Xavier, Governance and Modern Welfare State, *International Social Science Journal*, 11(5), March 1998.

Sartori, Giovanni, Re-thinking Democracy: Bad Polity and Bad Politics, *International Social Science Journal*, 43 (2), May 1991.

Stoker Gerry, Governance as Theory: Five Propositions, *International Social Science Journal*, 11(5), March 1998.

Seminar

Coalition Politics, *Seminar*, 437, January 1996, pp.53-57.

Datt, Bhaskar, in Search of Political Stability, *Seminar*, 454, September 1997.

Khare, Harish, Coalition Politics, *Seminar*, 377, January 1991.
Khare, Harish, Regional Parties Reduced Efficiency, *Seminar*, 399, November 1992.
Kothari, Rajni, Era of Darkness, *Seminar*, 399, November 1992.
Kothri Rajni, Institution Building, *Seminar*, 361, September 1989.
Mehta, Pratap Banu, Is Electoral and Institutional Reform the Answer? *Seminar*, 506, October 2001.
Mishra, Amresh, Beyond Coalition Politics, *Seminar*, 454, June 1997.
Mitra, Chandan, Unholy Alliance, *Seminar*, 454, June 1997.
Singh, Mahendra Prasad, After Congress What?, *Seminar*, 440, April 1996.
Unges, Robert, Towards a High Energy Democracy, *Seminar*, 506, October 2001.
Wilkinson Steven, Cleansing Political Institutions, *Seminar*, 506, October 2001.
Yadav, Yogendra, Electoral Prospects, *Seminar*, 417, May 1994.

Business India

Bhatt, Mayank, Rejoicing of Democracy, *Business India*, 507, 11th August 1997.
Roy, Anjan, New Election Expertise, *Business India*, 22, 2nd March 1998.

Teaching Politics

Bhalla, R.P., The Electoral System, Its Operation and Implications for Democracy in India, *Teaching Politics*, 15 (3-4), 1989.
Bhambri, C.P., Dynamics of Tenth Lok Sabha Elections, *Teaching Politics*, 17 (1-2), 1991.
Narang, A.S., Democracy Developments and Power Shifts: Reflections on 1991 Lok Sabha Elections, *Teaching Politics*, 17 (1-2), 1991.
Prasad, Poonam, Issues Before 10th General Election, *Teaching Politics*, 17 (1-2), 1991.

Radical Humanist

Coalition Government At the Center, *Radical Humanist*, 60 (4), July 1996
Devraj, P.I., Party System-The Bedrock of Indian Democracy, *Radical Humanist*, 62 (2), May 1998.
Gani, H.A., Political Parties and Degeneration of Democratic and Moral Virtues, *Radical Humanist*, 62 (2), May 1998.
Godbole, Madhav, Democracy at the Cross Roads, *Radical Humanist*, 62 (2), May 1998.
Good Governance? Fairness? Or Vice Versa, Or Both, *Radical Humanist*, 57 (7), October 1993.

Khan, Arshi, Regional Political Parties and the New Coalition, *Radical Humanist*, 62 (3), June 1998, pp.14-19.

Kumar, Ravindra, India—The Prospect Ahead, *Radical Humanist*, 62 (3), June 1998.

Ramamurthy, M.V., Role of Violence in Politics, *Radical Humanist*, 54 (3), June 1990.

Rane, M.A., Political Parties and Preservation of Democracy, *Radical Humanist*, 62 (3), June 1998.

Sinha, Shivendra K., Elections Sans Ideological Issues: Can We Afford It? *Radical Humanist*, 60 (5), August 1996.

Tarakunde, V.M., Fifty Years After Freedom: New Opportunities and Challenges, *Radical Humanist*, 61 (9), December 1997.

Tarakunde, V.M., Democracy and The Party System, *Radical Humanist*, 62 (3), June 1998.

Varde, Sadanand, Reform The Present Electoral System, *Radical Humanist*, 57 (7), October 1993.

Venkatraman, R., For a Stable Government in India, *Radical Humanist*, 62 (10), January 1999.

Wariawalla, Bharat, Coalitional Form of Governance, *Radical Humanist*, 54 (1), April 1990.

Ill Weekly India

Kapoor, Coomi and Saroj Nagi, Inner Party Democracy: Barren Promise, Ill *Weekly India*, 111 (22), 3rd January 1990.

Kapoor, Coomi, Crisis After Crisis, Ill *Weekly India*, 111 (44), 4th November 1990.

Kothari, Rajni, The Bottom Line, Ill *Weekly India*, 111 (36), 9th September 1990.

Shekhar, Chandra, The Age of Uncertainty, Ill *Weekly India*, 112 (28), 13th July 1991.

Janata

Bhargava, G.S., Party System and Democracy, *Janata*, 52 (14), 29th June 1997.

Dandavate, Madhu, Anarchical Style of Governance, *Janata*, 53 (14), 31st May 1998.

Dandavate, Madhu, Political Polarisation—Which Way?, *Janata*, 46 (30), 27th October 1991.

Devdutt, Post Election Scenario: The Real Empowerment of People Begins, *Janata*, 51 (11), 16th June 1996.

Dhar, Sisir K., The Ailing Political Life of India, *Janata*, 53 (23), 13th September 1998.

Dwivedy, Surendranath, Indian Political Scenario, *Janata*, 51 (21), 13th October 1996.

Kothari, Rajni, Institution Building in India Retrieving Lost Ground, *Janata*, 52 (1), 1997.

Kothari, Rajni, Interpreting 1996-II, *Janata*, 51 (15), 18th August 1996.

Mohan, Surendra, Non-Party Contribution to Election Issues, *Janata*, 51 (4), 17th March 1996.

Mohan, Surendra, Rising Factionalism in Political Parties, *Janata*, 49 (15), 19th June 1994.

Mohan, Surendra, The Emerging Threat to Democracy, *Janata*, 49 (12), 22nd May 1994.

Mohan, Surendra, Third Force Needs a Long Perspective, *Janata*, 52 (17), 3rd August 1997.

Mohan, Surendra, What Next?, *Janata*, 53 (4), 8th March 1998.

Nayar, Kuldip, Contradictions at the Center, *Janata*, 53 (18), 5th July 1998.

Varde, Sadananda, A Hung Lok Sabha Again? What Then?, *Janata*, 53 (1-3), 1998.

Asian Survey

Ganguly, Summit, Asia in 1997: Another Year of Turmoil, *Asian Survey*, 38 (2), February, 1998.

K Bajpai, Shankar, India in 1991: New Beginnings, *Asian Survey*, 32 (2), February 1992.

Kapur, Devesh and Mehta Pratap Bhanu, India In 1998: The Travails of Political Fragmentation, *Asian Survey*, 39 (1), January-February 1999.

Malik, Yogendra, Bharatiya Janata Party: An Alternative to the Congress (I), *Asian Survey*, 32 (4), April 1992.

Pai, Sudha, Party System Under Transformation, *Asian Survey*, 38 (9), September 1998.

Roy, Ramashray, *India in 1993:* The Struggle of Economic Reform, *Asian Survey*, 34 (2), February, 1994.

Singh, Mahendra Prasad, The Dilemmas of New Indian Party System: To Govern or Not to Govern, *Asian Survey*, 32 (4), April 1992.

Thakur, Ramesh, A Changing of the Guard in India, *Asian Survey*, 38 (6), June, 1998.

Otherside

Namboodripad E.M.S., Fifty Years of Indian Independence, *Otherside*, 17 (10), November 1997.

Rajesham, N., Fifty Years of Opportunistic Politics, *Otherside*, 17 (7), August 1997.

Shourie, H.D., Reforming the Political Parties, *Otherside*, 144, May 1996.

Frontier

Purohit, Vinayak, Final Doom of the Congress, *Frontier*, 28 (52), 3rd August 1996.

Roy, Himanshu, Party System in India, *Frontier*, 30 (23), 17 January, 1998.

Shukla, I.K., Post-Congress India: A Prospect, *Frontier*, 28 (47), 29th June 1996.

Southern Economist

Hegde, Ramakrishna, Parliament and Political Culture, *Southern Economist*, 32 (11), October 1993.

Ramaswamy, M.C., Congress or BJP: to Say Nothing About United Front, *Southern Economist*, 36 (21), 1st March 1998.

Ramaswamy, M.C., Governance by Consensus, Politically and Economically, *Southern Economist*, 35 (3), 1st June 1996, pp.5-6.

Singh, Karan, Fifty Years of Independence, *Southern Economist*, 37 (8), 15th August 1998.

Monthly Commentary On Indian Economic Conditions

Policies and Parties in Mid-Term Polls, *Monthly Commentary on Indian Economic Conditions*, 39 (5), December 1997.

Political Alignments and Popular Aspirations, *Monthly Commentary on Indian Economic Conditions*, 39 (8), March 1998.

Turbulent Coalition Politics, *Monthly Commentary On Indian Economic Conditions*, 39 (12), July 1998, pp.5-6.

Link

Atmosphere of Uncertainty, Suspense and Anxiety, *Link*, 33 (45), 16th June 1991.

Consensus Building?, *Link*, 34 (5), 15th September 1991.

Other Journals

Bhimik, Sabha Naqui, Fable of the Rooster, *Outlook*, 44 (3), January 26, 2004.

Buruma, Ian, India: The Peril as of Democracy, *New Quest*, 126, November-December 1997.

Gangrade, K.D., 50 Years of "Azadi": Disenchantment with Leaders, *IASSI Quarts*, 16 (1), July-September 1997.

Gujral, I.K., India the Redefining of Political Process, *Indian Author*, 18 (1-2), January-June 1993.

Jotwani, Nandlal, Preparing India for the Next Century: Review Article, *USI Journal*, 128 (531), January-March 1998.

Kanetkar, Supriya R., India at Fifty: In a Transition, *Humanscape*, 5 (2), February 1998.

Kumar, Ravindra, The Roots of Democracy in India, *Indian Horizons*, 41 (1-2), 1992.

Malikarjunaiah, S., Our Democracy and Constitution at Work, *Journal of Constitutional and Parliamentary Studies*, 27 (1-4), January-December 1994.

Paipanandikar, V.A., Vibrancy of Indian Democratic System, *Mahila Vidhi Bharati*, 16-17, July-December 1998.

Saxena, Rekha, Democratic Government in India, *Indian History Review*, 21 (1-2), July 1994-January 1995.

Simha, S.L.M., Towards More Efficient Democracy, *Southern Economics*, 31 (12), 15th October 1992.

Singh, Mahendra Prasad, From Centrist Predominance to Polarized Pluralism: The Post 1989 Party System in India, *Punjab Politics*, 16 (12), 1992.

Yadav, R.S., Democratization of Central Asian Republics and India, *Kurukshetra*, 28-29, 1994-1995.

Encyclopedias and Dictionary

Gould, Julius and Kolb, William L. (ed.), *A Dictionary of Social Science*, The Free Press, New York, 1969

Lipset, Seymour Martin, *The Encyclopedia of Democracy*, Vol. III, Routledge, London, 1995.

McClosky, Herbert, Political Participation, *International Encyclopedia of Social Science*, Vol. XII, Coller MacMillan Company, New York, 1968.

Sills David L. (ed.), *International Encyclopaedia of Social Science*, MacMillan Company and The Free Press, Vol. IV, U.S.A., 1968.

News Papers

Deccan Herald
The Hindu
The Navhind Times
The Times of India
The Vijay Times

Index